Cream of Cabbage Soup

1 medium cabbage, chopped
" onion
1/3 c carrot grated
2 c Soya milk
Smashed potato
2 (10 oz) cream of chicken soup.

365 plus one Vegan Recipes

Delicious meals and ideas for
every day of the year

Leah Leneman

Thorsons

An Imprint of HarperCollins*Publishers*

Thorsons
An Imprint of HarperCollins*Publishers*
77–85 Fulham Palace Road,
Hammersmith, London W6 8JB

1160 Battery Street,
San Francisco, California 94111-1213

Published by Thorsons 1993
3   5   7   9   10   8   6   4

A catalogue record for this book
is available from the British Library

ISBN 0 7225 2617 2

Printed in Great Britain
by The Bath Press, Avon

Contents

Acknowledgements

My thanks to all who helped with this book – many friends, in particular: Kath Macdonald who suggested ideas for recipes; Alison Crawford who typed the existing recipes into the word processor; and Graham Sutton who tasted most of the dishes.

Some of the recipes in this book have previously appeared in the following: *Vegan Cooking, Soya Foods Cookery, Vegetarian Pitta Bread Recipes,* and *The Amazing Avocado.*

Introduction

Vegetarianism is entering a new and dynamic phase. A cuisine based on vegetables, fruits, nuts and grains, flavoured with the herbs and spices of the world, is taking the place of a diet reliant on dairy products. This has come about primarily because of the growing realization that everyone in the world could be fed if a switch were made to a completely vegetarian diet. Britain could be self-sufficient if grazing lands were used to grow pulses and grains were fed direct to humans instead of being diverted to animals. Since dairy farming is almost as inefficient a way of using land as beef farming, the switch must be complete if it is to be effective.

It is not only human beings who would benefit for slaughterhouses would disappear. Lacto-vegetarians are beginning to realize that drinking cows' milk contributes to animal slaughter. Cows are kept continually pregnant and lactating, their calves usually taken away very shortly after birth (many ending their brief lives as veal), so that the milk can all be sold for human consumption. Even if factory farming were to be abolished, male calves would still have to be slaughtered to maintain the dairy industry. Similarly, in order for hens to lay there must be fertile eggs, and all of the male chicks will be killed. Thus, while free-range hens do not have to endure the inhumane battery system, eating any kind of eggs still contributes to animal slaughter.

There are so many second, third and even fourth generation lacto-vegetarians in this country now that no one could convincingly claim that flesh foods are necessary for health. Many people still fear, however, that to give up all animal produce is dangerous (and anyone who embarks on a vegan diet while riddled with apprehensions may well become ill from sheer anxiety). In fact, many lacto-vegetarians consume an excessive amount of dairy produce, thereby clogging up their arteries with saturated fat – a far greater health risk than a vegan diet.

The biggest worry seems to be protein. Giving up cheese and eggs, it is feared, will mean eating only 'inferior', and therefore insufficient, protein. Fortunately it has become more generally known that cereals can be combined with pulses or nuts to obtain all the necessary amino acids (the building blocks of protein) in required proportions. This combination forms the basis of many of the recipes in this book, making it virtually impossible for anyone using it to become deficient in protein. It is certainly not necessary to eat foods high in protein at every meal, or to worry about food combining.

The one and only nutrient which does not occur naturally in a vegan diet is vitamin B_{12}. Although some pioneering vegans who had never heard of this vitamin appear to have been able to synthesize it in their intestines, the effects of a deficiency are too drastic to make it worth the risk. Most of the plant milks now available in Britain are fortified with vitamin B_{12}, as are most textured vegetable protein (t.v.p.) products and a number of other foods. Yet only a small amount of this vitamin is required, which makes it very easy to incorporate into a vegan diet by eating any of the above foods regularly. (Note, however, that nearly all of the breakfast cereals found at supermarkets which contain vitamin B_{12} also contain vitamin D derived from an animal source and are not therefore vegan.) For those who prefer not to use processed foods, vegan vitamin B_{12} tablets are available in health food stores. Incidentally, anyone who argues that a vegan diet cannot be a truly natural one since it lacks an essential vitamin, should realize that the answer lies in our perhaps 'unnatural' level of hygiene, since an all-vegetable diet in a country where produce is not so rigorously cleaned would certainly contain that elusive vitamin.

Honey is a contentious issue as, strictly speaking, it is

an animal product, but whether it causes suffering is matter for disagreement. In 1992 the Vegan Society did not admit those who consumed honey as full members, and honey is not used in any of the recipes in this book, although many vegans do eat it.

The concern with animal products usually spills over into other areas as well. Most vegans do not wear leather or use soaps or cosmetics which contain animal products or are tested on animals. Wool production can be cruel, and as for lanolin, the idea of putting sheep fat on one's face is not appealing.

Some vegetarians who are vegan at home find it difficult to maintain the diet elsewhere. This is understandable in view of British restaurants' obsession with animal produce, but it is possible to get delicious vegan meals in many Indian and Chinese restaurants, and any good Italian restaurant can prepare pizzas without cheese.

Vegans have varied eating patterns. Some eat only raw foods, some stick strictly to unprocessed wholefoods, while others rely mainly on t.v.p. and vegan convenience meals. Variety is the key-note of this book. The philosophy here is that if the basic diet is one of natural unrefined foods, then there is no harm at all in using a certain amount of good quality processed and packaged foods to add different tastes and textures, as well as to save time.

Vegan cookery can be as quick as any other kind. After all, one of the most popular foods in Britain is baked beans on toast – a quick and nutritious vegan snack, particularly if the bread is wholewheat. A number of the recipes in this book can be prepared in half an hour or less. It is simply a question of gearing oneself to the use of a completely different set of foods; once you become used to the idea then no great mental effort is required to prepare tasty, healthy vegan meals. And should anyone still think that vegan food lacks variety, this book will prove just the opposite.

Clarification of some ingredients, quantities etc

- All recipes serve four unless otherwise stated, but do keep in mind that appetites vary a good deal. I am often astonished at the quantities that are supposed to provide 'four generous servings' in some cookery books, and I am aware that on days when I am feeling very hungry the recipes I create are likely to be more substantial than on days when I have no desire for a big meal; a certain amount of independent judgment is necessary.

- Many cookery books state that Imperial and metric measurements should not be mixed. As far as I am concerned, the recipes in this book are robust enough for imperial, metric and American measurements to be mixed at will. This is home cooking, not biochemistry.

- Onions and other vegetables are assumed to be 'medium-sized' unless otherwise stated.

- Breadcrumbs are always fresh. I never use dried ones since I always keep sliced bread in the freezer which defrosts very quickly.

- It is a good idea to cook double quantities of rice and potatoes and refrigerate half; many of my recipes call for cooked rice or potatoes.

- When a recipe calls for mashed potato that means mashed with a little soya (soy) milk and vegan margarine added. Many dried mashed potato mixes are vegan; they contain undesirable additives, but the time they can save may justify their occasional use.

- For deep frying I strongly recommend a deep-fat fryer for both health and safety reasons. It heats the oil to the right temperature so that the food immediately seals up and does not absorb the oil.

- It will be clear that eggs are not a necessary item in cooking, but if you want to use existing recipes that call for egg as a binder there are two vegan egg substitutes available in Britain. The British-made one, by GF Dietary, is available at many health food stores; I find it can go a bit lumpy and therefore usually blend it with the water in a liquidizer. The American-made one – *Ener-G Egg Replacer* – can be ordered at the dispensary of Boots or Unichem chemists.

- American readers may be puzzled by the ingredient 'yeast extract' while British readers might be puzzled by 'nutritional yeast'. Yeast extract is a salty brown paste which some American health food stores stock, most likely under its Australian brand name of Vegemite. If it cannot be found then soy sauce may be substituted, though the flavour will be different. Nutritional yeast comes in powdered or flaked form and is sold in British health food stores under the *'Engevita'* brand. As will be gathered by its use in many of my recipes, I have become an enthusiastic user of this product.

1

The Vegan 'Dairy'

Adult animals have no need for milk, either their own or that of another species, but in the western world people have become so accustomed to cows' milk and the products made from it that it becomes difficult to imagine a diet without such foods. Thus, while there is no physical need for dairy products – in the Far East much of the population is lactose-intolerant and never uses milk – the dishes which have evolved in the west require substitutes.

Over the past decade the growth in soya (soy) milks available has grown astonishingly, with some supermarkets offering own brand products. Although the ingredients on the different cartons appear similar, they are actually quite different in taste so if you try soya (soy) milk for the first time and don't like it then do try other brands. Soya (soy) milks come either unsweetened or sweetened (either with sugar or apple juice and/or barley malt). I find that for savoury dishes the unsweetened ones are much better; indeed the sweetened ones can even spoil such dishes. However, over cereals and in sweet dishes I definitely prefer sweetened soya (soy) milk. The only brand containing vitamin B_{12} is the British-made Plamil. The main lack at present (ironically, at one time it was nearly all one could get) is of a dried soya (soy) milk, which is particularly convenient when travelling.

Soya (soy) milks can be added to tea or coffee; they will curdle slightly but that does not affect the taste. An alternative is a true non-dairy creamer (but note that the so-called non-dairy creamers sold in supermarkets actually contain casein, a dairy derivative), which can be found in Jewish delicatessens.

Home-made Soya Milk

1 Bring about 570ml (1 pint/2½ cups) of water to the boil, add 115g (4 oz) soya (soy) beans, boil for 1 minute, then remove from the heat, cover and leave to soak overnight.

2 Drain the beans and wash them thoroughly. Put 1 cupful of beans in a liquidizer, add about 570ml (1 pint/2½ cups) hot water and blend them thoroughly. Pour through a clean tea towel (dish towel) or muslin, squeezing to extract all the liquid (the pulp can be used for savoury dishes if desired). Repeat until all the beans are used up.

3 Bring the milk to the boil, stirring frequently. (It has a tendency both to burn on the bottom of the pan and to boil over if not watched carefully!)

4 Simmer the milk over the lowest possible heat for 15-20 minutes. Set aside to cool and then keep in the refrigerator.

5 This can be made more palatable by adding pure vanilla essence or sweetening to taste.

Note: This recipe is for those who wish to make their own soya (soy) milks at home, although with such a choice now available few people need to.

Cashew or Almond Milk

115g (4 oz)	cashews or blanched almonds	¾ cup
285ml (½ pt)	water	1⅓ cups
As required	raw cane sugar or chopped dates	As required
2 tsp	vegetable oil	2 tsp

1 Put the cashews into the liquidizer and grind finely. Add the other ingredients and blend thoroughly.

Note: In southern Spain a popular summer drink is horchata, which is basically a nut milk. A milk made from either cashews or almonds is very pleasant over cereal. This recipe can be made thicker or thinner, if preferred, by increasing or decreasing the proportion of nuts and oil to water.

There are now delicious soya creams available at many health food stores and supermarkets in Britain. At Jewish delicatessens it is possible to find a vegan whipping cream, called Snowwhip Topping, and also, in canisters, a Canadian product called Richwhip Topping. These are very sweet and not particularly nutritious, but for special occasions when a whipped 'cream' is required I have found them invaluable. It is also possible to make some delicious vegan creams at home.

Mock Cream

1-2 tbs	cornflour (cornstarch)	1-2 tbs
285ml (½ pt)	soya (soy) milk	1⅓ cups
30-55g (1/2 oz)	vegan margarine	2 tbs-¼ cup

1 Blend the cornflour (cornstarch) to a smooth mixture with a little of the milk, then add the rest of the milk; pour the mixture into a saucepan and bring slowly to the boil, stirring constantly. Cook until thickened, then remove from the heat and set aside to cool.
2 Cream the margarine and sugar until very soft, but on no account warm the margarine.
3 Gradually beat in spoonsful of the cornflour mixture – the more you beat this, the better it becomes.

Cashew Cream

115g (4 oz)	cashews	¾ cup
425ml (¼ pt)	water	⅔ cup
1 tbs	vegetable oil	1 tbs
As required	raw cane sugar or chopped dates	As required
1 tsp	pure vanilla essence (optional)	1 tsp

1 Grind the cashews finely in a liquidizer. Add the rest of the ingredients and liquidize thoroughly.

Note: The thickness of this cream may be adjusted according to taste by altering the proportion of cashews and oil to water.

Coconut Cream

55-115g (2/4 oz)	creamed coconut	¼-½ cup
140ml (¼ pt)	very hot water (or to taste)	⅔ cup
As required	sweetening	As required

1 Grate the creamed coconut into a liquidizer or jar. Add the hot water and sweetening and liquidize or shake until the coconut has completely dissolved. Chill in the refrigerator. This can be made as a pouring cream or as a thick cream. It will thicken up when chilled so always make it a bit thinner than desired.

Note: Canned coconut milk from the Far East is now available (but read the label carefully as some contain preservative which is unnecessary and undesirable, and others contain coconut 'extract' which is not the same at all). This is really more like a cream than a milk. When you open the can you will probably find a thick almost solid chunk and a very watery remainder. The secret is to empty the whole thing into the liquidizer and blend thoroughly. Any coconut milk not used at the time can be refrigerated for a few days and is unlikely to separate again. The above is made from the solidified creamed coconut available at most delicatessens and many health food stores. It makes a particularly good topping for fresh strawberries or raspberries.

One product which vegans previously thought they had to do without was yogurt, but in fact the lactobacillus bulgaricus which so loves cows' milk is equally keen on soya (soy) milk, and soya yogurt is delicious. Without paying attention to the extravagant 'health' claims for yogurt, I would still urge vegans to include this in their diet. A high-fibre vegan diet is not necessarily the easiest thing for a delicate digestion to adjust to, and the friendly bacteria in soya yogurt can make a big difference. Most of the vegan yogurts now available in Britain (there are none, to my knowledge, in America) are long-life ones which means that though they may taste pleasant and be a reasonable source of protein, they are not 'live' and therefore will have no beneficial effects on the intestinal flora. The exception is a French line called Sojasun, which offers unsweetened natural vegan yogurt.

However, it is very easy to make soya yogurt at home. Sojasun unflavoured yogurt can be used as a starter or a dried ferment may be purchased at a health food store (but read the ingredients before buying – not all are vegan). Any soya milk can be used, even, surprisingly, the unsweetened ones. A yogurt maker is not necessary; I have always used a wide-rimmed thermos flask. Heat the milk to lukewarm (it is no longer necessary to heat it to boiling and then cool it down), mix in the starter or ferment and leave for several hours. A friend of mine mixes concentrated Plamil and boiling water and finds that that turns out to be the right temperature for yogurt (though she adds sweetening to the unsweetened kind). The yogurt can be used as a starter for the next batch and so on. The first batch is not usually that good, but it gets progressively better, and when it is at its best I usually freeze a little to be used as a starter later.

It is now well known that animal fats are not good for human beings, and however much the dairy industry attempts to disguise the fact, butter is an animal fat. Annoyingly, most supermarket 'vegetable' margarines still contain unnecessary dairy derivatives, but the own-brand 'soya margarine' found at many of them (and in the USA corn oil margarine) are vegan, and all of the health food store brands are 100% vegetable. Most of them are soft margarines, but Tomor (available also in Jewish delicatessens) is more similar in texture to butter and is the one I prefer for pastry. Vitaquell is the only unsalted one I know of in the UK, and I use it for spreading on bread.

Cheese was originally just a way of using extra cows' milk, but it has become so much a part of the western diet that the lack of it can be felt keenly. Vegan 'cheeses' are gradually coming on the market, and more can be expected in the future. The USA produces some under the Soymage brand which, through plasticky and not particularly palatable, are, in cooked dishes at least, very like dairy cheese. (Note that some American brands all contain casein, a dairy derivative.) British versions are certainly better: look out for Green Dragon 'Scheese' and the Redwood Company's 'Tofucheese'. By using one of these cheeses, soya (soy) milk, and a dried vegan egg substitute it is possible to make a facsimile of any of the popular British savoury dairy dishes. There are also spreads like Plamil Veeze or Fromsoya which can also be used in cooked dishes to give a 'cheesey' tang. Nutritional yeast can also add a mildly 'cheesey' flavour to various dishes.

Alternatively, any of the following can be made at home.

Soya Flour Cheese

Equal quantities of soya (soy) flour
and vegan margarine
Yeast extract to taste

1 Melt the margarine, add the flour and yeast extract and mix well.
2 Pour on to a greased tin and refrigerate until required. If a soft margarine is used then the resulting 'cheese' is easy to spread. If Tomor margarine is used then the 'cheese' can be sliced for sandwiches or grated and sprinkled over a hot savoury to be grilled (broiled) or baked.

Pimento 'Cheese' Spread

115g (4 oz)	cashew nuts	¾ cup
1 tin (200g)	pimentos	1 can (8 oz)
1 tbs	sesame seeds	1 tbs
1 tsp	nutritional yeast	1 tsp
½ tsp	onion salt	½ tsp
4 tbs	vegetable oil	4 tbs
2 tsp	lemon juice	2 tsp

1 Grind the cashews and sesame seeds finely in a liquidizer.
2 Add the pimentos (including the juice) and the rest of the ingredients and blend thoroughly.

Yogurt Cheese

Place some thick soya yogurt in a square of muslin or cheesecloth and tie securely; hang the muslin or cheesecloth over a tap to drip for several hours or overnight, then refrigerate. This is a soft cheese similar to a cream cheese texture.

Cashew Cottage Cheese

Cover some cashew nuts with lukewarm water. Leave undisturbed in a warm spot for three or four days. Drain off the liquid and grind the fermented cashews in a Mouli or grinder. (A liquidizer can be used, but the texture will be different.) Use with salads, particularly those with fruit.

2
American Breakfast and
British Afternoon Tea

It was difficult to know what to call this chapter because eating habits differ within the English-speaking world. In Britain scones and muffins would be eaten in the afternoon while in America they are eaten in the morning, as are pancakes, waffles and pastries, most of which the British would eat as dessert. I have put all such dishes in this chapter.

Quick and Easy Coffee Cake

Cake

225g (½ lb)	wholewheat flour	1 cup
Pinch	sea salt	Pinch
4 tsp	baking powder	4 tsp
3 tbs	raw cane sugar	3 tbs
2 tbs	vegan margarine	2 tbs
285ml (½ pt)	soya (soy) milk	1½ cups

Topping

3 tbs	wholewheat flour	3 tbs
4 tbs	raw cane sugar	4 tbs
3 tsp	ground cinnamon	3 tsp
55g (2 oz)	vegan margarine	¼ cup

1 Melt the margarine for the cake ingredients.
2 In a bowl combine the flour for the cake ingredients, salt, baking powder and sugar. Stir in the melted margarine and milk.
3 In a small bowl combine the topping flour, sugar and cinnamon. Rub in the margarine.
4 Pour the batter into a cake tin and spread the topping over it. Bake at 400°F/200°C (Gas Mark 6) for about half an hour. Serve warm, split and spread with additional margarine.

Note: In Britain something called a coffee cake will be flavoured with coffee, but Americans have adopted this kind of cake from the Continent, i.e. it is a cake served with coffee. It is not as sweet as the cakes in Chapter 17, and it is best served warm.

Apple Coffee Cake

Topping

55g (2 oz)	raw cane sugar	⅓ cup
1 tsp	cinnamon	1 tsp
30g (1 oz)	vegan margarine	2 tbs
3 tbs	wholewheat flour	3 tbs

Cake

225g (½ lb)	wholewheat flour	2 cups
Pinch	sea salt	Pinch
4 tsp	baking powder	4 tsp
½ tsp	bicarbonate of soda (baking soda)	½ tsp
55g (2 oz)	raw cane sugar	⅓ cup
285ml (½ pt)	soya milk	1⅓ cups
4 tbs	vegetable oil	4 tbs
340g (¾ lb)	apples	¾ lb

1 Mix the topping ingredients in a small bowl until crumbly and set aside.
2 Mix the flour, salt, baking powder, soda and sugar in a bowl. Stir in the milk and oil. Spoon into a greased pan.
3 Peel, core and slice the apples. Press them on top of the batter. Sprinkle with the topping.
4 Bake at 350°F/180°C (Gas Mark 4) for about half an hour.

Waffles

225g (½ lb)	wholewheat flour	2 cups
1½ tsp	baking powder	1½ tsp
Pinch	sea salt	Pinch
425ml (¾ pt)	soya (soy) milk	2 cups
4 tbs	vegetable oil	4 tbs

Optional

| As required | chopped pecans | As required |

1 Add the baking powder and salt to the flour in a large mixing bowl.
2 Gently stir in the milk and oil (and pecans if using). Prepare on a waffle iron.

Note: This is a fairly conventional waffle recipe but of course without the unnecessary eggs. Serve the waffles with maple syrup.

Oat and Cashew Waffles

225g (½ lb)	rolled oats	2 cups
85g (3 oz)	cashews	½ cup
Pinch	sea salt	Pinch
1 tbs	vegetable oil	1 tbs
225ml (8 fl oz)	water	1 cup

1 Put the oats and cashews in a liquidizer and grind. Add the salt, oil and water and blend thoroughly.
2 Pour the batter in a waffle iron and leave for a few minutes until cooked.

Note: This more unusual waffle recipe, which requires no raising agent, is still best served with maple syrup.

Hot Cakes

225g (½ lb)	wholewheat flour	2 cups
1 tsp	baking powder	1 tsp
1 tsp	bicarbonate of soda (baking soda)	1 tsp
Pinch	sea salt	Pinch
170g (6 oz)	soya (soy) yogurt	¾ cup
225ml (8 fl oz)	water	1 cup
2 tbs	vegetable oil	2 tbs

1 Mix the flour, baking powder, soda and salt in a bowl. Add the yogurt, water and oil, and stir briefly.
2 Fry the hot cakes in a heated frying pan or griddle, flipping them over when done on one side.

Note: I used to think this kind of pancake originated in the U.S.A. until I discovered 'Scotch' pancakes, which I think are the same, except the latter are served cold and these are served piping hot, with maple syrup.

American-style Muffins

225g (½ lb)	wholewheat flour	2 cups
1 tsp	baking powder	1 tsp
1 tsp	bicarbonate of soda (baking soda)	1 tsp
Pinch	sea salt	Pinch
1-2 tbs	raw cane sugar	1-2 tbs
3 tbs	vegan margarine	3 tbs
425ml (¾ pt)	soya (soy) yogurt	2 cups

1 Put all the dry ingredients in a bowl and mix them well.
2 Melt the margarine (I often do this in the muffin tins in the oven, thereby greasing them at the same time). Add it to the dry ingredients along with the yogurt. Stir the mixture until it is a smooth batter.
3 Pour the batter into greased muffin tins and bake at 425°F/225°C (Gas Mark 7) for 15-20 minutes.

Note: Nowadays American muffins are almost as sweet as cake, but in their original form they were only slightly sweetened and served with jam. This recipe makes about 2 dozen small muffins or a dozen large ones.

Crêpes

170g (6 oz)	wholewheat flour	1½ cups
3 tbs	soya (soy) flour	3 tbs
1 tsp	baking powder	1 tsp
2 tsp	vegetable oil	2 tsp
1 tsp	sea salt	1 tsp
As required	water	As required

1 Combine the flour, baking powder and sea salt. Make a well in the centre, pour in the oil, then pour in the water gradually, stirring constantly with a fork. The consistency should be like thick cream. Leave to stand for about half an hour. If it is too thick then add more water; if it is too thin, add more flour.
2 Melt some vegan margarine or vegetable oil and fry the crêpes on both sides.

Note: For breakfast, tea or dessert fill these with jam. They can also be used for savoury pancakes.

Banana and Lemon Pancakes

30g (1 oz)	raw cane sugar	2 tbs
1 tsp	cinnamon	1 tsp
Grating	nutmeg	Grating
Pinch	sea salt	Pinch
1-2 tbs	lemon juice	1-2 tbs
455g (1 lb)	ripe bananas	1 lb
As required	vegetable oil	As required
	Crêpe batter made from 225g (½ lb/2 cups) wholewheat flour (see above)	
30g (1 oz)	melted vegan margarine	2 tbs
As required	icing (powdered) sugar or finely ground raw cane sugar	As required
As required	lemon wedges	As required

1 Mix the sugar, cinnamon, nutmeg, salt and lemon juice in a small bowl. Slice the bananas and mix them gently in the lemon mixture.
2 Heat a frying pan and add a little vegetable oil. Fry each of the crêpes on both sides, and spread them with melted margarine and some of the banana mixture. Keep everything warm.
3 Serve the crêpes sprinkled with icing (powdered) or finely ground raw cane sugar. Garnish with lemon wedges.

Note: In Britain pancakes like these would probably be served as a dessert, but Americans might prefer them for breakfast.

Blintzes

	Crêpe batter made from 225g (½ lb/2 cups) wholewheat flour (see above)	
455g (1 lb)	tofu	2 cups
2 tbs	soya (soy) yogurt plus additional as required	2 tbs
2 tbs	raw cane sugar plus additional as required	2 tbs
¼ tsp	vanilla essence	¼ tsp
As required	vegan margarine	As required

1 Put the tofu into a tea towel (dish towel) and squeeze to extract the water. Transfer the dry tofu to a mixing bowl. Stir in the yogurt, sugar and vanilla essence.
2 Fry each pancake in margarine on one side only. Fill with the tofu mixture on the cooked side and roll up.
3 When all the pancakes are filled, heat a little margarine in the frying pan and fry the blintzes, turning them so that they are lightly browned on both sides.

Note: This is a vegan version of a traditional Jewish dish (makes 15-20 blintzes). Serve them topped with additional sugar and yogurt.

Tofu French Toast

340g (12oz)	soft or medium tofu	1½ cups
230ml (8 fl oz)	water	1 cup
4 tbs	vegetable oil	4 tbs
Pinch	sea salt	Pinch
1 tsp	vanilla essence	1 tsp
3-4 tsp	raw cane sugar	3-4 tsp
8 slices	wholewheat bread	8 slices
As required	margarine for frying	As required

1 Put the tofu, water, oil, salt, vanilla and sugar in a liquidizer and blend thoroughly. Pour the mixture into a shallow bowl, and dip the slices of bread in it.
2 Heat a little margarine in a frying pan, and fry the bread over a moderate heat until browned on both sides.

Note: 'French toast' is actually American, traditionally made with an eggy batter. Tofu gives the same effect. Serve with maple syrup, or jam, or a mixture of raw cane sugar and cinnamon.

Nutty French Toast

55g (2 oz)	cashews	⅓ cup
55g (2 oz)	almonds	⅓ cup
285ml (½ pt)	soya (soy) milk	1⅓ cups
8 slices	wholewheat bread	8 slices
As required	vegan margarine or vegetable oil	As required

1 Grind the cashews and almonds in a liquidizer. Add the milk and blend thoroughly.
2 Pour the nut and milk mixture into a shallow bowl and dip the bread slices in it.
3 Heat the margarine or oil and fry the coated bread, turning once so that it is golden brown on both sides. Serve immediately.

Note: This is a variant on the traditional French toast. Serve with the same toppings.

Queen Scones

255g (9 oz)	wholewheat flour	2¼ cups
2 tsp	baking powder	2 tsp
Pinch	sea salt	Pinch
45g (1½ oz)	raw cane sugar	3 tbs
60ml (2 fl oz)	vegetable oil	¼ cup
85g (3 oz)	sultanas (golden seedless raisins)	½ cup
115g (4 oz)	medium or soft tofu	½ cup
120ml (4 fl oz)	water	½ cup

1 Combine the flour, baking powder, salt and sugar in a bowl. Mix well. Stir in the oil and then the sultanas (golden seedless raisins).
2 Put the tofu and water in a liquidizer and blend well. Pour into the dry mixture and stir well.
3 Turn out on to a floured board, roll the dough out and cut it into scones. Place the scones on an oiled baking sheet and bake at 425°F/220°C (Gas Mark 7) for 15 minutes.

Note: Scones are a close relation to American biscuits.

Treacle Scones

225g (½ lb)	wholewheat flour	2 cups
2 tsp	baking powder	2 tsp
Pinch	sea salt	Pinch
½ tsp	ground cinnamon	½ tsp
½ tsp	ground ginger	½ tsp
½ tsp	ground allspice	½ tsp
55g (2 oz)	raw cane sugar	⅓ cup
55g (2 oz)	vegan margarine	¼ cup
1 tbs	black treacle or molasses	1 tbs
140ml (¼ pt)	soya (soy) milk	⅔ cup

1 Mix the dry ingredients together in a bowl. Rub in the margarine.
2 Soften the treacle a little and add it with the milk to make a fairly soft dough. Turn on to a floured board, roll out to about ½ inch thick, and cut into rounds.
3 Place the scones on a greased baking tray and bake in a hot oven 425°F/220°C (Gas Mark 7) for 10-15 minutes.

Potato Scones

455g (1 lb)	potatoes	1 lb
½ tsp	sea salt	½ tsp
115g (4 oz)	wholewheat flour	1 cup

1 Cook the potatoes (or use leftover cooked potatoes). Peel and mash them.
2 Add the salt and flour to the potatoes and knead the mixture. Roll it out thinly on a floured board and cut into rounds or triangles.
3 Bake in a very hot oven 500°F/240°C (Gas Mark 9) for 10 minutes, turning the scones after 5 minutes.
4 Serve warm with golden syrup or jam.

3
Soups

Lentil and Barley Soup

115g (4 oz)	brown lentils	⅔ cup
50g (2 oz)	pot barley	⅓ cup
1 large	onion	1 large
2 sticks	celery	2 sticks
2	carrots	2
1140ml (2 pts)	water	5 cups
2 tsp	dried mixed herbs	2 tsp
1 tbs	miso	1 tbs

1 Cover the lentils and barley with boiling water and leave to soak for a few hours or overnight. Drain well and rinse thoroughly.

2 Chop all the vegetables finely.

3 Mix together the lentils, barley and chopped vegetables and cover them with water. Bring to the boil, adding the herbs.

4 Simmer for 30-40 minutes until the lentils and barley are tender. Remove a little of the liquid and mix thoroughly with miso until smooth. Return this to the saucepan, mix thoroughly and serve. (Miso is quite salty, but extra salt can be added if desired.)

Note: The combination of lentil and pot barley (the unrefined version of pearl barley) makes this a high-protein, sustaining soup, perfect for a winter day. It is also good for slimmers as it is fat free.

Avocado Vichyssoise

3	leeks	3
1 large	onion	1 large
2 tbs	vegetable margarine	2 tbs
455g (1 lb)	potatoes	1 lb
850ml (1½ pts)	water	3¾ cups
½	vegetable stock cube	½
1	avocado	1
140ml (¼ pt)	soya (soy) milk	⅔ cup
¼ tsp	freshly grated nutmeg	¼ tsp
As required	sea salt	As required
Sprinkling	paprika	Sprinkling

1 Chop the leeks and onion. Sauté for 3-4 minutes in the margarine.

2 Peel and slice the potatoes thinly. Add to the leek and onion.

3 Pour in the water and add the stock cube. Bring to the boil, then cover and simmer for about 15 minutes until tender. Set aside to cool.

4 Peel and chop the avocado. Place in liquidizer and add the leek, potato mixture and milk. Also add the nutmeg and salt. Blend thoroughly.

5 Place in the refrigerator until thoroughly chilled. Sprinkle with paprika before serving.

Note: This is an unusual variant on an old favourite. Suitable for a dinner party.

Chilled Carrot Soup

455g (1 lb)	carrots	1 lb
140ml (½ pt)	water	1⅓ cup
2 tbs	grated onion	2 tbs
4 tbs	peanut butter	4 tbs
570ml (1 pt)	soya (soy) milk	2½ cups
As required	sea salt	As required
As required	freshly ground black pepper	As required

1 Clean and slice the carrots, cover them with the water and boil gently for 20 minutes.
2 Add the grated onion and peanut butter and simmer for 20 minutes more.
3 Cool slightly, add milk and seasoning, then blend the soup in a liquidizer.
4 Chill for several hours before serving.

Note: This is a pleasant soup for a hot summer day.

Curried Sweetcorn Soup

2 tins (c.340g) each	creamed-style sweetcorn (corn)	1½ lb canned
425ml (¾ pt)	soya (soy) milk	2 cups
1 tbs	grated onion	1 tbs
1 heaped tsp	curry powder	1 heaped tsp
1 tbs	vegan margarine	1 tbs
Sprinkling	paprika	Sprinkling

1 Combine all the ingredients except the last two in a liquidizer and blend thoroughly.
2 Pour the soup into a saucepan and heat gently. Simmer for 10 minutes.
3 Add the margarine and mix well.
4 Sprinkle paprika on the top when serving.

Note: This is a delicious creamy soup which is quick and easy to make.

Miso Soup

1	onion	1
1 large	carrot	1 large
1 small or ½ large head	white cabbage	1 small or ½ large head
1 tbs	vegetable oil	1 tbs
3 tbs	miso	3 tbs
1140ml (2 pts)	water	5 cups

1 Slice the onions thinly, cut the carrot into matchsticks, and shred the cabbage.
2 Sauté the onions for 2 minutes, then add the carrot and cabbage and sauté them for 5-10 minutes more, stirring constantly.

3 Add the water, bring to the boil and simmer for 20 minutes.
4 Remove some of the liquid and mix it in a cup with the miso until it is dissolved. Add this to the soup, mix thoroughly and serve.

Note: This is a version of a Japanese classic.

Avocado and Cashew Soup *good.*

85g (3 oz)	cashews	⅔ cup
1 large	avocado	1 large
340ml (⅔ pt)	water	1½ cups
1 tsp	dried oregano	1 tsp
As required	sea salt	As required

1 Grind the cashews finely in a liquidizer. Add the water and blend thoroughly.
2 Peel and dice the avocado. Add the liquidizer, along with the seasonings and blend well.
3 Pour into a saucepan and heat until just below simmer point.

Note: In this soup the ingredients are not cooked but only heated slightly.
Quick and Easy.

Potato and Carrot Soup *good.*

680g (1½ lb)	potatoes	1½ lb
455g (1 lb)	carrots	1 lb
1 small	onion	1 small
85g (3oz)	vegan margarine	⅓ cup
1140ml (2 pts)	water	5 cups
As required	sea salt	As required
As required	freshly ground black pepper	As required
As required	grated nutmeg	As required
As required	chopped parsley	As required

1 Peel the potatoes and cut them into slices. Slice the onion and carrots.
2 Melt half the margarine, add the onion and cook until softened but not brown. Add the potatoes and carrots and stir well.
3 Add a little salt and the water and cook until the vegetables are tender.
4 Cool slightly, then put into a liquidizer and purée.
5 Return the soup to the pan, reheat and season to taste. Stir in the remaining margarine and a little freshly chopped parsley.

Note: For those who like a blended soup, this one should prove a favourite, as the potatoes give it a pleasant creaminess.

Vegetable Soup

2	onions	2
3	carrots	3
2 sticks	celery	2 sticks
1 tbs	vegan margarine	1 tbs
1 small tin (c.5 oz)	tomato purée (paste)	5 oz canned
1	vegetable stock cube	1
As required	sea salt	As required
As required	freshly ground black pepper	As required
30g (1 oz)	wholewheat spaghetti	1 oz
55g (2 oz)	fresh or frozen green beans	⅛ cup
115g (4 oz)	cabbage	1 cup
2 heaped tbs	wholewheat flour	2 heaped tbs
1140ml (2 pts)	water	5 cups

1 Slice the onions, carrots and celery.
2 Melt the margarine and add the vegetables, sautéeing gently for 3-4 minutes without browning. Stir in the tomato purée (paste), stock cube, water, salt and pepper.
3 Bring to the boil and simmer for 10 minutes.
4 Break the spaghetti into small pieces, add them to the soup and simmer for a further 10 minutes.
5 Shred the cabbage and beans. Add them to the soup and simmer for 5-10 minutes longer until the spaghetti is tender.
6 Mix the flour with a little cold water in a cup. Add this to the soup, stirring well, and cook for another minute before serving.

Note: This soup is ideal for those who prefer a soup in which the ingredients remain recognisable.

Vegetable Soup with Miso

2	carrots	2
115-170g (4-6 oz)	white turnip	4-6 oz
4 sticks	celery	4 sticks
2	onions	2
850ml (1½ pts)	water	3¾ cups
30g (1 oz)	broken cashews	3 tbs
2 tbs	miso	2 tbs
1 tsp	garlic salt	1 tsp
2 tbs	parsley	2 tbs
1 tsp	dried basil	1 tsp

1 Chop the carrots, turnip, celery and onion. Put them in the water in a saucepan. Bring to the boil, then lower heat, cover and simmer for about 15 minutes.
2 Pour about half the liquid and vegetables (the precise quantity does not matter at all) into a liquidizer, leave to cool slightly. Add the cashews, miso, garlic, salt, parsley and basil and blend well.

3 Pour the blended mixture into the unblended soup, stir well and reheat very gently. Serve immediately.

Note: This soup is a compromise between a blended and unblended one, offering the texture of the vegetables in a creamy base.

Curried Pea Soup

1 tin (c.400g)	peas	1 can (c.14-16g)
1 tbs	grated onion	1 tbs
1 heaped tsp	curry powder	1 heaped tsp
As required	sea salt	As required
30g (1 oz)	vegan margarine	2 tbs
570ml (1 pt)	soya (soy) milk	2½ cups

1 Blend all the ingedients together in a liquidizer except the margarine.
2 Pour the mixture into a saucepan and heat gently. Add the margarine and mix in well.
3 Serve when well heated.

Note: This is about the fastest soup I know. It tastes better if superior quality tinned peas are used.
Quick and Easy.

Cream of Peanut Butter Soup

2 tops	celery	2 tops
285ml (½ pt)	water	1⅓ cups
1 tsp	sea salt	1 tsp
4 sticks	celery	4 sticks
1 tbs	grated onion	1 tbs
30g (1 oz)	vegan margarine	2 tbs
2 tbs	wholewheat flour	2 tbs
3 tbs	peanut butter	3 tbs
425ml (¾ pt)	soya (soy) milk	2 cups
As required	freshly ground black pepper	As required
Sprinkling	paprika	Sprinkling

1 Chop the celery tops and cook them in the water with the salt for about 10 minutes. Strain, reserving the water but discarding the celery tops.
2 Chop the celery finely. Sauté this with the onion in the margarine for 2 minutes.
3 Stir in the flour. When well blended, add the peanut butter and mix well.
4 Stir in the milk and celery water. Stir over a low heat until the mixture boils. Simmer for 2-3 minutes.
5 Season to taste with black pepper. When serving, sprinkle with paprika.

good

Chilled Avocado and Tomato Soup

2	tomatoes	2
1 small	onion	1 small
½ small	green pepper	½ small
1 large	avocado	1 large
570ml (1 pt)	tomato juice	2½ cups
2 tsp	lemon juice	2 tsp

1 Peel and chop the tomatoes. Quarter the onion. Dice the green pepper. Peel and dice the avocado.
2 Pour the tomato and lemon juice into the liquidizer, add the remaining ingredients and blend well.
3 Chill before serving.

Note: This is a good choice for a hot summer's day. Quick and Easy.

Lentil and Dulse Soup

2	onions	2
2 cloves	garlic	2 cloves
2 tbs	vegetable oil	2 tbs
170g (6 oz)	red lentils	1 cup
1140ml (2 pts)	water	5 cups
1	vegetable stock cube	1
30g (1 oz)	dulse	1 oz
As required	sea salt	As required
As required	freshly ground black pepper	As required

1 Chop the onions and garlic finely. Sauté in the oil in a saucepan 3-4 minutes.
2 Rinse and add the lentils and water; bring to the boil. Crumble and stir in the stock cube. Chop the dulse and add it to the saucepan. Turn heat as low as possible, cover pan, and simmer for 20-30 minutes, stirring occasionally. Taste for seasoning, add sea salt if necessary (some stock cubes are quite salty) and freshly ground black pepper to taste.

Note: Dulse is a home-grown sea vegetable which gives a lovely flavour to soup.

Curried Avocado Soup

2	avocados	2
2 tsp	curry powder	2 tsp
140ml (¼ pt)	soya (soy) milk	⅔ cup
Juice of 1	lemon	Juice of 1
570ml (1 pt)	water	2½ cups
½	vegetable stock cube	½
As required	sea salt	As required
As required	freshly ground black pepper	As required
2 tbs	finely chopped parsley	2 tbs

1 Peel the avocados and put the flesh into a liquidizer.
2 Add the curry powder, milk and lemon juice and blend.
3 Heat the water to boiling point and pour half of it into the liquidizer, together with the half vegetable stock cube. Blend again.
4 Add the avocado mixture to the remainder of the hot water in a saucepan and stir over a gentle heat until mixture is warmed through. Taste and season.
5 Sprinkle with parsley before serving.

Note: As with other avocado soups, it is not advisable to bring this to the boil, but just warm it gently. This recipe does not make a large quantity, but it is rich. Quick and Easy.

Wakame and Miso Soup

30g (1 oz)	dried wakame	1 oz
1 large	onion	1 large
2 tbs	vegetable oil	2 tbs
1 litre (1¾ pts)	water	4 cups
2-3 tsp	miso	2-3 tsp

1 Soak the wakame in cold water for about 10 minutes. Drain and chop.
2 Chop the onion finely and sauté in the oil until lightly browned. Pour in the water and bring to the boil. Add the wakame, lower the heat, then cover the pan and simmer for 10-15 minutes.
3 Remove a little of the liquid from the pan and mix it in a small bowl with the miso. Return it to the pan, leave the pan uncovered on the lowest possible heat for a minute or two then serve immediately.

Note: Wakame is a sea vegetable traditionally used in Japanese miso soups.

Cream of Mushroom Miso Soup

455g (1 lb)	mushrooms	8 cups
1	onion	1
2 sticks	celery	2 sticks
55g (2 oz)	vegan margarine	¼ cup
425ml (¾ pt)	water or vegetable stock	2 cups
2 tbs	miso	2 tbs
2 tbs	wholewheat flour	2 tbs
425ml (¾ pt)	soya (soy) milk	2 cups
As required	freshly ground black pepper	As required
3 tbs	finely chopped parsley	3 tbs

1 Chop the mushrooms, onion and celery. Melt half the margarine in a saucepan and add the vegetables. Sauté for about 3 minutes.
2 Add the water or stock, bring to the boil, then lower the heat, cover and simmer for about 10 minutes.
3 Pour the mixture into a liquidizer along with the miso, and leave to cool slightly. Blend thoroughly.
4 Meanwhile, melt the remainder of the margarine and stir in the flour. Gradually stir in the milk, very slowly to avoid lumps, and bring to the boil. Boil for a minute or two, then lower heat to the barest minimum and pour in the contents of the liquidizer.
5 Season with pepper, and serve topped with the parsley.

Note: Traditional miso soups are not creamy, but there is no reason why this ingredient should not be used in a non-traditional soup. It should not boil after the miso is added.
Suitable for a dinner party.

Split Pea and Wakame Soup

115g (4 oz)	split peas	¾ cup
1140ml (2 pts)	water	5 cups
30g (1 oz)	wakame	1 oz
2	onions	2
225g (½ lb)	carrots	½ lb
2 tbs	tahini	2 tbs
As required	sea salt and/or soy sauce	As required

1 Cover the split peas with cold water and leave to soak overnight.
2 Drain the peas, then cover with the water and bring to the boil. Lower the heat, then cover and simmer for 15-20 minutes. Meanwhile, cover the wakame with cold water and leave to soak.
3 Chop the onion and carrot finely. Drain and chop the wakame, discarding the tough centre. Add these ingredients to the saucepan.
4 Continue simmering the soup for a further 20-25 minutes. Remove from the heat, add the tahini and soy sauce (plus sea salt if desired) to taste. Serve immediately.

Note: Split pea soup is an old favourite; the addition of a sea vegetable (wakame) makes it even more nutritious – and delicious.

Creamy Chestnut and Celery Soup

2	onions	2
4 sticks	celery	4 sticks
30g (1 oz)	vegan margarine	2 tbs
425ml (¾ pt)	vegetable stock or water	2 cups
225g (½ lb)	dried chestnuts which have been soaked in a thermos flask (see p.77)	½ lb
285ml (½ pt)	soya (soy) milk	1⅓ cup
As required	sea salt	As required
As required	freshly ground black pepper	As required

1 Chop the onions and celery finely. Heat the margarine in a saucepan and sauté them for a few minutes.
2 Add the stock or water and bring to the boil. Chop the chestnuts coarsely and add them to the pan. Lower the heat, cover, and simmer for 10-15 minutes.
3 Pour the milk into a liquidizer and add about half the soup mixture. Blend thoroughly and return to the pan, stirring well. Season to taste. Simmer over a low heat for a few minutes longer before serving.

Note: The combination of chestnut and celery has long been popular, and also works well as a soup.

Coconutty Sweetcorn and Red Pepper Soup

2	onions	2
3 tbs	vegetable oil	3 tbs
1	red pepper	1
2 cloves	garlic	2 cloves
1-2 tsp	powdered ginger	1-2 tsp
850ml (1½ pts)	water	2 cups
225g (½ lb)	fresh, frozen or tinned (canned) sweetcorn (corn)	½ lb
115g (4 oz)	creamed coconut	½ cup
As required	sea salt	As required
As required	freshly ground black pepper	As required

1 Chop the onions finely. Sauté in the oil for a few minutes.
2 Chop the red pepper finely and add it to the saucepan. Crush the garlic and stir it in. Sauté for a few minutes longer.
3 Add the ginger to the pan and stir well. Pour in the water, and bring to the boil. Add the corn and creamed coconut (chopped or grated). Add seasoning to taste. Cover the pan and simmer for a few more minutes before serving.

Note: I was trying for a Malaysian flavour with this soup, but my partner thought it was Caribbean!
Quick and Easy.

White Bean and Black Olive Soup

2	onions	2
3 cloves	garlic	3 cloves
3 tbs	olive oil	3 tbs
850ml (1½ pts)	vegetable stock or water	3¾ cups
455g (1 lb) or 2 tins (425g each)	cooked drained haricot (navy) beans	3 cups or 14-16 oz canned
16	black olives	16
Juice of 1 small	lemon	Juice of 1 small
As required	sea salt	As required
As required	freshly ground black pepper	As required

1 Chop the onions finely. Crush the garlic. Sauté them in the oil for a few minutes until they begin to go brown.
2 Add the stock and beans. Chop the olives and add them to the pan. Bring to the boil, then lower the heat and simmer, uncovered, for a few minutes.
3 Add the lemon juice and season to taste. (Taste before adding salt as olives can be salty enough for this soup to require no more.) Serve piping hot.

Note: This soup has a Mediterranean flavour.
Quick and Easy.

Curried Lentil Soup with Mushrooms

2	onions	2
2-3 cloves	garlic	2-3 cloves
2 tbs	vegetable oil	2 tbs
115g (4 oz)	mushrooms	2 cups
½ tsp	ground coriander	½ tsp
½ tsp	turmeric	½ tsp
½ tsp	ground cumin	½ tsp
½ tsp	ground ginger	½ tsp
185g (6 oz)	red lentils	1 cup
850ml (1½ pts)	water	4 cups
30g (2 oz)	creamed coconut	¼ cup
As required	sea salt	As required
As required	freshly ground black pepper	As required

1 Chop the onions and garlic finely. Heat the oil in a saucepan and sauté them for a few minutes. Chop the mushrooms and add them to the pan; cook for a few minutes longer.
2 Stir in the spices and cook for a minute or two more, then add the lentils and water, plus a little sea salt. Bring to the boil, then lower the heat, cover and cook for 15-20 minutes, until the lentils are soft.
3 Chop or grate the creamed coconut and stir it into the pan. Taste for seasoning and add more salt if required and black pepper.

Note: Curry powder can be used instead of the suggested spices for this soup, but the results will not be nearly as nice.

4
Salads

Cabbage and Apple Salad

1 small	white cabbage	1 small
3	sweet apples	3
2 sticks	celery	2 sticks
2 small	raw beetroots (beets)	2 small
2	carrots	2
2 tbs	raisins	2 tbs
2 very ripe	bananas	2 very ripe
As required	vegetable oil	As required
As required	lemon juice	As required

1 Chop the celery finely, grate the apple and beetroot and shred the cabbage.
2 Mix the vegetables together with the raisins in a bowl.
3 Mash the bananas. Add the oil and lemon juice, beating well after each addition until the texture resembles that of mayonnaise.
4 Mix the dressing well with the salad and serve.

Note: This is a vitamin-packed winter salad.

Macaroni and Kidney Bean Salad

455g (1 lb) or 2 tins (c.400g each)	cooked, drained kidney beans	2½ cups or 2 cans (c.14-16 oz each)
225g (½ lb)	wholewheat macaroni	2 cups
4 sticks	celery	4 sticks
½	green pepper	½
4	spring onions (scallions)	4
As required	sea salt	As required
As required	freshly ground black pepper	As required
5 tbs	vegetable oil	5 tbs
3 tbs	cider vinegar or wine vinegar	3 tbs
85g (3 oz)	walnuts	⅔ cup
2 (or more) tbs	Smokey Snaps (soy bakon bits)	2 (or more) tbs
As required	crisp lettuce leaves	As required

1 Drain the beans. Cook the macaroni, rinse in cold water and drain. Combine the macaroni and beans.
2 Chop the celery, green pepper and spring onions (scallions) finely. Chop the walnuts coarsely.
3 Add the vegetables and nuts to the macaroni and bean mixture.
4 Combine the oil, vinegar and seasoning. Add this to the salad and mix well.
5 Turn the mixture into a lettuce-lined bowl, sprinkle with Smokey Snaps (soy bakon bits) and serve.

Note: This is a high-protein, filling main dish salad.

Italian Bread Salad

455g (1 lb)	stale wholewheat bread	1 lb
140ml (¼ pt)	water	⅔ cup
1 clove	garlic	1 clove
1	onion	1
200g (6 oz)	tomatoes	¾ cup
3 tbs	vegetable oil	3 tbs
1 tbs	cider vinegar or wine vinegar	1 tbs
As required	sea salt	As required
As required	freshly ground black pepper	As required
2 tsp or 2 tbs	dried basil fresh basil	2 tsp or 2 tbs

1 Dice the bread, soak it in the water for 10 minutes or more. Drain out the surplus moisture.
2 Crush the garlic and rub the salad bowl with it.
3 Chop the onion finely and peel and dice the tomatoes.
4 Combine the bread with the onion and tomatoes. Add the oil and vinegar with the seasoning and mix lightly together.
5 Sprinkle with basil and serve.

Note: This salad provides a good way of recycling bread that has not been eaten while fresh.

Caribbean Salad

1 tin (c.400g)	pineapple chunks	1 can (14-16 oz)
½	green pepper	½
½	red pepper	½
4 sticks	celery	4 sticks
4 tbs	coarsely chopped walnuts	4 tbs
4-6 tbs	vegan mayonnaise	4-6 tbs
As required	lemon juice	As required

1 Chop the peppers and celery and drain the pineapple.
2 Combine all the ingredients and serve.

Note: This salad is best served as a starter or accompaniment rather than a main dish.
Quick and Easy.

Chick Pea and Walnut Salad

455g (1 lb) or 2 tins (c.400g each)	cooked drained chick peas (garbanzo beans)	2½ cups or 2 cans (c.14-16 oz each)
115g (4 oz)	walnuts	¾ cup
6 tbs	lemon juice	6 tbs
4 tbs	vegetable oil	4 tbs
2 cloves	crushed garlic	2 cloves
1 tsp	sea salt	1 tsp
Hearts of 2 heads	Cos (Romaine) lettuce	Hearts of 2 heads

1 Drain the beans. Mash them until they are the consistency of coarse crumbs.
2 Chop the walnuts finely and combine them with the mashed beans.
3 Combine the lemon juice, oil, garlic and salt and mix this dressing with the walnuts and beans.
4 Serve at room temperature, spooned into the centre of a shallow dish. Surround with lettuce leaves to use as scoopers.

Note: This is a high-protein Middle-Eastern mixture which serves four as a luncheon dish or eight as a starter. Quick and Easy.

Green Bean and Almond Salad

455g (1 lb)	fresh or frozen green beans	1 lb
55g (2 oz)	almonds	½ cup
4	tomatoes	4
1 small	onion	1 small
30g (1 oz)	vegan margarine	2 tbs
55g (2 oz)	raisins or sultanas golden seedless raisins	⅓ cup
2 tbs	vegetable oil	2 tbs
2 tbs	cider vinegar or wine vinegar	2 tbs
As required	sea salt	As required
As required	freshly ground black pepper	As required

1 Wash, string and slice the beans and cook them until tender. Drain them well and leave to cool.
2 Shred the almonds finely. Peel and chop the tomatoes and onions.
3 Melt the margarine in a saucepan, add the onion, almonds and sultanas and sauté them until the onion is tender.
4 Combine the oil, vinegar and seasoning.
5 Mix together the beans, onion mixture, tomatoes and dressing in a bowl.
6 Chill and serve.

Note: In Mediterranean countries cooked vegetables are often dressed with oil and vinegar and served cold as salads, but the addition of nuts and raisins in this recipe makes it distinctive and gives it more substance. It serves four as a light luncheon dish or eight as a starter.

Brussels Sprouts Salad

455g (1 lb)	Brussels sprouts	1 lb
4	carrots	4
2 tbs	lemon juice	2 tbs
4 tbs	vegan mayonnaise	4 tbs
4 tbs	chopped dates	4 tbs
1 bunch	watercress	1 bunch

1 Coarsely grate the sprouts and finely grate the carrots.
2 Mix these together with the lemon juice, dates and dressing.
3 Serve on a bed of watercress.

Note: While cabbage is well known as a salad ingredient, people rarely think of using Brussels sprouts, which are just as nutritious.
Quick and Easy.

Potato and Artichoke Heart Salad

455g (1 lb)	potatoes	1 lb
1 tin (c.400g)	artichoke hearts	1 can (14-16 oz)
4 tbs	olive oil	4 tbs
As required	sea salt	As required
As required	freshly ground black pepper	As required
2 tsp	lemon juice	2 tsp
55g (2 oz)	walnuts	½ cup
As required	crisp lettuce leaves	As required

1 Cook the potatoes until tender. (They can be peeled if desired, but this is not necessary.) Quarter them and sprinkle with 1 tbs olive oil while still warm.
2 Chop the walnuts and combine them with the potatoes.
3 Drain the canned artichoke hearts and arrange them on lettuce leaves with the potatoes and walnuts.
4 Combine the remaining olive oil with the lemon juice and seasoning and pour over the salad.

Note: Canned artichokes are quite expensive, but they make this Mediterranean style salad something special. Cold-pressed extra virgin olive oil should, of course, be used.

Salad Niçoise

455g (1 lb)	fresh or frozen French beans	1 lb
6 large	tomatoes	6 large
2 large	potatoes	2 large
4 tbs	olive oil	4 tbs
2 tbs	cider vinegar or wine vinegar	2 tbs
¼ tsp	mustard powder	¼ tsp
As required	sea salt	As required
As required	freshly ground black pepper	As required
1 tbs	capers	1 tbs
55g (2 oz)	olives	½ cup

1 Cook the beans and potatoes (separately) until tender. Leave to cool and slice them.
2 Quarter the tomatoes and arrange them with the beans and potatoes on individual salad plates.
3 Combine the olive oil, vinegar, mustard and seasoning and pour this over the salad.
4 Chop the olives finely, combine them with the capers and sprinkle over the salad.

Note: In restaurants this traditional salad is normally barred to vegetarians because it contains anchovies: here the capers add a piquant, salty taste which is vegan.

Green Bean and Pimento Salad

1 tin (c.225g)	pimentos	1 can (c.8 oz)
455g (1 lb)	fresh or frozen sliced green beans	1 cup
2	carrots	2
4 tbs	vegan mayonnaise	4 tbs

1 Drain the pimentos and slice them into thin strips.
2 Cook the beans until just tender; drain and leave to cool.
3 Grate the carrots coarsely.
4 Combine all the ingredients and serve.

Note: Canned pimentos are rarely used for anything more than a garnish, though they have a lovely, sweetish flavour. This is a side salad rather than a main dish.

Curried Butter Bean Salad

455g (1 lb)	cooked butter beans	2½ cups
or 2 tins	(lima beans)	or 2 14-16
(c.400g)		oz cans
140ml (¼ pt)	vegan mayonnaise	⅔ cup
1 heaped tbs	mango chutney	1 heaped tbs
1 heaped tbs	desiccated (shredded)	1 heaped tbs
	coconut	
2 heaped tsp	curry powder	2 heaped tsp

1 Drain the beans.
2 Combine the mayonnaise, chutney, curry powder and coconut. Add the beans, mix and serve.

Note: Nothing could be simpler than this dish.
Quick and Easy. Suitable for One.

Stuffed Pear Salad

4	ripe pears	4
170g (6 oz)	dates	1 cup
85g (3 oz)	walnuts	⅔ cup
3 tbs	vegetable oil	3 tbs
1½ tbs	lemon juice	1½ tbs
As required	crisp lettuce leaves	As required

1 Chop the dates and walnuts. Peel and halve the pears, remove the cores and some of the flesh to leave a hollow for the filling. (The flesh can be chopped into the filling.)
2 Combine the dates, walnuts, oil and lemon juice with the chopped flesh and pile the mixture into the pear halves.
3 Serve on crisp lettuce leaves.

Note: This nutritious dish is sweet enough to act as main dish and dessert at the same time.
Quick and Easy. Suitable for One.

Stuffed Banana Salad

4 small	bananas	4 small
55g (2 oz)	peanut butter	2 oz
30g (1 oz)	raisins or sultanas	1/6 cup
	(golden seedless raisins)	
2 tbs	vegan mayonnaise	2 tbs
2 tbs	salted peanuts	2 tbs
As required	crisp lettuce leaves	As required

1 Chop the raisins finely. Mix them together with the peanut butter.
2 Peel and split the bananas lengthwise and fill them sandwich fashion with the peanut butter-raisin mixture.
3 Spoon the dressing over the bananas and top with the salted peanuts.
4 Serve on crisp lettuce leaves.

Note: When I lived on my own I often made this for lunch.
Quick and Easy. Suitable for One.

Mexican-style Potato Salad

455g (1 lb)	new potatoes	1 lb
1 tbs	vegetable oil	1 tbs
1 tbs	cider vinegar or wine	1 tbs
	vinegar	
1 tin	sweetcorn (corn)	1 can
(c.340g)		(12 oz)
140ml (¼ pt)	soya (soy) yogurt	⅔ cup
As required	sea salt	As required
As required	freshly ground black	As required
	pepper	
1 bunch	watercress	1 bunch
2 tbs	Smokey Snaps	2 tbs
	(soy bakon bits)	

1 Cook the potatoes until tender, drain and dice them.
2 Combine the oil and vinegar, pour this over diced potatoes and leave until cold.
3 Drain the corn and mix it with the yogurt and seasoning. Combine this with the potatoes.
4 Pile on to a serving dish and surround with sprigs of watercress. Sprinkle Smokey Snaps (soy bakon bits) over the salad just before serving.

Note: It is better to use freshly cooked potatoes for this so that the vinaigrette can soak into them, but if you have leftover potatoes, use these instead.

Christmas Salad

115g (4 oz)	hazelnuts or almonds	¾ cup
As required	Chinese leaves	As required
2	avocados	2
As required	lemon juice	As required
4	kiwi fruits	4
8	fresh lychees	8
4 tbs	vegetable oil	4 tbs
1 tbs	cider vinegar or wine vinegar	1 tbs
As required	sea salt	As required
As required	freshly ground black pepper	As required
1 small	onion	1 small

1 Toast the nuts and set aside.
2 Slice the Chinese leaves to make a bed on a large platter or four individual plates.
3 Peel and cube the avocados, sprinkling them with lemon juice at the same time. Arrange on the bed of leaves.
4 Peel and slice the kiwi fruits and arrange with the avocado cubes.
5 Peel the lychees and cut into small pieces. Scatter them among the avocado and kiwi fruit.
6 Mix the oil and vinegar together and sprinkle over the salad. Season to taste.
7 Scatter the toasted nuts on top.
8 Chop the onion very finely and scatter over the salad. Serve.

Note: This salad is perfect for the holiday season.

Tabbouleh

225g (½ lb)	bulgur wheat	1⅓ cups
55g (2 oz)	fresh parsley	2 cups
4 or 5	spring onions (scallions)	4 or 5
2 tbs	fresh mint or	2 tbs
or 2 tsp	dried mint (optional)	or 2 tsp
Juice of	lemon	Juice of
1 small		1 small
4 tbs	olive oil	4 tbs
As required	sea salt	As required
As required	freshly ground black pepper	As required

1 Cover the wheat with plenty of cold water and leave to soak for 45 minutes to one hour.
2 Line a colander with a clean tea towel (dish towel) and pour the bulgur wheat into it, allowing the water to drain through. Gather up the edges of the towel and squeeze the wheat, to expel as much of the liquid as possible. Place in a large mixing bowl.
3 Mince the parsley, spring onions (scallions), and the fresh mint if used. Add to the wheat. Pour in the lemon

juice and olive oil and stir well.
4 Season to taste and serve.

Note: No vegan cookery book would be complete without a version of this Middle-Eastern classic.

American-style Tabbouleh

170g (6 oz)	bulgur wheat	1⅓ cups
55g (2 oz)	fresh parsley	2 cups
1	tomato	1
3	spring onions (scallions)	3
1 stick	celery	1 stick
4 tsp	dried mint	4 tsp
or 2 tbs	fresh	or 2 tbs
⅛	cucumber	⅛
455g (1 lb) or 2 tins (c.400g each)	cooked drained chick peas (garbanzo beans)	2½ cups or 2 cans (c.14-16 oz each)
Juice of 2	lemons	Juice of 2
4 tbs	olive oil	4 tbs
As required	sea salt	As required
As required	freshly ground black pepper	As required

1 In a large bowl put the bulgur wheat with lots of cold water to cover it, and leave to soak for about an hour.
2 Drain well and squeeze out as much of the water as possible. (For an efficient way of doing that see the previous recipe.)
3 Chop the parsley, tomato, spring onions (scallions), celery, mint and cucumber finely. Add to the bulgur wheat, along with the beans. Mix well.
4 Pour the lemon juice and olive oil over everything and mix in thoroughly. Season to taste.
5 Serve chilled.

Note: The addition of beans turns this into a substantial and filling dish.

Lentil Salad

2	onions	2
2 cloves	garlic	2 cloves
225g (½ lb)	brown lentils	1⅓ cups
Juice of 1	lemon	Juice of 1
2 tsp	cumin seeds	2 tsp
As required	sea salt	As required
As required	freshly ground black pepper	As required

1 Chop the onions. Heat the oil in a large saucepan, and sauté the onions until lightly browned.
2 Crush the garlic.
3 Add the lentils, garlic, lemon juice, and enough water

to cover the lentils, about ¾-1 inch (2-2.5 cm) over the surface. Cover, bring to the boil, then lower the heat and simmer.

4 Crush the cumin seeds. After the lentils have been cooking for about 15 minutes add the cumin, salt and pepper. Cover the saucepan again, and leave to simmer for a further 10-15 minutes, by which time the water should be absorbed and the lentils tender (if not, then raise the heat and uncover the saucepan).

5 Leave to cool, then chill in the refrigerator.

Note: This is another traditional Middle-Eastern dish. There is no need to soak the lentils beforehand.

Chick Pea Salad with Tahini Dressing

455g (1 lb) or 2 tins (c.400g each)	cooked drained chick peas (garbanzo beans)	2½ cups or 2 cans (c.14-16 oz each)
3-4 tbs	tahini	3-4 tbs
Juice of 2	lemons	Juice of 2
4-6 tbs	water	4-6 tbs
1-2 cloves	garlic	1-2 cloves
4	spring onions (scallions)	4
2 tsp	whole cumin	2 tsp
3 tbs	finely chopped parsley	3 tbs
As required	sea salt	As required
As required	freshly ground black pepper	As required

1 In a small mixing bowl cream the tahini with the lemon juice and water.

2 Crush the garlic, chop the spring onions (scallions) finely, and grind the cumin. Add these ingredients to the tahini and mix well.

3 Pour the dressing ingredients over the cooked and drained chick peas (garbanzo beans). Season and sprinkle with parsley.

Note: This has basically the same ingredients as hummus, but the beans are left whole for an interesting contrast of textures.

Quick and Easy. Suitable for One.

Black-eyed Bean Salad

170g (6 oz)	dried black-eyed beans	1 cup
Juice of 1	lemon	Juice of 1
3 tbs	olive oil	3 tbs
45g (1½ oz)	fresh parsley	1½ cups
As required	sea salt	As required
As required	freshly ground black pepper	As required

1 The night before, cover the beans with boiling water and leave to soak overnight.

2 In the morning, drain them, cover with lots of fresh water, bring to the boil, then lower the heat. Sprinkle in a little lemon juice, then cover and leave to simmer until tender, about 45 minutes. After about half an hour add a little more lemon juice (this keeps the white colour of the beans from becoming brown), and a few minutes before the end of the cooking time add a little sea salt.

3 Drain the beans, and while still hot, pour the remainder of the lemon juice and the olive oil over them. Stir well. Leave to cool, then chill.

4 Chop the parsley finely. Just before serving stir the parsley into the beans, and add salt and pepper to taste.

Note: This is a French-style salad. Other fresh herbs can be used in addition to, or instead of, parsley.

Three Bean Salad

225g (½ lb)	fresh or frozen green beans	½ lb
1	onion	1
225g (½ lb)	cooked drained kidney beans	1⅓ cups
225g (½ lb)	cooked drained chick peas (garbanzo beans)	1⅓ cups
4 tbs	olive oil	4 tbs
4 tbs	cider vinegar or wine vinegar	4 tbs
As required	sea salt	As required
As required	freshly ground black pepper	As required

1 Cook the green beans in a little salted water until just tender. Drain and cool. (If the beans are whole then slice them.)

2 Slice the onion very thinly.

3 Combine the kidney beans, chick peas (garbanzo beans), and green beans in a bowl. Add the onion. Pour over the oil, vinegar and seasoning and mix well.

4 Cover the bowl and refrigerate for several hours to marinate before serving.

Note: This is a version of the American classic.

Millet Salad

170g (6 oz)	millet	¾ cup
As required	sea salt	As required
As required	freshly ground black pepper	As required
½	green pepper	½
4	spring onions (scallions)	4
2 sticks	celery	2 sticks
30g (1 oz)	sunflower seeds	⅓ cup
2 tbs	olive oil	2 tbs
1 tbs	cider vinegar or wine vinegar	1 tbs
2 tbs	minced parsley	2 tbs

1 Cook the millet until tender in three times its volume of water, with a little sea salt added (about 20 minutes). Cool, then chill.
2 Chop finely the green pepper, spring onions (scallions) and celery. Toast the sunflower seeds under a grill (broiler) until lightly browned.
3 Fluff the millet with a fork. Add the oil and vinegar and mix in.
4 Stir in the chopped vegetables and parsley and the toasted sunflower seeds. Adjust the seasoning as required.

Note: Millet is a very nutritious grain and in this recipe forms the basis of a tasty salad.

Fruit and Nut Coleslaw

1 small	white cabbage	1 small
2	dessert apples	2
1 tin (c.225g)	pineapple chunks	1 can (c.8 oz)
4 oz (115g)	salted peanuts	¾ cup
115g (4 oz)	vegan mayonnaise	½ cup

1 Shred the cabbage and dice the apple.
2 Combine with all the remaining ingredients in a salad bowl and serve.

Note: Now that vegan mayonnaise is readily available in health food shops, lovers of coleslaw can easily ring the changes.
Quick and Easy.

Piquant Coleslaw

1 head (900g/2 lb)	white cabbage	1 head (about 2 lb)
4 sticks	celery	4 sticks
1	green pepper	1
1 small	onion	1 small
A dozen	green olives	A dozen
4-6 tbs	vegan mayonnaise	4-6 tbs
A few drops	Tabasco sauce	A few drops

1 Grate the cabbage coarsely. Chop the celery and green pepper. Chop the onion and olives finely.
2 Combine all the ingredients in a large bowl and mix thoroughly.

Apple and Mushroom Coleslaw

1 small head (565-680g/ 1¼-1½ lb)	white cabbage	1 small head (1¼-1½ lb)
1 small	onion	1 small
2	sweet apples	2
115g (4 oz)	mushrooms	2 cups
4-6 tbs	vegan mayonnaise	4-6 tbs
Juice of 1	lemon	Juice of 1
As required	sea salt	As required
As required	freshly ground black pepper	As required

1 Grate the cabbage and onion.
2 Peel the apples if desired. Dice the apples and mushrooms.
3 Combine all the ingredients and chill.

High Protein Vegetable Salad

225g (½ lb)	white cabbage	2 cups
1 large	carrot	1 large
55g (2 oz)	mushrooms	1 cup
1 stick	celery	1 stick
¼	cucumber	¼
2 tbs	chopped parsley	2 tbs
115g (4 oz)	cooked red kidney beans	⅔ cup
55g (2 oz)	chopped cashews	½ cup
30g (1 oz)	sunflower seeds	1/5 cup
3 tbs	vegetable oil	3 tbs
Juice of 1	lemon	Juice of 1

1 Grate the cabbage and carrot coarsely. Chop the mushrooms, celery and cucumber finely.
2 In a bowl combine the cabbage, carrot, mushrooms, cucumber, parsley, beans, cashews and sunflower seeds.
3 Pour the oil and lemon juice over the mixture and combine thoroughly.
4 Cover the bowl and leave in refrigerator until serving time.

Vegetable-stuffed Avocados

115g (4 oz)	cooked red kidney beans	⅔ cup
115g (4 oz)	fresh (shelled) or frozen peas	⅔ cup
115g (4 oz)	carrots	⅔ cup
115g (4 oz)	celery	⅔ cup
6 tbs	vinaigrette dressing	6 tbs
4	avocados	4
As required	lettuce leaves	As required
1 tbs	minced parsley	1 tbs

1 Drain the beans. Cook the peas until tender. Dice the carrot and cook until tender. Cool.
2 Chop the celery. Combine with the beans, peas and carrots.
3 Mix in the vinaigrette. Leave to marinate for several hours.
4 Halve, stone and peel the avocados. Place on lettuce leaves.
5 Fill the avocados with the vegetable mixture, sprinkling parsley on top.

Note: The hollows of an avocado are perfect for filling with a mixture of beans and other vegetables. The vinaigrette can be a bought one or a simple mixture of olive oil and wine vinegar, with a pinch of mustard powder if desired.

Avocado and Mushroom Salad

225g (½ lb)	mushrooms	4 cups
1 clove	garlic	1 clove
Juice of 2 small	lemons	Juice of 2 small
90ml (3 fl oz)	olive oil	⅓ cup
2 tsp	mustard	2 tsp
4 medium	avocados	4 medium
4 boxes	mustard and cress	4 boxes

1 Slice the mushrooms thinly.
2 Crush the garlic and mix with the lemon juice, olive oil and mustard to make a dressing.
3 Combine the mushrooms and dressing and leave to marinate for about half an hour, turning occasionally.
4 Peel the avocados and slice into long thin pieces.
5 Arrange a bed of cress on four plates and arrange the avocado slices on top.
6 Spoon the mushroom mixture over the avocados.

Note: As a main dish for lunch this serves four, but it stretches to eight as a starter.
Suitable for a dinner party.

Avocado and Butter Bean (Lima Bean) Salad

1	red pepper	1
2 sticks	celery	2 sticks
½	cucumber	½
1 medium	carrot	1 medium
3 tbs	olive oil	3 tbs
1 tbs	lemon juice	1 tbs
As required	sea salt	As required
As required	freshly ground black pepper	As required
1 large or 2 small	avocado	1 large or 2 small
225g (½ lb) or 1 tin (c.400g)	cooked butter (lima) beans	½ lb or 1 can (14-16 oz)
1 large	firm tomato	1 large
6	black olives	6

1 De-seed and slice thinly the red pepper. Slice the celery and cucumber. Grate the carrot coarsely. Mix together.
2 Mix the oil, lemon juice and seasoning together.
3 Peel and dice the avocado. Add to the vegetable mixture, along with the beans. Pour the dressing over and mix thoroughly.
4 Pour the dressing over and mix thoroughly.
5 Slice the tomato. Chop the olives finely.
6 Sprinkle the chopped olives on top of the salad. Arrange the tomato slices in a border around the edge and serve at once.

Note: Avocados are very nutritious, and in this salad they are combined with other vegetables and beans, for a dish that is high in both vitamins and protein.

Macaroni and Avocado Salad

225g (½ lb)	wholewheat macaroni	2 cups
2	avocados	2
As required	lemon juice	As required
1	cucumber	1
1 or 2	spring onions (scallions)	1 or 2
140ml (¼ pt)	vegan mayonnaise	⅔ cup
2 tbs	finely chopped parsley	2 tbs
1 tbs	cider vinegar or wine vinegar	1 tbs
1 tsp	mustard	1 tsp
½ tsp	oregano	½ tsp
As required	sea salt	As required
As required	freshly ground black pepper	As required
2 tbs	Smokey Snaps (soy bakon bits)	2 tbs

1 Cook, drain and rinse the macaroni. Set aside.
2 Peel the avocado and dice. Sprinkle with lemon juice and set aside.
3 Dice the cucumber and set aside. Finally chop the spring onions (scallions).
4 In a bowl combine the mayonnaise, chopped spring onions (scallions), parsley, vinegar, mustard and seasoning. Mix thoroughly.
5 Add the macaroni, avocado, cucumber and Smokey Snaps (soy bakon bits). Mix well and serve.

Note: In this salad the avocado is rich and creamy, while the Smokey Snaps (soy bakon bits) add a crispy salty contrast.
Quick and Easy.

Mediterranean-style Pasta Salad

225g (½ lb)	wholewheat pasta shapes	½ lb
2-3	spring onions (scallions)	2-3
1 large	green or red pepper	1 large
A dozen	olives	A dozen
170g (6 oz)	smoked tofu	¾ cup
3 slices	wholewheat bread	3 slices
2 tbs	olive oil	2 tbs
2 tsp	cider vinegar or wine vinegar	2 tsp
Pinch	dried oregano	Pinch
¼ tsp	garlic salt	¼ tsp
As required	freshly ground black pepper	As required

1 Cook the pasta until tender, drain, place in a large salad bowl and cool.

2 Chop the spring onions (scallions) finely. Halve the olives and remove the stones. Chop the green or red pepper. Dice the tofu. Toast the bread lightly and cube it. Add all of these ingredients to the pasta in the bowl.
3 In a small cup combine with a fork the oil, vinegar, oregano, garlic salt and pepper. Pour the dressing over the salad, toss well, and serve.

Note: This can be made with pasta shells or any other pasta shape. The smoked tofu adds an appealing flavour, and an interesting texture, as well as protein.
Quick and Easy.

Mexican Frosted Cauliflower Salad

1 large	cauliflower	1 large
90ml (3 fl oz)	olive oil	⅓ cup
3 tbs	cider vinegar or wine vinegar	3 tbs
Pinch	garlic salt	Pinch
2	avocados	2
2 large	tomatoes	2 large
1 small	onion	1 small

1 Trim, wash and cook the cauliflower whole until just tender.
2 Chill the cooked cauliflower.
3 Combine the oil, vinegar, and garlic salt. Set aside.
4 Peel and mash the avocados. Peel and chop the tomatoes. Chop the onion finely.
5 Mix together the mashed avocado, tomato and onion and beat well.
6 Place the cauliflower on a serving plate. Pour the oil and vinegar dressing over it, then cover with the avocado mixture and serve at once.

Note: This is an impressive dish, with a complete cauliflower coated with an avocado dressing.

5
Starters, Spreads and Snacks

Tomato and Onion Savoury

55g (2 oz)	vegan margarine	¼ cup
2 large	onions	2 large
1 dozen medium-sized or large	very ripe tomatoes	1 dozen medium-sized or large
Pinch	dried oregano	Pinch
2 tsp	raw cane sugar	2 tsp
As required	sea salt	As required
As required	freshly ground black pepper	As required
8 slices	wholewheat toast spread with vegan margarine	8 slices

1 Slice the onions and chop the tomatoes coarsely.
2 Heat the margarine and sauté the sliced onions until golden. Add the tomatoes and seasonings.
3 Simmer gently for approximately 15 minutes until the tomatoes are tender.
4 Serve immediately on hot 'buttered' toast.

Note: For a quick lunch or snack, nothing could be simpler or tastier than this.
Quick and Easy.

Curry Spread

1	onion	1
2 cloves	garlic	2 cloves
55g (2 oz)	vegan margarine	¼ cup
1 tbs	curry powder	1 tbs
285ml (½ pt)	tomato ketchup	1⅓ cups
1 tsp	cider vinegar or wine vinegar	1 tsp
2	bay leaves	2
12	whole cloves	12

1 Slice the onions and chop the garlic finely.
2 Heat the margarine and sauté the onion and garlic until brown.
3 Stir in the curry powder and add the tomato ketchup, vinegar, cloves and bay leaves. Simmer for 20 minutes until thick then remove cloves and bay leaves.

Note: This is best served hot on wholewheat toast or chilled on crispbread or biscuits (crackers). It is quite a rich mixture, so spread it thinly.

Mushroom Spread

455g (1 lb)	mushrooms	8 cups
2	onions	2
1 tbs	vegetable oil	1 tbs
1 tbs	vegan margarine	1 tbs
1-2 tbs	soya (soy) yogurt	1-2 tbs
As required	sea salt	As required
As required	freshly ground black pepper	As required

1 Chop the mushrooms and onions.
2 Sauté them in the oil and margarine until tender.
3 Finely chop, mash, or blend the mixture in a liquidizer.
4 Add the yogurt and seasoning to taste. Chill.

Note: The flavour of mushrooms is so good that few additional ingredients are needed for this spread. Serve it chilled on wholewheat bread or toast.
Quick and Easy.

Grilled Garlic Mushrooms

455g (1 lb)	mushrooms	2 cups
115g (4 oz)	vegan margarine	4 oz
2 cloves	garlic	2 cloves
8 small slices	wholewheat toast	8 small slices

1 Clean the mushrooms and remove the stems.
2 Crush the garlic and sauté it in the margarine over a very low flame.
3 Fill the mushroom caps with the garlic-margarine mixture. Place in a shallow baking pan and grill (broil) for 5-7 minutes.
4 Soak up the margarine which has run out of the caps with the toast; place the mushrooms on the toast and serve hot.

Note: This is an ideal light lunch or snack for lovers of mushrooms and garlic.
Quick and Easy. Suitable for One.

Hummus

2 cloves	garlic	2 cloves
455g (1 lb) or 2 tins (c.400g each)	cooked chick peas (garbanzo beans)	2½ cups or 2 cans c.14-16 oz each)
Juice of 1	large lemon	Juice of 1
2 tbs	tahini	2 tbs
2 tbs	cumin seeds	2 tbs
3-5 tbs	bean liquid	3-5 tbs
As required	sea salt	As required

1 Drain the beans, reserving the liquid.
2 Put all the ingredients into a liquidizer and blend well. It will usually be necessary to scrape the sides a few times to get an even blend. For a thick solid hummus add only about 3 tbs of the cooking liquid from the beans; for a thin runny dip add more.

Note: It may be easy to find ready-made hummus these days, but nothing beats the home-made one. After experimenting a lot I have decided that it is the cumin seeds that make this version superior.
Quick and Easy

Haricot Bean and Olive Dip

455g (1 lb) or 2 tins (c.400g each)	cooked drained haricot (navy beans)	2½ cups or 2 cans c.14-16 oz each)
Juice of 2 small or 1 large	lemon(s)	Juice of 2 small or 1 large
8	black olives	8
4 tbs	olive oil	4 tbs
As required	sea salt	As required
As required	freshly ground black pepper	As required

1 Drain the beans and blend them thoroughly in a liquidizer, with the lemon juice.
2 Chop the olives finely and add them to the puréed beans, along with the olive oil and seasoning to taste. Stir well so that the mixture is thoroughly amalgamated.
3 Cover and refrigerate until serving time.

Note: Although hummus is the only bean-based dip known in Britain, in the Middle East you will find many others, as in this and the following recipe.
Quick and Easy.

Brown Lentil Dip

170g (6 oz)	brown lentils	1 cup
1	onion	1
285ml (½ pt)	water	1⅓ cups
Juice of ½	lemon	Juice of ½
As required	sea salt	As required
½ tsp	cayenne pepper	½ tsp
2 tbs	finely chopped parsley	2 tbs

1 Pour boiling water over the lentils, cover the pan and leave to soak for an hour or longer. Drain.
2 Chop the onion. Put the lentils into a saucepan with the chopped onion, and cover with the ½ pint (285ml/1⅓ cups water. Cover the saucepan, bring to the boil, lower the heat and leave to simmer until the lentils are tender and the water is absorbed – about 20-25 minutes.
3 Cool the lentils slightly, then liquidize with the lemon juice, sea salt and cayenne pepper.
4 Pour the lentil mixture into a shallow bowl, and garnish with the parsley. Serve chilled or at room temperature.

Aubergine and Tahini Dip

4 small or 2 large (about 900g (2 lb)	aubergines (eggplants)	4 small or 2 large (about 2 lb)
3 cloves	garlic	3 cloves
2 tbs	tahini	2 tbs
Juice of 2	lemons	Juice of 2
As required	sea salt	As required
As required	freshly ground black pepper	As required
3 tbs	finely chopped parsley	3 tbs

1 Prick the aubergines (eggplants) all over with a fork. Place them under a hot grill (broiler) and grill (broil) them, turning when necessary, until they are

thoroughly charred on all sides (a fork should pierce right through them with no resistance). An alternative method is to bake them in a very hot oven 450°F/230°C (Gas Mark 8) for about an hour. This is obviously the longer and more costly method in fuel, but the grill (broiler) method works best for small aubergines (eggplants) and the oven for large ones.

2 Rinse the aubergines (eggplants) under cold water and peel the charred skins off. (This does not have to be done immediately; if preferred they can be left to cool first.)

3 Chop the aubergine (eggplant) flesh. Chop the garlic. Put both into the liquidizer along with the tahini, lemon juice, salt and pepper. Blend thoroughly.

4 Stir the parsley in last. Serve either chilled or at room temperature.

Note: This is another Middle-Eastern classic, which appears under various names (baba ganoush is one) and with variants of ingredients in different countries. Charring the aubergines (eggplants) is essential for the flavour of this dish.
Suitable for a dinner party.

Falafel

225g (½ lb)	*chick peas (garbanzo beans)*	*1⅓ cups*
6	*spring onions (scallions)*	*6*
2 tsp	*coriander seeds*	*2 tsp*
2 tsp	*cumin seeds*	*2 tsp*
1 clove	*garlic*	*1 clove*
2 tsp	*chopped parsley*	*2 tsp*
1 tsp	*sea salt*	*1 tsp*
1 tsp	*bicarbonate of soda (baking soda)*	*1 tsp*
As required	*freshly ground black pepper*	*As required*
As required	*vegetable oil for frying*	*As required*

1 Cover the chick peas (garbanzo beans) with cold water and leave to soak overnight. Drain well and grind the beans – in a food processor, liquidizer (do them in at least 4 separate batches), or mincer.

2 Chop the spring onions (scallions) finely. Grind the coriander and cumin. Crush the garlic.

3 Combine all the remaining ingredients with the chick peas (garbanzo beans) in a large bowl. Mix thoroughly.

4 Form the mixture into small balls, about the size of a walnut (or smaller if desired). Deep-fry them in oil which has been heated to 350-375°F/180-190°C (or in a deep-fat fryer) until they are golden. Drain thoroughly on paper towels.

Note: The secret of this recipe is to use raw beans, not cooked ones. Serve them in pitta bread pockets with shredded lettuce and finely chopped cucumber and

tomato, with some tahini creamed with lemon juice and crushed garlic.

Cauliflower Sandwich Spread

1 medium	*cauliflower*	*1 medium*
4	*spring onions (scallions)*	*4*
2 tbs	*minced parsley*	*2 tbs*
4-5 tbs	*vegan mayonnaise*	*4-5 tbs*

1 Wash and break the cauliflower into florets. Steam in a small amount of water until just tender (only a few minutes).

2 Mash the cauliflower coarsely or chop it finely. Cool it. (Alternatively the cauliflower can be cooked the day before and left in the refrigerator overnight, to be mashed just before eating.)

3 Chop the spring onions (scallions) finely.

4 Combine all the ingredients and if they are not already chilled then chill before serving.

Note: Americans like to chop up white flesh of a fowl or fish and mix it with mayonnaise as a sandwich filling. This recipe uses the same method but with a white vegetable instead.

Chick Pea Spread

455g (1 lb) or 2 tins (c.400g each)	*cooked drain chick peas (garbanzo beans)*	*2½ cups or 2 cans (c.14-16 oz each)*
3 sticks	*celery*	*3 sticks*
4	*spring onions (scallions)*	*4*
4 tbs	*vegan mayonnaise*	*4 tbs*
As required	*sea salt*	*As required*
As required	*freshly ground black pepper*	*As required*

1 Drain the beans. Place them in a large bowl and mash them (a potato masher or pastry blender is useful for this). They do not have to be particularly smooth.

2 Chop the celery and spring onions (scallions) finely.

3 Combine all the ingredients, and use immediately or chill before serving.

Note: This is a variant on the same theme as above. Quick and Easy.

Tempeh Spread

225g (½ lb)	tempeh	1 cup
1 large	onion	1 large
2 cloves	garlic	2 cloves
2 tbs	vegetable oil	2 tbs
4 tbs	Smokey Snaps (soy bakon bits)	4 tbs
1 tsp	oregano	1 tsp
5 tbs	finely chopped parsley	5 tbs
5-6 tbs	vegan mayonnaise	5-6 tbs

1 Steam the tempeh, then mash it in a mixing bowl.
2 Chop the onion finely, crush the garlic and sauté together in the oil in a frying pan for 3-5 minutes until lightly browned.
3 Add the fried onion and garlic to the tempeh, together with the Smokey Snaps (soy bakon bits), oregano, parsley, and mayonnaise. Mix thoroughly. Chill before serving.

Note: This is a more elaborate variant on the same theme.

Guacamole

2	avocados	2
1 tsp	grated onion	1 tsp
1 tsp	lemon juice	1 tsp
2 tsp	olive oil	2 tsp
As required	Tabasco sauce, cayenne or chilli powder	As required
Pinch	sea salt	Pinch

1 Mash the avocados well.
2 Combine all the ingredients and beat thoroughly.

Note: For a rough texture mix the ingredients with a fork; for a smooth one use a liquidizer.
Quick and Easy.

Curried Avocado Spread

2	avocados	2
Juice of ½	lemon	Juice of ½
½-1 tsp	curry powder	½-1 tsp
1 tbs	vegan mayonnaise	1 tbs
3 tbs	Smokey Snaps (soy bakon bits)	3 tbs

1 Mash the avocados.
2 Add the rest of the ingredients and mix thoroughly.

Note: This is nice served on crispbread.
Quick and Easy.

Lentil Pâté

115g (4 oz)	wholewheat bread	2 cups
115g (4 oz)	red lentils	½ cup
285ml (½ pt)	water	1⅓ cups
1	onion	1
2 tbs	vegetable oil	2 tbs
1 tbs	tahini	1 tbs
1 tsp	dried rosemary	1 tsp
½ tsp	dried thyme	½ tsp
Pinch	nutmeg	Pinch
1 tbs	finely chopped parsley	1 tbs
1 tbs	miso	1 tbs

1 Break the bread up into pieces, cover with water, and leave to soak for about an hour.
2 Cook the lentils in the 285ml (½ pt/1⅓ cups) water for about 15 minutes until tender.
3 Chop the onion. Sauté it in the oil for about 5 minutes, until tender and beginning to brown.
4 Add the onions to the lentils. Drain the bread and squeeze as much moisture out as possible; add to the lentils and onions.
5 Stir in the tahini, rosemary, thyme and nutmeg, and cook over a low heat for about 5 minutes.
6 Stir in the parsley and miso, beating well to amalgamate it into the mixture.
7 Turn into an oiled baking dish, and bake for about half an hour at 350°F/180°C (Gas Mark 4). Serve warm or cold.

Note: it is difficult to know when something is a pâté rather than a spread but the texture and richness of this and the recipe which follows seem to demand the pâté label.

Pecan Pâté

115g (4 oz)	pecans	1 cup
115g (4 oz)	wholewheat breadcrumbs	2 cups
1 large or 2 small	carrot	1 large or 2 small
1 small	onion	1 small
1 tbs	chopped parsley	1 tbs
2 tsp	tomato purée (paste)	2 tsp
1 tsp	Vecon	1 tsp
1 tbs	hot water	1 tbs

1 Grind the pecans.
2 Grate the carrot(s) finely. Chop the onion finely. Dissolve the Vecon in the hot water.
3 Combine all the ingredients in a bowl and using fingers mix them well. Cover the bowl and refrigerate for two hours or longer.

Note: This pâté can be served on toast or crispbread, or alternatively, the mixture can be formed into little balls and served with salad. (Vecon is a concentrated vegetable stock paste.)

Wakame Fritters

115g (4 oz)	wholewheat flour	1 cup
2 tsp	baking powder	2 tsp
1 tsp	cream of tartar	1 tsp
140ml (¼ pt)	water	⅔ cup
1 tsp	soya (soy) sauce	1 tsp
1 tsp	vegetable oil	1 tsp
55g (2 oz)	wakame	2 oz
As required	oil for deep-frying	As required
As required	slices of lemon	As required

1 Mix the flour with the baking powder and cream of tartar. Whisk in the water, soy sauce and vegetable oil. Let the batter stand for at least half an hour.
2 Soak the wakame for about 10 minutes. Drain and chop into pieces, discarding any tough central rib. Coat the pieces with the batter and deep-fry until crisp.
3 Drain the fritters well, keeping them warm, and serve with lemon slices.

Note: Chapter 13 gives main dish recipes for this sea vegetable, but this makes a tasty snack.

Kombu Fritters

	Fritter batter (see recipe for Wakame fritters above)	
115g (2 oz)	kombu	2 oz
As required	oil for deep-frying	As required
As required	slices of lemon	As required

1 Make the batter as described in the recipe for Wakame Fritters. Leave for at least half an hour.
2 Soak the kombu for about 10 minutes. (If a less chewy texture is desired then cook it for 20-30 minutes, drain and cool before using.) Chop the kombu into small pieces, coat with batter and deep-fry until crisp.
3 Drain well, keeping the fritters warm, and serve with lemon slices.

Note: Kombu has a very different taste and texture from wakame but also makes lovely fritters.

Hijiki Tofu Balls

55g (2 oz)	hijiki	2 oz
565g (1¼ lb)	tofu	2½ lb
4 tbs	soya (soy) sauce	4 tbs
1-2 (about 115g/4 oz)	carrots	1-2 (about ¼ lb)
As required	sesame seeds	As required
As required	oil for deep-frying	As required

1 Rinse the hijiki well by covering with water and draining two or three times. Soak it in enough water to cover for about 20 minutes.
2 Bring the water to the boil, lower the heat and simmer the hijiki for about 20 minutes. Add 2 tablespoons soya (soy) sauce and simmer for a further 15-20 minutes. Drain and cool.
3 Drain the tofu, put it into a large bowl, and mash thoroughly. Grate the carrot. Chop the hijiki finely. Add the carrot and hijiki to the tofu, along with the remaining soya (soy) sauce. Knead the mixture with the hands, then form into balls about the size of golf balls.
4 Spread sesame seeds on to a plate and roll each ball in them so that they are coated with the seeds.
5 Deep fry the balls until lightly browned.

Note: This is a more substantial sea vegetable-based snack. The balls are particularly nice served with a dip made from soy sauce and finely grated fresh ginger, diluted with water to taste.

Eggless 'Egg' Sandwich Spread

225g (½ lb)	tofu	½ lb
¼ tsp	turmeric	¼ tsp
1 stick	celery	1 stick
1 small	onion	1 small
1 tbs	vegan mayonnaise	1 tbs
1 tbs	finely chopped parsley	1 tbs
1 tsp	nutritional yeast	1 tsp
½ tsp	mustard powder	½ tsp
As required	sea salt (or celery salt)	As required

1 Mash the tofu. Finely chop the onion and celery.
2 Combine all the ingredients and store in the fridge.

Note: In Chapter 11 there are recipes using tofu in place of scrambled eggs. Here it is used raw as a sandwich filling.
Quick and Easy.

Ful Medams with Tahini

2	onions	2
4 cloves	garlic	4 cloves
4 tbs	olive oil	4 tbs
2 tins	Egyptian brown beans	2 cans
Juice of 1	lemon	Juice of 1
2 tsp	cumin seeds	2 tsp
2 tbs	tahini	2 tbs
1 tsp (or to taste	Tabasco sauce	1 tsp (or to taste
As required	freshly ground black pepper	As required

1 Chop the onions finely. Crush the garlic. Fry them in half the oil for a few minutes until lightly browned.
2 Drain the beans, retaining the liquid. Add them to the pan with the lemon juice, mashing them with a fork while doing so.
3 Grind the cumin seeds and add them to the pan with the tahini, Tabasco sauce and pepper. Add as much of the bean liquid as desired to get a thicker or thinner texture. Stir in the mixture and simmer over a low heat until hot.

Note: The cans of beans used for this dish will already be labelled 'Ful Medams'. I once went to a restaurant in Cairo which offered at least half a dozen 'ful medam' dishes so I have tried to replicate my favourite one. Serve with pitta bread.

Indian Potato Balls in Batter

680g (1½ lb)	potatoes	1½ lb
2	onions	2
1 tbs	vegan margarine	1 tbs
2	fresh green chillies	2
2.5cm (1 in) piece	fresh ginger	1 inch piece
2 tsp	mustard seeds	2 tsp
2 tbs	broken cashews	2 tbs
As required	sea salt	As required
Juice of ½	lemon	Juice of ½
170g (6 oz)	gram (chick pea) flour	1½ cups
225ml (8 fl oz)	water	1 cup

1 Cook the potatoes; cool, peel and mash.
2 Chop the onions finely. Heat the margarine in a large saucepan and sauté them for a few minutes. Peel and chop the chillies (making sure to discard all the seeds) and ginger finely. Add them to the pan and cook for a couple of minutes longer. Add the mustard seeds and cashews and continue cooking for a few minutes more.
3 Remove the pan from the heat and add the mashed potatoes, a little salt, and the lemon juice. Mix well, then form little balls (about the size of walnuts).
4 Mix the gram (chick pea) flour and water and add a

pinch of salt. Coat the potato balls in the batter and deep-fry them until they are golden. Serve immediately.

Note: This traditional Indian dish is usually found in restaurants as a starter but makes a pleasant lunch dish. It is a good way of using up leftover cooked potatoes and serves four for lunch or eight to ten as a starter. Serve with chutney.

Indian Potato Cutlets

680g (1½ lb)	potatoes	1½ lb
1	onion	1
2 cloves	garlic	2 cloves
2	fresh chillies	2
3 tsp	cumin seeds	3 tsp
Juice of ½	lemon	Juice of ½
2 tbs	gram (chick pea) flour	2 tbs
2 tbs	water	2 tbs
As required	sea salt	As required
As required	freshly ground black pepper	As required
As required	wholewheat flour	As required
As required	vegetable oil	As required

1 Cook the potatoes (or use leftover cooked potatoes). Peel and mash them in a large mixing bowl.
2 Grate the onion. Crush the garlic. Chop the chillies finely. Grind the cumin seeds. Add all of these ingredients, and the lemon juice, to the potatoes and mix well.
3 Put the gram (chick pea) flour and water in a cup and mix well with a fork. Add this to the potato mixture and mix well.
4 Spread some flour on a plate. Form the potato mixture into balls and flatten the balls on the flour, turning to coat both sides.
5 Heat some oil in a frying pan and shallow-fry the cutlets, turning once so that they are golden brown on both sides.

Note: This is my version of a traditional dish. Serve it with chutneys.

Vegan Rarebit

2 jars (c.135g each)	vegan cheese spread	2 jars
140ml (¼ pt)	soya (soy) milk	⅔ cup
1 tsp	vegan Worcestershire sauce	1 tsp
Pinch	mustard powder	Pinch
Pinch	cayenne pepper	Pinch

1 Gently heat all the ingredients in a saucepan. Serve as soon as it is blended, smooth and bubbling.

Note: Several different kinds of vegan 'cheese spread' (Plamil, Fromsoya, and Marigold) are available in British health food shops. As well as using them straight you can heat them to make this familiar favourite. Serve over toast.
Quick and Easy. Suitable for One.

Fried Peanut Butter Sandwiches

8 slices	wholemeal bread	8 slices
As required	peanut butter	As required
As required	vegan margarine or vegetable oil	As required

1 Spread half the slices of bread thickly with peanut butter. Cover with the dry slices.
2 Heat the margarine or oil in a frying pan and fry the sandwiches, turning them once so they are lightly browned on both sides. Serve immediately.

Note: You may have already thought of this simple recipe, but for those of you who haven't it is one of my favourite quick lunches. Serve with crisp lettuce leaves.
Quick and Easy. Suitable for One.

6
Rice and Other Grains

Introduction

There are so many dishes in this book which are best served over rice that it is perhaps the food which appears most often. Its usefulness as a base is obvious, and it complements protein-rich foods like beans or tofu for maximum nutritional benefit. Of course, in this book I have used only brown rice.

Many different varieties of brown rice are available from various parts of the world. In most of the recipes I have not distinguished short-grain from long-grain (for one thing Italian long-grain is shorter than some varieties of short-grain). Short-grain brown rice is perhaps more suitable for Oriental cooking than long-grain, but long-grain has more general appeal. Cooking some varieties of brown rice can take as long as 45 minutes; however, by covering the rice with boiling water and leaving it to soak for several hours it should take only 20-25 minutes to cook. The soaking water should be discarded, and the rice rinsed and then covered with water with a little salt added. After bringing the water to the boil the pan should be covered, and the rice left to simmer until the water is absorbed. There are now some varieties which do not require pre-soaking but call for a much greater volume of salted water; the pan is left uncovered and the water kept boiling rather than simmering. Those varieties usually take only 20-25 minutes to cook so no advance planning is necessary. The other grains and cereals in this chapter include the following:

Barley – a pleasantly 'nutty' grain which can be used as a base for many dishes in place of rice. The barley called for is pot barley which is to pearl barley what brown rice is to white. To cook, cover with boiling water for several hours, discard the soaking water, rinse the barley and cover with fresh water and a little salt. Bring to the boil, then cover the pan, lower the heat and simmer for about 25 minutes until the water is absorbed.

Oats – the staple food of Scotland for centuries. Oats are not eaten in grain form but come in various thicknesses of 'meal' as well as flakes. Although most usually eaten as porridge, oats will be found in main meal recipes in this chapter.

Maize – the staple food for much of Africa. The word 'corn' originally meant any kind of grain (and still does in some European languages), but as maize was the only grain which the first white settlers found in America the word corn came to mean maize, with the British eventually calling it sweetcorn. Unlike any other grain in this chapter, 'corn' is eaten fresh as a vegetable, while dried it is used only for popcorn (a nutritious food). However, as 'cornmeal' it comes into its own as the basis for main dishes.

Millet – for non-vegetarians this is strictly birdfood, but in fact it is a highly nutritious (and delicious) grain. It needs no pre-soaking although before being cooked it can be briefly dry-roasted in a stainless steel pan for extra flavour. It should be covered with about three times its quantity of water, with a little salt added and simmered in a covered pan for about half an hour, by which time the water should be absorbed and the millet soft.

Wheat – most commonly eaten as bread, although it comes in various other forms as well. Wheat 'berries' are the equivalent of brown rice or pearl barley, but their stronger flavour and chewier texture make them less versatile. They should be pre-soaked and cooked in the same way as rice or barley. Bulgur wheat is wheat which has been cracked and briefly precooked. It can be soaked in cold water for at least half an hour, then drained and eaten raw, or it can be covered with about three times its quantity of boiling water, then simmered for just a few minutes until the water is absorbed and the wheat is soft. Cous-cous is similar but the wheat has been somewhat 'refined'. Semolina – or farina, as it is called in America – is the wheaten equivalent to oatmeal. It can now be found at wholefood stores in its unrefined form, which is suitable for some savoury dishes, though rather coarse in texture. Although 'refined' semolina obviously lacks the fibre content of wholemeal semolina, it is actually higher in protein. The most usual commercial use of semolina is to make pasta, but pasta is such a versatile food that it has a chapter to itself.

Many types of wholewheat (wholemeal) flour are available providing a choice between 'strong' flour suitable for bread and 'soft' flour which is better for other uses. It is also possible to find 81% or 85% flours, which have the bran removed but not the germ.

Recipes

Wholewheat Shortcrust Pastry

225g (½lb)	wholewheat flour	2 cups
Pinch	sea salt	Pinch
115g (4oz)	vegan margarine	½ cup
As required	water	As required

1 Put the flour in a bowl and add a little salt. Add the margarine in small pieces. (I prefer using a hard margarine like Tomor, but a soft one can be used instead.) A hard margarine is best rubbed in with a pastry blender while a fork is more suitable for a soft margarine.
2 Add water (amount will vary according to the type of flour used). There should be enough to make a *soft* dough (a firm dry one will make a hard chewy pastry). If it is a little too soft then sprinkle a lot of flour on the board which will then be absorbed by the pastry, but be sure to err on the side of soft and moist.
3 Handle the dough as little as possible and roll it out on a floured board. For a pre-baked case (shell) prick the pastry all over with a fork and bake at 425°F/225°C (Gas Mark 7) for 5-10 minutes, then for about 15 minutes at 350°F/180°C (Gas Mark 4).

Note: this basic recipe for wholewheat pastry will be found in many of the recipes which follow.

Tomato and Rice Loaf

225g (½lb)	brown rice	1¼ cup
225g (½lb)	tomatoes	½lb
2 sticks	celery	2 sticks
85g (3oz)	wholewheat breadcrumbs	1½ cups
200ml (⅓ pint)	soya/(soy) milk	¾ cup
1 tbs	vegetable oil	1 tbs
½ tsp	garlic salt	½ tsp
½ tsp	onion salt	½ tsp

1 Cook the rice until tender.
2 Chop the tomatoes and celery and sauté them in the oil under tender.
3 Combine all of the ingredients, including the rice, and mix well.
4 Pour the mixture into an oiled loaf tin and bake in a moderate oven at 350°F/180°C (Gas Mark 4) for about half an hour.

Note: serve this as the centrepiece of a meal, accompanied by seasonal vegetables.

Creamy Banana Risotto

225g (½lb)	brown rice	1¼ cup
55g (2oz)	vegan margarine	¼ cup
1 small	onion	1 small
1	green pepper	1
30g (1oz)	wholewheat flour	¼ cup
570ml (1 pint)	soya/(soy) milk	2½ cups
30g (1oz)	soya/(soy) flour 'cheese' (see p.13)	¼ cup
455g (1lb)	green-tipped bananas	1lb

1 Cook the rice until tender.
2 Chop the onion, slice the green pepper into thin strips and sauté them in 1oz (30g) (2 tbs) margarine until tender.
3 Stir this mixture into the cooked rice.
4 Melt the rest of the margarine and stir in the flour. Slowly add the milk, stirring constantly to avoid lumps. Bring to the boil and simmer for 1 minute. Add the 'cheese' and stir until melted.
5 Peel and slice the bananas thinly and mix in with the rice mixture. Season to taste.
6 Put a layer of the rice mixture into a greased baking dish. Cover with a layer of sauce. Repeat the layers until all the ingredients are used up, ending with the sauce.
7 Bake in a moderate oven at 350°F/180°C (Gas Mark 4) for about half an hour.

Note: this is an unusual combination but tastes delicious.

Rice and Vegetable Savoury

285g (10oz)	brown rice	1¾ cups
285ml (½ pint)	tomato juice	1⅓ cups
As required	water	As required
2 large	aubergines (eggplants)	2 large
455g (1lb)	fresh or frozen shelled peas	1lb
4 large	carrots	4 large
4-6 tbs	vegetable oil	4-6 tbs

1 Pour boiling water over the rice and leave to soak for several hours. Drain, place in a saucepan and add the tomato juice, 1 tablespoon of oil and enough water to cover. Bring to the boil, lower the heat and simmer until the liquid is absorbed and the rice is tender.

2 Dice the carrots and cook them with the peas in boiling salted water until just tender. Set aside to drain.

3 Dice the aubergines (eggplants) and fry them in the rest of the vegetable oil until tender.

4 Place half the rice in a greased baking dish. Cover this with the vegetables and top with another layer of rice. Press down slightly.

5 Bake in a moderate oven at 350°F/180°C (Gas Mark 4) for 15-20 minutes.

Note: in this dish the rice absorbs the tomato juice, forming a pleasant contrast to the layered vegetables.

Pilau Rice

225g (½lb)	brown rice	1¼ cups
425ml (¾ pint)	water	2 cups
1	onion	1
2 tbs	vegetable oil	2 tbs
2 cloves	garlic	2 cloves
2 tsp	finely chopped fresh ginger	2 tsp
115g (4oz)	green beans	¼ cup
115g (4oz)	mushrooms	2 cups
1 tsp	turmeric	1 tsp
2 tsp	ground coriander	2 tsp
1 tbs	garam masala	1 tbs
2	bay leaves	2
225g (4oz)	fresh (shelled) or frozen peas	⅔ cup
As required	sea salt	As required

1 Cover the rice with boiling water and leave to soak for several hours. Drain.

2 Chop the onion and sauté in the vegetable oil for 3-4 minutes.

3 Chop the garlic finely, and add it to the saucepan, along with the ginger. Sauté for a further minute or two.

4 Top and tail the beans; break in half or into smaller pieces if necessary. Chop the mushrooms. Add the beans and mushrooms to the saucepan, along with the rice, turmeric, coriander, garam masala, and bay leaves. Stir briefly, then add water. Bring to the boil then lower and leave to simmer.

5 After 15-20 minutes, when most of the water has been absorbed, add the peas. Cook for a further 3 minutes, then serve.

Note: pilau rice is usually served with a curry, but this is nice enough to serve on its own, with chapatis and chutney if desired.

American-style 'Mexican' Rice

225g (½lb)	brown rice	1¼ cups
2 tbs	vegan margarine	2 tbs
2	onions	2
1	green pepper	1
2 sticks	celery	2 sticks
1 tin (c.440g)	tomatoes	1 can (c.14oz)
1 tbs	tomato purée (paste)	1 tbs
2 tsp	paprika	2 tsp
2	bay leaves	2
As required	sea salt	As required
As required	freshly ground black pepper	As required
140ml (¼ pint)	water	⅔ cup
2 tbs	Smokey Snaps (soy bakon bits)	2 tbs

1 Cover the rice with boiling water and soak for several hours. Drain well.

2 Slice the onions thinly and sauté in the margarine for 2-3 minutes.

3 Chop the pepper and celery and add it to the saucepan. Continue sautéing for a further 2-3 minutes.

4 Add the rice and stir well. Add the tomatoes, purée (paste), paprika, bay leaves, and seasoning. Stir well. Add the water and bring to the boil. Lower the heat and leave to simmer until the liquid is absorbed and the rice is tender (about 25-30 minutes).

5 Just before serving, remove the bay leaves and stir in the Smokey Snaps (soy bakon bits).

Note: this style of preparing rice is called 'Mexican' in the USA, though the rice in Mexican restaurants is not at all like this. The Smokey Snaps (soy bakon bits) give it extra flavour and 'crunch'.

Curried Vegetable Rice

285-340g (10-12oz)	brown rice	1½-2 cups
455g (1lb)	tomatoes	1lb
225g (½lb)	carrots	½lb
225g (½lb)	mushrooms	4 cups
115g (4oz)	shelled (or frozen) peas	¼lb

2 large	onions	2 large
2-3 cloves	garlic	2-3 cloves
2 tbs	vegetable oil	2 tbs
2 tbs (or to taste)	curry powder	2 tbs (or to taste)
115g (4oz)	broken cashews	1 cup
170-240ml (6-8 fl oz)	water	¾-1 cup
As required	sea salt	As required

1 Cook the rice or, if already cooked, remove from refrigerator.
2 Skin and chop the tomatoes. Chop the carrots and mushrooms. Set aside.
3 Chop the onions and garlic finely. Heat the oil in a large saucepan and sauté the onion and garlic for 3-4 minutes.
4 Sprinkle in the curry powder and stir over a low heat for a minute or two. Add the tomatoes, carrots, mushrooms, peas, and cashews and stir well. Pour in the water, bring to the boil, then lower the heat and simmer, covered, for 4-5 minutes. Stir in the rice and salt to taste and cook for 4-5 minutes longer.

Note: it is always useful to cook double quantities of rice, refrigerate half and use it later in the week for a dish like this one.
Quick and Easy. Suitable for One.

Deep-fried Rice Balls with Sweet and Sour Vegetables

For the balls:

285g (10oz)	short-grain brown rice	1¾ cups
4-5	spring onions (scallions)	4-5
2 cloves	garlic	2 cloves
3 tbs	miso	3 tbs
3 tbs	tahini	3 tbs
3 tsp	finely chopped fresh ginger	3 tbs
As required	cornflour (cornstarch)	As required
As required	vegetable oil for deep frying	As required

For the sauce:

1 large	onion	1 large
2 tbs	vegetable oil	2 tbs
1	green pepper	1
1	carrot	1
1 tin (c.225g)	pineapple	1 can (c.8oz)
3-4 tsp	raw cane sugar	3-4 tsp
1 tbs	cider vinegar or wine vinegar	1 tbs
2 tbs	soy sauce	2 tbs
6 tbs	water	6 tbs
1 tbs	cornflour (cornstarch)	1 tbs

1 To make the balls, cook the rice until tender and cool slightly.
2 Finely chop the spring onions (scallions) and crush the garlic, then add them, along with the miso, tahini and ginger, to the rice. Mix very thoroughly.
3 Cover the bottom of a plate with cornflour (cornstarch). Form the rice mixture into balls about the size of a walnut or a little larger, and roll in the cornflour (cornstarch). As the mixture is rather sloppy and sticky, it is easier to transfer a spoonful at a time of moisture to the plate, then roll it into a ball with the help of the cornflour (cornstarch) adhering to it. Deep-fry the balls until brown and crisp.
4 To make the sauce, chop the onion finely and sauté in the oil for about 2 minutes.
5 Chop the green pepper and grate the carrot coarsely. Add them to the saucepan and continue cooking for a further 2-3 minutes.
6 Add the pineapple juice from the tin, the sugar, vinegar, soy sauce and 3 tbs of the water. Bring to the boil, then lower the heat, cover and simmer for a few minutes.
7 Dissolve the cornflour (cornstarch) in the remaining 3 tablespoons water and stir it into the vegetables until thickened.

Note: this is a different way of serving rice, a bit fiddly perhaps but worth it for the results.

Jambalaya

285g (10oz)	brown rice	2½ cups
225g (½lb)	tofu	1 cup
2	onions	2
3 tbs	vegetable oil	3 tbs
4 sticks	celery	4 sticks
1	green pepper	1
115g (4oz)	mushrooms	2 cups
2	tomatoes	2
2 tbs	miso	2 tbs
2 tsp	paprika	2 tsp
A few drops	Tabasco sauce	A few drops
30g (1oz)	parsley	1 cup

1 Cook the rice until tender.
2 Cube the tofu and deep-fry the cubes until golden brown.
3 Chop the onions and sauté in the oil for 2-3 minutes.
4 Chop the celery, green pepper and mushrooms, and add to the onion. Cook for a further minute or two.
5 Chop the tomatoes and add to the pan; cook for 2-3 minutes longer. Then stir in the deep-fried tofu cubes.
6 Remove the saucepan from the heat, and stir in the cooked rice, miso, paprika, and Tabasco sauce. Mix well and turn into an oiled casserole. Bake at 300°F/150°C (Gas Mark 2) for about 45 minutes.
7 Chop the parsley finely, and sprinkle over the dish just before serving.

Note: Deep-fried tofu adds a 'chewy' texture (and protein) to this rice dish.

Avocado and Mushroom Pilaff

340g (12oz)	brown rice	2 cups
1 large	onion	1 large
1 clove	garlic	1 clove
115g (4oz)	vegetable margarine	½ cup
As required	sea salt	As required
As required	freshly ground black pepper	As required
170g (6oz)	mushrooms	3 cups
6 large	tomatoes	6 large
½ tsp	dried oregano	½ tsp
2	avocados	2
1 tbs	minced parsley	1 tbs

1 Soak the rice overnight or for several hours.
2 Chop the onion and finely chop the garlic.
3 Melt half the margarine in a saucepan and sauté the onion and garlic until golden brown.
4 Drain the rice and add it to the saucepan, stirring well. Add sea salt to taste and enough water to cover the rice. Bring to the boil, turn the heat down to low and simmer until cooked.
5 Meanwhile, slice the mushrooms, and peel and chop the tomatoes.
6 Melt the remainder of the margarine in a frying pan and add the mushrooms. Sauté for 2 or 3 minutes, then add the tomatoes, oregano, sea salt and black pepper and cook for 3 or 4 minutes longer.
7 Peel and dice the avocados. Stir into the tomato and mushrooms mixture.
8 Arrange the rice on a serving dish in a ring and fill the centre with the avocado mixture. Sprinkle the parsley over the top.

Note: avocados are not often found in cooked dishes, but here they fill a ring of cooked rice.

Nasi Goreng

2	onions	2
2 tbs	vegetable oil	2 tbs
2 tbs	tomato ketchup	2 tbs
2 tbs	soya (soy) sauce	2 tbs
2 tsp	Tabasco sauce	2 tsp
340g (¾lb)	brown rice, cooked	2 cups
1 small or ½ large	cucumber	1 small or ½ large

1 Chop the onions. Heat the oil in a wok or frying pan and fry them until turning brown.
2 Add the ketchup, soya (soy) sauce and Tabasco sauce to the wok and stir well. Add the rice and stir-fry until heated through.
3 Dice the cucumber and spinkle it over the top.

Note: nasi goreng simply means fried rice in Malaysian/Indonesian. This is a vegan adaptation of the basic recipe and can be eaten on its own as a light lunch with added stir-fried vegetables, peanuts, tofu etc for a substantial main course. If you have cooked a double amount of rice for a previous meal and kept the leftover rice in the refrigerator, this is a really speedy dish.
Quick and Easy.

Short-cut Risotto

2	onions	2
2 tbs	olive oil	2 tbs
1 tbs	vegan margarine	1 tbs
225g (½ lb)	mushrooms	4 cups
3-4 cloves	garlic	3-4 cloves
285-340g (10-12 oz)	brown rice, cooked	1¾-2 cups
285ml (½ pt)	water or vegetable stock	1⅓ cup
3 tbs	tomato purée (paste)	3 tbs
2 tbs	minced parsley	2 tbs
225g (½ lb)	fresh (shelled) or frozen peas	½ lb
As required	sea salt	As required
As required	freshly ground black pepper	As required
Optional	nutritional yeast	Optional

1 Chop the onions. Heat the oil and margarine in a large saucepan and sauté them for 2-3 minutes.
2 Crush the garlic and add it to the pan. Chop the mushrooms and stir them in. Cook for a few minutes until the mushrooms are tender.
3 Stir in the water or stock and tomato purée (paste). Bring to the boil. Add the cooked rice, parsley and peas. Lower the heat and cook for a few minutes until the water is absorbed and the peas are tender. Season to taste. Sprinkle nutritional yeast on top if desired.

Note: A traditional risotto is made by cooking rice in a flavoured stock, but by using leftover rice it is possible to make a pretty good imitation which takes no time at all.
Quick and Easy. Suitable for One.

Millet Casserole

225g (½ lb)	millet	1 cup
As required	sea salt	As required
2	onions	2
850ml	boiling water	3¾ cups
(1½ pts)		
2	carrots	2
1 small	cabbage	1 small
90ml	vegetable oil	⅓ cup
(3 fl oz)		
30g (1 oz)	wholewheat flour	¼ cup
285ml (½ pt)	water	1⅓ cups
1-2 tbs	soya (soy) sauce	1-2 tbs
30g (1 oz)	wholewheat breadcrumbs	½ cup

1 Chop the onion, cut the carrots into slivers and shred the cabbage.
2 Sauté the millet in 2 tbs of the oil until it is beginning to brown. Cover with the boiling water and salt. Simmer for about 20 minutes.
3 Sauté the vegetables in 2 tbs of the oil until tender.
4 In a separate saucepan, heat the remaining oil, add the flour and stir well. Slowly add the water, stirring constantly to avoid lumps. Add the soy sauce and bring to the boil. Simmer for 2-3 minutes.
5 In a greased baking dish, place alternate layers of millet, vegetables and sauce, ending with a layer of sauce. Sprinkle with the breadcrumbs.
6 Bake in a moderate oven at 350°C/180°F (Gas Mark 4) for about 20 minutes until the top is lightly browned.

Note: This is a good introduction to a tasty, rarely-used grain.

Millet and Vegetable Savoury

225g (½ lb)	millet	1 cup
850ml	water	3¾ cups
(1½ pts)		
As required	sea salt	As required
4 small or	leeks	4 small or
2 large		2 large
2	carrots	2
4 sticks	celery	4 sticks
55g (2 oz)	vegan margarine	¼ cup
340g (¾ lb)	tofu	1½ cups
2 tbs	tahini	2 tbs
1½ tbs	miso	1½ tbs
Juice of	lemon	Juice of
1 small		1 small
2 tsp	soy sauce	2 tsp
4 tbs	soya (soy) yogurt	4 tbs
6 tbs	water	6 tbs

1 Wash the millet, cover with the water (lightly salted to taste), bring to the boil, lower the heat, cover and simmer until all the water is absorbed (about 30 minutes).
2 Meanwhile, chop the leeks and grate the carrots coarsely. Melt the margarine in a frying pan and sauté the vegetables for about 10 minutes, stirring frequently.
3 Put the tofu, tahini, miso, lemon juice, soy sauce, yogurt and water in a liquidizer and blend thoroughly.
4 Mix the vegetables into the millet. Pour about three-quarters of the tofu mixture in and mix thoroughly. Pour this mixture into a greased casserole, and pour the remainder of the tofu mixture over the top.
5 Bake at 375°F/190°C (Gas Mark 5) for 20-30 minutes, until the top is nicely browned.

Note: This millet dish is high in protein.

Creamy Curried Sauce on Bulgur

225g (½ lb)	bulgur wheat	1 cup
3 tbs	vegetable oil	3 tbs
As required	sea salt	As required
4 small	leeks	4 small
4 sticks	celery	4 sticks
225g (½ lb)	mushrooms	4 cups
285ml (½ pt)	soya (soy) yogurt	1⅓ cups

1 Cook the bulgur wheat in salted water until tender.
2 Heat the oil and add the curry powder. Cook over a gentle heat for 1 minute.
3 Slice the leeks finely and chop the celery and mushrooms, then stir-fry them in the seasoned oil for a few minutes, until just tender.
4 Turn off the heat, stir in the yogurt and mix well.
5 Serve the sauce over the cooked bulgur wheat.

Note: This and the following three recipes use wheat in various forms. The contrast of a creamy sauce and bulgur wheat is very pleasing.
Quick and Easy. Suitable for One.

Gnocchi alla Romana

1140ml (2 pts)	soya (soy) milk	5 cups
As required	sea salt	As required
As required	freshly ground black pepper	As required
As required	nutmeg	As required
225g (½ lb)	wholewheat semolina (farina)	2 cups
55g (2 oz)	nutritional yeast	2 oz
85g (3 oz)	vegan margarine	⅓ cup
As required	tomato sauce	As required

1 Heat the milk in a saucepan, seasoning it with salt, pepper and a good grating of nutmeg. Sprinkle in the semolina (farina) and bring to the boil. Stir continuously over a low heat until thickened.
2 Stir half the yeast flakes or powder and 55g (2 oz/¼ cup) of the margarine into the semolina, then spread it on an oiled dish or board and smooth it down to about ½ inch. Cool and then chill until ready to prepare.
3 Cut the mixture into small squares and put the squares, overlapping if desired, into a greased shallow ovenproof dish. Sprinkle with the other half of the yeast, and top with small pieces of the remaining margarine.
4 Bake at 400°F/200°C (Gas Mark 6) for about 20 minutes.
5 Serve with tomato sauce.

Note: This is my vegan adaptation of a traditional Italian dish. The sauce can be either home-made or a good quality sauce from a shop.
Quick and Easy. Suitable for One.

Bulgur Wheat and Chestnut Bake

225g (½ lb)	dried chestnuts	½ lb
225g (½ lb)	bulgur wheat	1⅓ cups
2	onions	2
2 tbs	vegetable oil	2 tbs
225g (½ lb)	soya (soy) yogurt	1 cup
½ tsp	dried marjoram	½ tsp
As required	sea salt	As required
As required	freshly ground black pepper	As required

1 Soak the chestnuts in a wide-rimmed Thermos flask until soft (see p.77).
2 Cover the bulgur wheat with about three times its volume in water, add a little salt, and cook until the water is absorbed.
3 Chop the onions. Heat the oil in a frying pan and fry the onions until lightly browned.

4 Stir the chestnuts and onions into the bulgur wheat. Add the yogurt, marjoram and seasoning, and mix thoroughly.
5 Turn the mixture into a greased oven dish and bake in a moderate oven 350°F/180°C (Gas Mark 4) for about half an hour.

Note: This is a very quick and easy dish, which allows the sweet flavour of chestnuts to dominate. Serve it with seasonal vegetables.
Suitable for One.

Quick Pizza

200g (7 oz)	wholewheat flour	1¾ cups
5 tbs	vegetable oil	5 tbs
Pinch	sea salt	Pinch
2 tsp	baking powder	2 tsp
1	onion	1
2 tbs	tomato purée (paste)	2 tbs
5 tbs	water	5 tbs
2 tsp	dried oregano	2 tsp
6	black olives	6
1 tbs	tahini	1 tbs
1 tbs	miso	1 tbs

1 Mix the flour with 1 tbs oil, salt and baking powder, then add sufficient water to make a soft dough. Roll out into two 7-inch circles for the bases.
2 Chop the onion finely. Fry in 2 tablespoons oil until tender.
3 Mix the tomato purée (paste), 2 tablespoons water, oregano and the onion in a small bowl.
4 Chop the olives finely.
5 Mix the tahini, miso and remaining 3 tablespoons water in a small bowl.
6 Heat 1 tablespoon oil in a large frying pan. Fry one of the bases for 4-5 minutes, then turn over. Spread with half the tomato mixture, sprinkle with half the olives, and top with half the tahini mixture. Cook for a further 4-5 minutes, then place under a medium grill (broiler) until the tahini is browned.
7 Repeat with the second base. Serve with a green salad.

Note: A traditional pizza dough is made with yeast, which of course requires time to rise and time to bake, whereas this requires neither. The topping is rich and full of flavour. Serve with a green salad.
Quick and Easy.

Stir-fried Vegetables with Barley

225g (½ lb)	pot barley	1¼ cups
As required	sea salt	As required
3 small	leeks	3 small
2	carrots	2
4 sticks	celery	4 sticks
225g (½ lb)	mushrooms	4 cups
4 tbs	vegetable oil	4 tbs
1 tsp	ground cumin	1 tsp
2 tbs	sunflower seeds	2 tbs

1 After soaking, cook the barley in salted water until tender.
2 Slice the leeks thinly, cut the carrots into matchsticks, chop the celery and mushrooms.
3 Heat the oil gently, add the cumin and stir well.
4 Add the vegetables to the oil and stir-fry for a few minutes until the vegetables are just tender.
5 Toast the sunflower seeds under the grill (broiler) until slightly roasted.
6 Combine the cooked barley, vegetables and sunflower seeds, stirring well, and serve.

Note: This recipe, and the two that follow, use barley as a change from rice.
Quick and Easy. Suitable for One.

Barley Lentil Savoury

225g (½ lb)	pot barley	1⅓ cups
225g (½ lb)	green lentils	1⅓ cups
1	vegetable stock cube	1
2 tbs	vegetable oil	2 tbs
2	onions	2
As required	sea salt	As required
As required	freshly ground black pepper	As required

1 Put the barley and lentils in a large saucepan, cover with boiling water and leave for several hours. Drain, cover with fresh water, add the stock cube, bring to the boil, then lower the heat and leave to simmer for 20-30 minutes.
2 Chop the onions and sauté them in the oil until tender. Add them to the barley mixture during the last few minutes of cooking. Season to taste.

Note: This is a very simple dish, with an ideal pulse and grain combination.
Quick and Easy. Suitable for One.

Barley and Cashew Casserole

225g (½ lb)	pot barley	1⅓ cups
Pinch	sea salt	Pinch
425ml (¾ pt)	water	2 cups
140ml (¼ pt)	soya (soy) milk	⅔ cup
2	onions	2
2	tomatoes	2
115g (4 oz)	mushrooms	2 cups
2 tbs	vegetable oil	2 tbs
115g (4 oz)	cashews	1 cup
1 tsp	yeast extract	1 tsp
As required	sea salt	As required
As required	freshly ground black pepper	As required

1 Soak the barley, then cook it with a little salt in the water and milk until nearly tender.
2 Chop the onions, tomatoes and mushrooms, and sauté in the oil until just tender. Place in the bottom of a greased baking dish.
3 Stir the cashews and yeast extract into the barley; add additional seasoning to taste. Put this over the onion mixture, and bake in a moderate oven 350°F/180°C (Gas Mark 4) for 20-30 minutes.

Note: In this recipe barley is combined with cashews and vegetables for a satisfying main dish.

Oaty Burgers

1	onion	1
2 cloves	garlic	2 cloves
2 tbs	vegetable oil plus additional as required	2 tbs
115g (4 oz)	rolled oats	1 cup
55g (2 oz)	soya (soy) flour	½ cup
2-3 tbs	peanut butter	2-3 tbs
2 tsp	yeast extract	2 tsp
1-2 tsp	caraway seeds	1-2 tsp
4-6 tbs	water	4-6 tbs

1 Chop the onion and garlic finely. Sauté in the oil until lightly browned.
2 In a mixing bowl combine the oats, flour, peanut butter, yeast extract and caraway seeds. Add the onion and garlic and just enough water to form into firm patties.
3 Add just a little more oil to the frying pan and fry the burgers until nicely browned on both sides.

Note: These are very simple to make and use ingredients found in most larders, so they are useful for emergencies (but pleasant any time). Serve in buns with lettuce and sliced tomatoes or ketchup if desired.
Quick and Easy. Suitable for One.

Savoury Oatmeal Pudding

115g (4 oz)	medium oatmeal	1 cup
55g (2 oz)	soya (soy) flour	½ cup
55g (2 oz)	wholewheat breadcrumbs	1 cup
1 tsp	baking powder	1 tsp
½ tsp	dried mixed herbs	½ tsp
1 small	onion	1 small
85g (3 oz)	hard vegetable fat	⅓ cup
As required	water	As required

1 Combine the oatmeal, soya (soy) flour, breadcrumbs, baking powder and herbs in a large mixing bowl.
2 Chop the onion finely and add to the bowl.
3 Grate the fat and mix it in. Add enough water to make a thick pouring consistency and turn the mixture into a greased pudding basin. Steam for two hours.

Note: This very simple dish is perfect for a cold winter's night. Serve with a vegan gravy and Brussels sprouts, broccoli, or Savoy cabbage.

Fried Polenta

225g (½ lb)	cornmeal	2 cups
570ml (1 pt)	cold water	2½ cups
Pinch	sea salt	Pinch
810ml (1¼ pt)	boiling water	3 cups
30g (1 oz)	vegan margarine	2 tbs
3 tbs	olive oil	3 tbs
As required	tomato sauce	As required
Optional	nutritional yeast	Optional

1 Mix the cornmeal and cold water in a saucepan and add a little salt. Pour in the boiling water, then stir continuously over a low heat until beginning to boil and thicken. Place the saucepan on top of another saucepan (or use a steamer or double boiler), cover it and leave it to steam for about 30 minutes. Remove from the heat and spoon the polenta on to an oiled plate or baking sheet, smoothing it down to about ½ inch in depth. Cool then chill.
2 Cut the chilled polenta into squares. Heat the margarine and oil in a large frying pan and fry the squares, turning so that they are lightly browned on both sides.
3 Serve topped with a well-flavoured tomato sauce and sprinkled, if desired, with nutritional yeast.

Note: Cornmeal in the form of polenta is very popular in Italy and France.
Quick and Easy. Suitable for One.

Tamale Pie

225g (1 lb) or 2 tins (c.425g each)	cooked drained Borlotti (pinto) beans	2½ cups or 28-32 oz canned
2	onions	2
3 tbs	vegetable oil	3 tbs
3 cloves	garlic	3 cloves
1 small	green pepper	1 small
3 sticks	celery	3 sticks
½ tsp (or to taste)	chilli powder	½ tsp
2 tsp	ground cumin	2 tsp
2 tsp	dried oregano	2 tsp
A dozen	black olives	A dozen
170g (6 oz)	sweetcorn (corn) (fresh, frozen or tinned/ canned)	6 oz
2 tbs	tomato purée (paste)	2 tbs
2 tbs	chopped parsley	2 tbs
4 tbs	water	4 tbs
As required	sea salt	As required
As required	freshly ground black pepper	As required
170g (6 oz)	cornmeal	1½ cups
570ml (1 pt)	water	2½ cups
Pinch	sea salt	Pinch
30g (1 oz)	vegan margarine	2 tbs
4 tbs	nutritional yeast	4 tbs

1 Drain the beans, mash them and set aside.
2 Chop the onion and sauté it in the oil in a large saucepan for a few minutes.
3 Crush the garlic. Chop the green pepper and celery. Add these ingredients to the pan and cook for a few minutes longer.
4 Add the spices to the pan. Chop the olives and add them, as well as the mashed beans, corn, tomato purée (paste), parsley, water, and seasoning. Cook over a low heat for several minutes.
5 In another pan add the cornmeal and salt to the water (if lumpy use an eggbeater or whisk). Bring to the boil, stirring constantly, until it thickens and comes to the boil. Stir in the margarine and yeast.
6 Grease a baking dish and spread about two-thirds of the cornmeal mixture on the bottom. Spoon the bean mixture over this and top with the remaining cornmeal. Bake at 350°F/180°C (Gas Mark 4) for about half an hour.

Note: Recipes with a long list of ingredients can look intimidating, but this one is really very simple and does not take long at all. The combination of beans and cornmeal is a traditional one in Mexico and western America. Serve with a fresh green salad.

7
Pasta

Introduction

I firmly believe pasta to be one of the greatest culinary inventions ever. It is so easy to prepare and it can be used in so many ways. The only thing a vegan has to avoid is 'pasta all uovo' (with eggs); fortunately most pasta is eggless.

In order to add variety to the pasta-based Italian diet there have evolved a large number of different pasta shapes, but to keep things simple I have specified only spaghetti (for which linguini could be substituted), macaroni (meaning elbow macaroni of whatever size), noodles (which could be egg-free tagliatelle), lasagne, and 'pasta shapes', meaning shells, wheels or whatever.

Wholewheat pasta is more nutritious and higher in fibre, but even 'white' pasta, which is made from high-protein durum semolina, is good for you. Since vegans already get plenty of fibre in their diet, one of the multi-coloured pastas, which contain tomato and spinach as well, might be chosen for a change.

The usual cooking time for pasta is about twelve minutes, and if the packet gives no instructions then that is the time to start tasting it, but cooking times vary a great deal so do read the instructions carefully. Pasta should always be cooked 'al dente', with a slight resistance to it rather than completely soft. I have found that wholewheat pasta is harder to overcook than the 'refined' kinds.

Recipes

Creole Style Noodles

340g (¾ lb)	wholewheat noodles	¾ lb
2	onions	2
55g (2 oz)	vegan margarine	¼ cup
2	green peppers	2
900g (2 lb)	tomatoes	2 lb
225g (½ lb)	green beans	½ lb
115g (4 oz)	fresh okra	¼ lb
As required	sea salt	As required

1 Cook the noodles for 10 minutes in boiling salted water, then leave them to drain.
2 Chop the onions and sauté them in the margarine until they begin to soften.
3 Peel and chop the tomatoes and chop the green pepper and green beans. Remove both ends of the okra, cut them into small pieces and cover with boiling water for 1 minute, then drain.
4 Add all of the vegetables to the onions, cover and simmer for 20 minutes.
5 Add the noodles and cook until they are tender, adding water if necessary. Season to taste and serve.

Note: Okra is more readily available now than it used to be and adds an exotic touch to this easy self-contained dish.

Oriental Macaroni

340g (¾ lb)	wholewheat macaroni	3 cups
2 tbs	vegetable oil	2 tbs
1 bunch	spring onions (scallions)	1 bunch
4 sticks	celery	4 sticks
115g (4 oz)	fresh or frozen green beans	¼ lb
285ml (½ pt)	water	1⅓ cups
½	vegetable stock cube	½
2 tbs	brown rice flour	2 tbs
1 tbs	soya (soy) flour	1 tbs
½ 225g tin	water chestnuts	½ ½ lb can
2 tbs	soya (soy) sauce	2 tbs
½ tsp	garlic salt	½ tsp
115g (4 oz) tinned	pimentos	¼ lb canned
1 tbs	sunflower seeds	1 tbs
4 oz (115g)	fresh bean sprouts	2 cups

1 Cook the macaroni until tender, drain and keep warm.
2 Chop the spring onions (scallions) and celery finely and sauté them in the oil for 2-3 minutes.
3 Slice the beans and add them to the saucepan together with most of the water (retaining about ¼ cupful) and the half broth cube. Bring to the boil, cover and simmer for 5 minutes.

4 Mix the rice flour and soya (soy) flour with the remaining water. Add this to the saucepan, stirring until thickened.
5 Slice the water chestnuts and dice the pimentos.
6 Add to the remaining ingredients and mix thoroughly. Stir until everything is heated through, then pour over the macaroni and mix well.

Note: Macaroni is traditionally associated with Italian dishes, but there is no reason why a Far-Eastern version should not be enjoyed. Another self-contained dish.

Banana and Spaghetti Curry

285g (10 oz)	wholewheat spaghetti	10 oz
3 large	bananas	3 large
55g (2 oz)	vegan margarine	¼ cup
55g (2 oz)	raisins or sultanas (golden seedless raisins)	⅓ cup
285ml (½ pt)	soya (soy) milk	1⅓ cups
1 small	onion	1 small
40g (1½ oz)	wholewheat flour	⅓ cup
2 tsp	curry powder	2 tsp
2 tsp	chutney	2 tsp
140ml (¼ pt)	water from spaghetti	⅔ cup

1 Cook the spaghetti in boiling salted water until tender, then drain, reserving 140ml (¼ pt/⅔ cup) of the water.
2 Chop the onion finely, melt the margarine and sauté the onion gently for 5 minutes.
3 Stir in the flour and curry powder, then add the milk and spaghetti water, stirring constantly to avoid lumps.
4 Bring to the boil, then add the raisins and chutney.
5 Cut the bananas into 1.5cm (½ inch) slices and add them to the sauce. Simmer gently for 10 minutes.
6 Place the spaghetti in a heated serving dish and pour the sauce over.

Note: This is an unusual combination. To avoid too much sweetness choose green-tipped bananas.

Mixed Vegetables with Pasta

4 tbs	olive oil	4 tbs
6-8 tbs	minced parsley	6-8 tbs
6	spring onions (scallions)	6
2 cloves	garlic	2 cloves
1	onion	1
1 tbs	basil	1 tbs
½ small head	cabbage	½ small head
225g (½ lb)	courgettes (zucchini)	½ lb
225g (½ lb)	tomatoes	½ lb
2	green peppers	2
285ml (½ pt)	water	1⅓ cups
½	vegetable stock cube	½

2 tsp	cider vinegar or wine vinegar	2 tsp
As required	sea salt	As required
As required	freshly ground black pepper	As required
340-395g (12-14 oz)	wholewheat noodles or spaghetti	12-14 oz
30g (1 oz)	vegan margarine	2 tbs
4 tbs	Smokey Snaps (soy bakon bits)	4 tbs

1 Chop the spring onions (scallions), garlic and onion finely. Sauté them in the oil for 3 minutes.
2 Shred the cabbage, dice the courgettes (zucchini) and green peppers, peel and slice the tomatoes and add these ingredients to the saucepan, together with the water, half stock cube, vinegar, basil and seasoning.
3 Simmer, uncovered, for 10 minutes.
4 Cook the pasta until just tender, then drain and toss with the margarine.
5 Add the vegetable mixture, mix well, and sprinkle with the Smokey Snaps (soy bakon bits).

Note: This highly nutritious, tasty dish requires no accompaniments.

Baked Noodles and Aubergine

680g (1½ lb)	aubergines (eggplant)	1½ lb
As required	sea salt	As required
395g (14 oz)	wholewheat noodles	14 oz
1 large	onion	1 large
1 clove	garlic	1 clove
3 tbs (or more if required)	vegetable oil	3 tbs (or more if required)
2 large	tomatoes	2 large
2 tbs	tomato purée (paste)	2 tbs
½ tsp	cinnamon	½ tsp
¼ tsp	grated nutmeg	¼ tsp
¼ tsp	cayenne pepper	¼ tsp

1 Slice the aubergines (eggplants), sprinkle with salt, and leave them in a colander for at least half an hour to allow the bitter juice to drain away. Rinse well and pat dry.
2 Cook the noodles in boiling salted water until just tender. Drain and keep warm.
3 Chop the onion and garlic and sauté them in the oil until golden.
4 Add the aubergine (eggplant) slices and fry until lightly browned on both sides, using a little more oil if necessary.
5 Skin and chop the tomatoes and add them to the aubergine (eggplant) mixture along with the tomato purée (paste). Season with the spices and add just a

little water, simmering gently until the aubergines (eggplants) are tender and you have a thick sauce.
6 Place alternate layers of pasta and sauce in a greased casserole.
7 Bake in a moderate oven at 350°F/180°C (Gas Mark 4) for about half an hour.

Note: This is my version of a traditional Middle-Eastern dish. It can be served on its own or with salad. Suitable for a dinner party.

Macaroni and Mushroom Loaf

225g (½ lb)	wholewheat macaroni	2 cups
55g (2 oz)	vegan margarine	¼ cup
1	onion	1
2 large	tomatoes	2 large
170g (6 oz)	mushrooms	3 cups
2 tbs	gram (chick pea flour)	2 tbs
4 tbs	water	4 tbs
As required	sea salt	As required
As required	freshly ground black pepper	As required
As required	wholewheat breadcrumbs	As required

1 Cook the macaroni until tender and leave to drain.
2 Chop the onions finely, peel and slice the tomatoes and chop the mushrooms.
3 Heat the margarine and sauté the vegetables until tender.
4 Combine the macaroni and vegetables.
5 Add the water to the gram (chick pea flour) and mix well. Add this to the macaroni mixture and mix well.
6 Add enough breadcrumbs to make a sticky consistency and season to taste.
7 Put into a greased loaf tin and bake with oven at 350°F/180°C (Gas Mark 4) for 30-40 minutes.

Note: Use small macaroni for this British dish. (If preferred it can be baked in a casserole dish rather than a loaf tin.) Serve it with seasonal vegetables.

Macaroni 'Cheese'

340-395g (12-14 oz)	wholewheat macaroni	3-3½ cups
115g (4 oz)	vegan margarine	½ cup
55g (2 oz)	wholewheat flour	¼ cup
285ml (½ pt)	hot water	1⅓ cups
570ml (1 pt)	soya (soy) milk	2½ cups
1-2 tbs	soya (soy) sauce or vegetarian Worcester sauce	1-2 tbs
As required	sea salt	As required
As required	freshly ground black pepper	As required
55g (2 oz)	nutritional yeast	½ cup

1 Cook the macaroni until tender then drain.

2 Melt 85g (3 oz/⅓ cup) margarine in a large saucepan and stir in the flour. Add the hot water, stirring constantly to avoid lumps. Slowly stir in the milk. Stir over a low heat until thickened and boiling. Add sauce and seasoning to taste and stir in ¾ of the yeast.

3 Stir the cooked macaroni into the sauce and transfer to an oiled casserole dish. Top with the remaining yeast and slivers of margarine. Bake at 350°F/180°C (Gas Mark 4) for 15-20 minutes.

Note: I confess to fond memories of traditional macaroni cheese and have experimented with vegan versions. This one uses nutritional yeast for the 'cheese'.

Macaroni 'Cheese' With a Difference

340g (¾ lb)	wholewheat macaroni	3 cups
225g (½ lb)	cashew pieces	2 cups
1 tin (c.400g)	pimentos	1 can (c.14 oz)
Juice of ½	lemon	Juice of ½
3 tbs	vegetable oil	3 tbs
4 tbs	nutritional yeast	4 tbs
2 tbs	water	2 tbs
1-2 tbs	soya (soy) sauce	1-2 tbs
As required	sea salt	As required
As required	freshly ground black pepper	As required

1 Cook the macaroni until just tender and drain.

2 Put the cashews into a liquidizer or food processor and grind them. Add all the remaining ingredients and blend thoroughly.

3 Mix the sauce with the macaroni, put into a greased casserole, and bake at 350°F/180°C (Gas Mark 4) for about half an hour.

Note: This is an adaptation of an American idea. The mixture is not all that 'cheesey' when it is raw, but the texture changes after cooking.

If you make twice the required quantity of the 'cheese' mixture in this recipe you can use the second half for the recipe below.

Pasta, Broccoli and Mushroom Casserole with Cashew/Pimento 'Cheese'

	'Cheese' mixture as in recipe above	
340g (¾ lb)	wholemeal pasta shells (or other shape)	3 cups
340g (¾ lb)	broccoli	¾ lb
2 tbs	vegetable oil	2 tbs
2	onions	2
2 cloves	garlic	2 cloves
340g (¾ lb)	mushrooms	6 cups

1 Make the mixture described in the recipe above.

2 Cook the pasta until just tender and drain.

3 Cook the broccoli until just tender and drain.

4 Heat the oil in a frying pan. Chop the onions and sauté them. Chop the garlic finely and add to the pan. Continue to cook for a few minutes while cleaning and chopping the mushrooms. Add the mushrooms and sauté for a few minutes longer.

5 In a large saucepan or bowl mix the pasta, broccoli, and contents of the frying pan with the 'cheese' mixture. Transfer to a greased casserole and bake at 350°F/180°C (Gas Mark 4) for about half an hour.

Spaghetti with Chestnut Sauce

225g (½ lb)	dried chestnuts soaked in a Thermos flask overnight (see p.77)	½ lb
2	onions	2
2 tbs	olive oil	2 tbs
455g (1 lb)	tomatoes	1 lb
2 tbs	water	2 tbs
As required	sea salt	As required
As required	freshly ground black pepper	As required
1 tsp dried or 1 tbs fresh	marjoram	1 tsp dried or 1 tbs fresh
340-395g (12-14 oz)	wholewheat spaghetti	12-14 oz

1 Drain the chestnuts.

2 Chop the onions. Heat the oil in a saucepan and sauté the onions for a few minutes. Add the chestnuts to the pan and cook 3-4 minutes longer.

3 Skin and chop the tomatoes. Add them to the saucepan together with the water, seasonings and marjoram. Cover the pan and cook over a very low heat for 10-15 minutes, stirring occasionally.

4 Cook the spaghetti until just tender; drain and top with the chestnut sauce.

Note: Chestnuts make a delicious basis for this pasta sauce.

Pasta in Forno

340-395g (12-14 oz)	wholemeal shells (or other shape)	3-3½ cups
2	onions	2
55g (2 oz)	vegan margarine	¼ cup
2 tbs	olive oil	2 tbs
2 cloves	garlic	2 cloves
1	green pepper	1
455g (1 lb)	aubergine (eggplant)	1 lb
680g (1½ lbs)	tomatoes	1½ lbs
1 tsp	dried oregano	1 tsp
1 tsp	dried basil	1 tsp
As required	sea salt	As required
As required	freshly ground black pepper	As required
4 tbs	water	4 tbs
30g (1 oz)	nutritional yeast	¼ cup

1 Cook the pasta until just tender.

2 Meanwhile, chop the onion and fry it in half the margarine and the oil for 2-3 minutes. Chop the garlic finely and add it to the pan for another 2-3 minutes.

3 Chop the green pepper finely. Dice the aubergine (eggplant). Skin and chop the tomatoes. Add these ingredients to the pan, together with the herbs, seasoning and water. Bring to the boil, then lower the heat, cover, and simmer for a few minutes until the vegetables are just tender.

4 Mix the pasta with the vegetables and transfer to a large greased casserole. Sprinkle the yeast on top and dot with the remainder of the margarine. Bake at 350°F/180°C (Gas Mark 4) for about half an hour.

Note: Pasta dishes cooked in the oven ('in forno') are the only kind which the Italians consider to be true main dishes. This is my adaptation of such a dish.

Spaghetti with Tahini Sauce

225g (½ lb)	wholewheat spaghetti	½ lb
2	onions	2
3 tbs	vegetable oil	3 tbs
4 tbs	tahini	4 tbs
4 tbs	tomato purée (paste)	4 tbs
285-425ml (½-¾ pt)	water	1½-2 cups
2 tsp	yeast extract	2 tsp
As required	freshly ground black pepper	As required

1 Cook the spaghetti.

2 Meanwhile, chop the onions and fry them in the oil in a saucepan for a few minutes until lightly browned.

3 Add the tahini and tomato purée (paste) and then the water (start with the smaller quantity and if the sauce is too thick, add the rest). Bring to the boil, stirring constantly until thickened. Stir in the yeast extract and add pepper to taste. Simmer, uncovered, for a few minutes.

4 When the spaghetti is tender, drain it and pour the sauce over it.

Note: In this recipe, tahini, which is high in protein and calcium, forms the basis of a rich, satisfying spaghetti sauce. If double quantities of all the ingredients are used, then half can be refrigerated and used for the following dish as well.
Quick and Easy.

Baked Tahini Pasta

340-395g (12-14 oz)	wholemeal macaroni or shells Ingredients for sauce from above recipe	3-3½ cups
55g (2 oz)	wholewheat breadcrumbs	1 cup

1 Cook the pasta.

2 Make the sauce as described in the recipe above.

3 Drain the pasta, and mix it with the sauce. Turn the mixture into an oiled casserole dish, and top with breadcrumbs. Bake at 350°F/180°C (Gas Mark 4) for about half an hour.

Note: When baked with pasta, tahini sauce (see recipe above) changes its texture and is quite different. Serve this dish with salad.

Tangy Noodle Casserole

285g (10 oz)	wholewheat noodles	10 oz
455g (1 lb)	tofu	2 cups
1½ tbs	lemon juice	1½ tbs
1 tbs	vegetable oil	1 tbs
2 tbs	miso	2 tbs
3	spring onions (scallions)	3
1 tbs	vegan margarine	1 tbs

1 Cook the noodles until tender in lightly salted water and drain.
2 Put half the tofu in a liquidizer along with the lemon juice, oil and miso, and blend thoroughly.
3 Put the other half of the tofu into a tea towel (dish towel) and squeeze as much of the moisture out as possible.
4 Chop the spring onions (scallions) finely.
5 In a large bowl combine the noodles, tofu/miso mixture, squeezed tofu and chopped spring onions (scallions). Mix well, then turn into an oiled casserole.
6 Dot the top of the casserole with small pieces of margarine, cover and bake at 350°F/180°C (Gas Mark 4) for 20 minutes, then uncover and bake for a further 10 minutes.

Note: The idea for this recipe is based on an Eastern European dish of noodles with cottage cheese. Serve it with seasonal vegetables.

Macaroni, Mushroom and Tofu Casserole

225g (½ lb)	tofu	1 cup
As required	vegetable oil for deep-frying	As required
225g (½ lb)	wholewheat macaroni	2 cups
225g (½ lb)	mushrooms	4 cups
4 tbs	vegan margarine	4 tbs
2 tsp	lemon juice	2 tsp
3 tbs	wholewheat flour	3 tbs
285ml (½ pt)	soya (soy) milk	1⅓ cups
2 tsp	miso	2 tsp
As required	freshly ground black pepper	As required
As required	nutritional yeast	As required

1 Cube the tofu and deep-fry until golden. Set aside.
2 Cook the macaroni until tender and set aside.
3 Slice the mushrooms and sauté them in 1 tablespoon margarine until just tender. Sprinkle the lemon juice over them and set aside.
4 Melt the remainder of the margarine in a saucepan, and stir in the flour. Slowly add the milk, stirring constantly to avoid lumps. Remove from the heat, and stir in the miso and pepper.

5 Add the cooked macaroni, fried tofu cubes, and sautéed mushrooms to the sauce, and mix well. Turn into an oiled casserole, sprinkle with Good-Tasting Yeast if used, and place in the oven at 350°F/180°C (Gas Mark 4) for about 15 minutes.

Note: Serve with either cooked seasonal vegetables or salad.

Spaghetti All' Alfredo

240-395g (12-14 oz)	wholewheat spaghetti	12-14 oz
55g (2 oz)	vegan margarine	¼ cup
2 cartons (120g each)	vegan cream	1-1½ cups
55g (2 oz)	nutritional yeast	½ cup
As required	sea salt	As required
As required	freshly ground black pepper	As required

1 Cook the spaghetti until just tender then drain.
2 Melt the margarine over a low heat in a large saucepan. Lower the heat to minimum and heat the cream until warm.
3 Add the spaghetti to the pan and sprinkle in the yeast, a little salt, and lots of pepper. Stir the spaghetti until it is coated with the sauce and serve immediately.

Note: Many Italian restaurants make a feature of pasta with a rich cream sauce. Now that there are good, not-too-sweet vegan creams available I thought I would try a vegan version – here is the result.
Quick and Easy. Suitable for One.

Tempeh Sauce for Spaghetti

2	onions	2
1-2 cloves	garlic	1-2 cloves
2 tbs	olive oil	2 tbs
2 sticks	celery	2 sticks
115g (4 oz)	mushrooms	2 cups
1 tin (c.400g)	tomatoes	1 can (14-16 oz)
4 tbs	tomato purée (paste)	4 tbs
140ml (¼ pt)	water	⅔ cup
3 tsp	dried basil	3 tsp
2 tsp	dried marjoram	2 tsp
As required	sea salt	As required
As required	freshly ground black pepper	As required
225g (½ lb)	tempeh	1 cup
340g (12 oz)	wholewheat spaghetti	12 oz

1 Chop the onions and garlic finely. Sauté in the oil for 2-3 minutes.
2 Chop the celery and mushrooms and add them to the saucepan. Stir well and cook for a further 2-3 minutes.

3 Add the tomatoes (mashing them with a spoon while doing so), tomato purée, water, herbs and seasoning. Crumble the tempeh into the saucepan. Stir well. Bring to the boil, then lower the heat and simmer for about 20 minutes, stirring occasionally while the spaghetti is cooking.

Note: This is a traditional 'Bolognese' sauce, made with tempeh instead of meat.

Tofu and Miso Sauce for Spaghetti

455g (1 lb)	tofu	2 cups
2 tbs	vegetable oil plus additional for deep-frying	1 tbs
2	onions	2
2 cloves	garlic	2 cloves
115g (4 oz)	mushrooms	2 cups
2 sticks	celery	2 sticks
340g (¾ lb)	tomatoes	¾ lb
2	carrots	2
120ml (4 fl oz)	tomato ketchup	½ cup
140ml (¼ pt)	water	⅔ cup
2	bay leaves	2
As required	freshly ground black pepper	As required
3 tsp	miso	3 tsp
2 tbs	hot water	2 tbs

1 Cut the tofu into small cubes and deep-fry until golden. Set aside.
2 Chop the onions coarsely and the garlic finely. Sauté in the oil for 2-3 minutes.
3 Chop the mushrooms, celery and tomatoes. Grate the carrots. Add to the onion, stir, and cook for a further 2-3 minutes.
4 Add the ketchup, water, bay leaves, pepper and tofu. Bring to the boil, then lower the heat and simmer for about 15 minutes.
5 Cream the miso in a cup with the hot water and add to the tofu sauce. Simmer for another minute, then remove from the heat and serve over spaghetti.

Lasagne al Forno

170g (6 oz)	wholewheat lasagne	6 oz
340g (12 oz)	tempeh	1½ cups
2	onions	2
2 cloves	garlic	2 cloves
2 tbs	vegetable oil	2 tbs
115g (4 oz)	mushrooms	2 cups
2 tins (c.400g each)	tomatoes	28-32 oz canned
4 tbs	tomato purée (paste)	4 tbs
2 tsp	oregano	2 tsp
As required	freshly ground black pepper	As required
455g (1 lb)	tofu	2 cups
3 tbs	tahini	3 tbs
1 tbs	soya (soy) sauce	1 tbs
2 tbs	soya (soy) yogurt	2 tbs
Juice of ½	lemon	Juice of ½

1 Cook the lasagne in boiling water until tender. Drain.
2 Steam the tempeh (according to the instructions on p.85 or in a mixture of 4 parts water to 1 part soy sauce). Cool.
3 Chop the onions. Crush the garlic. Sauté in the oil in a saucepan for 3-4 minutes.
4 Chop the mushrooms finely. Add to the saucepan, together with the tomatoes, tomato purée (paste), and oregano. Bring to the boil, then lower the heat and simmer, uncovered, for about 10 minutes.
5 Crumble the tempeh into the saucepan, and continue simmering for about 10 minutes longer. Season to taste (additional salt should not be required).
6 Meanwhile, put the tofu, tahini, soya (soy) sauce, yogurt and lemon juice in a liquidizer and blend thoroughly.
7 Put alternate layers of lasagne, tempeh sauce, and blended tofu in a casserole, finishing with a layer of tofu. Bake at 350°F/180°C (Gas Mark 4) for about half an hour.

Note: Tempeh makes a good filling for lasagne, and tofu adds low-fat creaminess.

8
Beans

Introduction

Pulses are a mainstay of a vegan diet. High in protein and high in fibre, they are also very versatile, and there are enough different kinds to provide plenty of variety. Beans have a bad reputation for causing flatulence, but if they are properly cooked and served not more than once a day this should not be a problem. Unlike other vegetables, beans should always be cooked until they are soft; 'al dente' beans are hard to digest. (The only beans I do find indigestible are soya (soy) beans, so I do not tend to use them.)

Most beans need to be soaked for many hours before cooking. Discard the soaking water, cover with fresh, bring to the boil and cook over a low heat for the amount of time needed. (Kidney shaped beans should be vigorously boiled for 10 minutes before simmering.) Do not add salt until near the end of the cooking time as salt retards the cooking process.

Unlike fresh vegetables, beans do not lose any of their food value when canned. Tinned beans tend to have far too much salt added to them, but it is easy enough to drain and rinse them thoroughly. Most British tinned beans have not only salt but also sugar added to them, but again it can be washed off. Buying beans in cans does, undeniably, cost considerably more than buying them dried, but much time is saved (and there is no need to remember to soak them). It will soon become evident to anyone reading the recipes which follow that I generally use tinned rather than dried beans myself. Therefore, for most of the recipes quantities are given in cooked weight rather than dried weight. Most dried beans will approximately double in weight when cooked. Below is a brief description of the pulses used in the recipes in this chapter and a note on their cooking times (obviously a pressure cooker will greatly shorten those

times, but pressure cookers terrify me, so I am unable to help with cooking times for them.)

Butter (lima) beans – these big white beans are the easiest to find in cans in Britain, though not only do they have sugar added they are also rather overcooked, so if you can find Continental ones (slightly different in size and shape) I would recommend them. Cooked after soaking from dried they should take about 1½ hours. American lima beans are similar but much smaller.

Haricot (navy) beans – these are little white beans, the kind found in British baked beans, without much distinguishing flavour but for that very reason, useful in highly seasoned dishes. In tins they are usually called by their Italian name, cannellini beans (not exactly the same variety but similar enough). Cooking them from dried after soaking should take 45 minutes to an hour.

Chick peas (garbanzo beans) – they have become remarkably well known in Britain of late if only as the main ingredient of hummus. The taste and texture of these beans makes them a great favourite in various parts of the world. As may be gathered from the number of recipes for them in this chapter, they are my favourite too. Cooking them from dried after soaking will take about 1½ hours.

Red kidney beans – it must be the slight sweetness of these beans (which certainly do not need the sugar added to them in British tins) that makes them so distinctive, and their texture is pleasing too. Cooking time after soaking should be about one hour.

Borlotti (pinto) beans – brown, often speckled, kidney-shaped beans which are used in America mainly for chilli;

they are not that well known in Britain where they are usually found under their Italian name. Although similar to red kidney beans they are less sweet and have a slightly different texture. Cooking time should be about an hour after soaking.

Aduki beans – in the Far East these are used primarily for desserts as they have a naturally sweet flavour. In Britain they are most often used in macrobiotic meals. They cannot be found in tins, but they take only about 45 minutes to cook after soaking.

Black-eyed beans – these lovely 'earthy' beans – much used in the American Deep South – also take no more than 45 minutes to cook after soaking. A secret to keep the white part of the bean white is to add a little lemon juice to the cooking water.

Split peas – both the yellow and green ones taste similar. They take less than half an hour if soaked and can be cooked, if preferred, without pre-soaking. They usually tend to be cooked to a mush, but I think they are much nicer cooked for a shorter time so that they are soft but still recognisable in their original shapes.

Brown/green/Continental lentils – brown and green lentils are similar, but I think the brown ones taste more interesting. If soaked (I usually pour boiling water over them and leave them for a couple of hours) they take 15-20 minutes to cook; they can also be cooked without pre-soaking and still won't take more than about half an hour. For many dishes it is better *not* to pre-soak them, as they are more likely to retain their texture and not go mushy.

Red (Egyptian) lentils – these are split and hulled brown lentils and are the easiest pulses to use, requiring no pre-soaking and only about 15 minutes cooking time (I have never understood why so many cookery book writers tell you to cook them for 30 to 45 minutes).

Recipes

Butter Bean (Lima Bean) and Potato Stew

680g (1½ lb)	potatoes	1½ lb
2	onions	2
2 tbs	vegetable oil	2 tbs
285ml (½ pt)	vegetable stock or water	1⅓ cups
1 tbs	finely chopped parsley	1 tbs
1 tsp	dried sage	1 tsp
455g (1 lb) or 2 tins (c.400g each)	cooked drained butter beans (lima beans)	2½ cups or 2 cans (c.14-16 oz each)
1 tsp	miso	1 tsp

1 Cook the potatoes in lightly salted boiling water until tender (or use leftover cooked potatoes). Drain and chop.
2 Slice the onions thinly. Sauté in the oil for a few minutes until lightly browned.
3 Stir in the stock or water, the parsley and the sage. Then stir in the drained beans. Bring to the boil and simmer for 2-3 minutes.
4 Stir in the potatoes and simmer for a further 2-3 minutes.
5 Remove a little of the stock from the saucepan and cream it with the miso in a cup before stirring it into the saucepan. Serve immediately.

Note: Stews usually take a long time to prepare, but if the beans and potatoes are cooked beforehand, this one is quick to make. Serve either over brown rice or in a bowl accompanied by wholewheat bread.
Quick and Easy. Suitable for One.

Vegetable and White Bean Casserole

680g (1½ lb)	mixed root vegetables (carrots, turnips, swedes)	1½ lb
225g (½ lb)	potatoes	½ lb
1 small head	celery	1 small head
3	onions	3
55g (2 oz)	vegan margarine	¼ cup
455g (1 lb) or 2 tins (c.400g each)	cooked drained butter beans (lima beans) or haricot (navy) beans	2½ cups or 2 cans c.14-16 oz each)
285ml (½ pt)	water	1⅓ cups
2 tsp	yeast extract	2 tsp
1 tin (c.400g)	tomatoes	1 can (c.14-16 oz)
55g (2 oz)	wholewheat breadcrumbs	1 cup

1 Dice the root vegetables and potatoes (peeled if desired). Trim and slice the celery and the onions.
2 Melt the margarine in a large saucepan. Add the diced vegetables, celery and onion. Stir over a moderate heat for 5 minutes.
3 Stir in the beans, water, yeast extract and the can of tomatoes. Bring to the boil, then transfer to a large casserole.
4 Cover and bake in the centre of a moderate oven at 350°F/180°C (Gas Mark 4) for 1¼-1½ hours until the vegetables are cooked.
5 Remove the lid from the casserole. Sprinkle the breadcrumbs over the vegetables and cook for a further 20-30 minutes in the oven until the topping is crisp and golden.

Note: Although this satisfying, old-fashioned casserole takes a long time to cook, it requires no attention for most of that time.

Spaghetti and Butter Bean Casserole

225g (½ lb)	wholewheat spaghetti	½ lb
225g (½ lb) or 1 tin (c.400g)	cooked drained butter beans (lima beans)	1¼ cup or 1 can (c.14-16 oz)
1 large	onion	1 large
2 cloves	garlic	2 cloves
1 small or ½ large	red pepper	1 small or ½ large
4 tbs	olive oil	4 tbs
1 tin (c.400g)	tomatoes	1 can (c.14-16 oz)
1 tin (c.140g)	tomato purée (paste)	1 can (c.5 oz)
1 tsp	raw cane sugar	1 tsp
½ tsp	oregano	½ tsp
½ tsp	thyme	½ tsp
2 tbs	chopped parsley	2 tbs
30g (1 oz)	vegan margarine	2 tbs
55g (2 oz)	wholewheat breadcrumbs	1 cup

1 Cook the spaghetti in boiling salted water until just tender.
2 Chop the onion, garlic and red pepper finely and sauté them in the olive oil until soft but not brown.
3 Blend the tomatoes in a liquidizer and add them to the saucepan together with the tomato purée, sugar and herbs. Mix well and simmer over a low heat for about 20 minutes.
4 Layer the spaghetti, cooked beans and tomato sauce in a greased casserole.
5 Melt the margarine and stir in the breadcrumbs.
6 Top the casserole with the breadcrumbs and bake for 45 minutes in a moderate oven at 350°F/180°C (Gas Mark 4).

Note: Spaghetti is rarely used in baked dishes. Here it is combined with butter beans (lima beans) for a pleasing mixture of tastes and textures. Serve with a salad if desired.

Haricot (Navy) Bean and Root Vegetable Pie

2	onions	2
455g (1 lb)	swede (rutabaga) - peeled	1 lb
225g (½ lb)	carrots	½ lb
2 tbs	vegetable oil	2 tbs
30g (1 oz)	vegan margarine	2 tbs
30g (1 oz)	wholewheat flour	¼ cup
425ml (¾ pt)	soya (soy) milk	2 cups
As required	sea salt	As required
As required	freshly ground black pepper	As required
455g (1 lb) or 2 tins (c.400g each)	cooked drained haricot (navy) beans	2½ cups or 2 cans (c.14-16 oz each)
900g (2 lb)	mashed potatoes	2 lb

1 Chop the onions. Peel and chop the swede (rutabaga) and carrots.
2 Heat the oil in a large saucepan. Add the vegetables and cover the pan, then leave to cook over a low heat until just tender (10-15 minutes).
3 Melt the margarine in another saucepan. Stir in the flour, and then slowly add the milk, stirring constantly to avoid lumps. When it has thickened remove from the heat. Season to taste.

4 Add the drained beans to the cooked vegetables. Season to taste. Transfer the mixture to a greased casserole dish. Spoon the white sauce over it and top with the mashed potatoes.

5 Bake at 375°F/190°C (Gas Mark 5) for 20-30 minutes until the top has begun to turn brown.

Note: This recipe offers a pleasant contrast of tastes and textures. It can be served with a green salad if desired but is fine on its own.

Haricot (Navy) Beans in a Mediterranean Style Sauce

2	onions	2
455g (1 lb)	courgettes (zucchini)	1 lb
1 large	green pepper	1 large
55g (2 oz)	vegan margarine	¼ cup
455g (1 lb)	ripe tomatoes	1 lb
1-2 cloves	garlic	1-2 cloves
30g (1 oz)	wholewheat flour	¼ cup
425ml (¾ pt)	soya (soy) milk	2 cups
1	bay leaf	1
1 tsp	dried basil	1 tsp
455g (1 lb) or 2 tins (c.400g each)	cooked drained haricot (navy) beans	2½ cups or 2 cans (c.14-16 oz each)
As required	sea salt	As required
As required	freshly ground black pepper	As required

1 Chop the onions, courgettes (zucchini), and green pepper. Heat the margarine in a large saucepan and sauté the vegetables for a few minutes.

2 Skin and chop the tomatoes. Crush the garlic. Add these ingredients to the pan and cook for a couple of minutes longer. Stir in the flour, then add the milk, stirring constantly until smooth. Add the bay leaf and basil and simmer over a low heat, uncovered, for 10-15 minutes.

3 Add the beans to the sauce and season to taste. Simmer for a few minutes longer, then remove bay leaf and serve.

Note: This sauce can be served over rice, pasta or a mashed potato ring.

Mediterranean-style Beans and Chestnuts

115g (4 oz)	dried chestnuts	¼ lb
2	onions	2
3 tbs	vegetable oil	3 tbs
2 cloves	garlic	2 cloves
2 tins (c.400g each)	chopped tomatoes	28-32 oz canned
2 tsp	dried oregano	2 tsp
As required	sea salt	As required
As required	freshly ground black pepper	As required
225-340g (½-¾ lb)	courgettes (zucchini)	½-¾ lb
225g (½ lb) or 1 tin (c.425g)	cooked drained haricot (navy) beans	1¼ cups or 1 can (14-16 oz)

1 Soak the chestnuts in a thermos flask until tender (see p.77).

2 Chop the onions. Heat the oil and sauté them for a minute or two while finely chopping the garlic. Add the garlic to the pan and continue cooking while chopping the courgettes (zucchini); add them to the pan and continue sautéing for a few minutes longer.

3 Add the tomatoes to the pan and bring to the boil. Stir in the oregano, salt (if required – tinned tomatoes are quite salty) and pepper. Add the drained beans and chestnuts. Lower the heat and simmer, uncovered, for about 15 minutes.

Note: Serve over brown rice or pasta or as a stew with crusty wholewheat bread.

Macaroni and Bean 'Hot-Pot'

225-340g (½-¾ lb)	wholewheat macaroni	2-3 cups
4 tbs	vegetable oil	4 tbs
1	onion	1
1	green pepper	1
170g (6 oz)	mushrooms	3 cups
2 large	tomatoes	2 large
1 tsp	dried mixed herbs	1 tsp
1 tsp	lemon juice	1 tsp
1 tin (c.400g)	curried baked beans	1 can (c.14-16 oz)

1 Cook the macaroni in salted water until tender.

2 Chop the onion and pepper finely and slice the mushrooms. Peel and chop the tomatoes and sauté all the vegetables in the oil for about 10 minutes.

3 Add the herbs and lemon juice. Then add the beans, mix well and heat thoroughly.

4 Add the cooked macaroni, mix well and serve.

Note: Canned haricot (navy) beans in a curry sauce combine with pasta in this speedy savoury. Quick and Easy. Suitable for One.

Chick Peas in Spanish Sauce

455g (1 lb) or 2 tins (c.400g each)	cooked drained chick peas (garbanzo beans)	2½ cups or 2 cans (c.14-16 oz each)
1	green pepper	1
1	red pepper	1
1	fresh chilli	1
1	onion	1
1 clove	garlic	1 clove
2 tbs	olive oil	2 tbs
1 tbs	chopped parsley	1 tbs
1 tsp	sea salt	1 tsp
455g (1 lb)	ripe tomatoes	1 lb

1 Chop the peppers, onions, garlic and tomatoes.
2 Lightly fry the peppers, onion and garlic in the olive oil for a few minutes.
3 Add the parsley, tomatoes and salt and cook on a low heat for about half an hour, stirring occasionally, until the tomatoes are pulped.
4 Combine this mixture with the cooked chick peas (garbanzo beans) and serve.

Note: This recipe makes a very pleasant, spicy mixture which can be served with potatoes or over rice.

Aubergine and Chick Pea 'Ragout'

1 large	aubergine (eggplant)	1 large
2 large	onions	2 large
100ml (4 fl oz)	olive oil	½ cup
455g (1 lb) or 2 tins (c.400g each)	chick peas (garbanzo beans)	2½ cups or 2 cans (c.14-16 oz)
2 tins (c.395-455g)	tomatoes	2 cans (c.14-16 oz)
1 tsp	dried mint	1 tsp
As required	sea salt	As required
As required	freshly ground black pepper	As required

1 Chop the aubergine (eggplant) into cubes and chop the onions coarsely. Heat the olive oil gently and sauté until tenderized. Add the cooked chick peas (garbanzo beans), tinned tomatoes, mint and seasoning.
2 Cook uncovered, over a low heat for half an hour.
3 Cool and serve at room temperature.

Note: This dish comes from Greece where food is generally served lukewarm. Of course, it could be served either hot or cold instead, but there are times when it is quite handy to have a dish that can be left on the table for people to help themselves to, without worrying about keeping it either hot or refrigerated.

Chick Pea Stroganoff

30g (1 oz)	vegan margarine	2 tbs
1	onion	1
225g (½lb)	mushrooms	4 cups
455g (1 lb) or 2 tins (c.400g each)	cooked drained chick peas (garbanzo beans)	2½ cups or 2 cans (c.14-16 oz each)
4 tbs	vegetable stock or water	4 tbs
¼ tsp	freshly ground nutmeg	¼ tsp
1 tsp	soya (soy) sauce	1 tsp
¼ tsp	mustard powder	¼ tsp
2 tsp	cider vinegar or wine vinegar	2 tsp
200ml (⅓ pt)	soya (soy) yogurt	¾ cup
285g (10 oz)	wholewheat noodles	2 cups

1 Chop the onion and mushrooms. Melt the margarine and sauté the vegetables until soft.
2 Add the stock, seasonings, chick peas (garbanzo beans) and vinegar. Cover and simmer on a low heat for about 10 minutes.
3 Meanwhile, cook the noodles for 10-15 minutes until soft.
4 Add the yogurt to the chick pea (garbanzo bean) mixture over the lowest possible heat, stirring constantly without bringing to the boil, until heated through.
6 Serve over the cooked noodles.

Note: This is one of my all-time favourite dishes. Quick and Easy. Suitable for One.

Chick Pea Burgers

225g (½lb) or 1 tin (c.400g each)	cooked drained chick peas (garbanzo beans)	2½ cups or 2 cans (c.14-16 oz)
1 small	onion	1 small
1 stick	celery	1 stick
85g (3 oz)	mushrooms	1½ cups
115g (4 oz)	sesame seeds	¾ cup
1 tbs	soy sauce	1 tbs
As required	vegetable oil	As required

1 Mash the chick peas (garbanzo beans) in a bowl.
2 Chop the onion, celery and mushrooms very finely. Grind the sesame seeds in a liquidizer.
3 Add the chopped vegetables and ground sesame seeds to the beans and knead with the hands. At this stage it will probably look as though the mixture can never be formed into burgers, but add the soy sauce and continue kneading and it should soon be easy to form into four burgers.
4 Sauté the burgers in a little oil on each side, starting out with a high heat, then lowering it, so that each side is browned but cooked through.

Note: Serve these in a bun with lettuce, and sliced tomatoes or ketchup.

Quick and Easy. Suitable for One.

Chick Pea Curry

2	onions	2
2 tbs	vegan margarine	2 tbs
2 cloves	garlic	2 cloves
2	fresh chillies	2
2.5cm (1 inch)	piece fresh ginger	1 inch
3 tsp	cumin seeds	3 tsp
2 tsp	coriander seeds	2 tsp
1 tsp	turmeric	1 tsp
1 tsp	paprika	1 tsp
455g (1 lb) or 2 tins (c.400g each)	cooked drained chick peas (garbanzo beans)	2½ cups or 2 cans (c.14-16 oz each)
285ml (½ pt)	vegetable stock	1⅓ cups

1 Chop the onions and sauté in the margarine for a minute or two. Chop the garlic finely and add to the saucepan. Continue sautéeing until the onion is lightly browned.

2 Seed and chop the chillies finely. Peel and chop the ginger finely. Add to the saucepan and cook for a minute or two longer.

3 Grind the cumin and coriander seeds. Add them to the saucepan, together with the turmeric and paprika, and stir well for a minute or so.

4 Add the chick peas (garbanzo beans) and stir well. Pour in the stock and bring to the boil. Lower the heat to moderately low, cover and cook for about 15 minutes, then uncover and, if necessary, turn the heat up a little, and cook for about 5 minutes longer, until virtually all the liquid has been absorbed.

Note: This can be made with curry powder instead of the suggested spices, but it is not nearly as nice. Even using whole seeds instead of ground ones makes a big difference to the flavour of a curry.

Chick Pea and Sesame Roast with Tomato Topping

Roast

2	onions	2
2 tbs	vegetable oil	2 tbs
455g (1 lb) or 2 tins (c.400g each)	cooked drained chick peas (garbanzo beans)	2½ cups or 2 cans (c.14-16 oz each)
2 tbs	water	2 tbs
1 tbs	gram (chick pea) flour	1 tbs
1 large or 2 small	carrots	1 large or 2 small
1 tsp dried or 2 tsp fresh	marjoram	1 tsp dried or 2 tsp fresh
55g (2 oz)	tahini	⅓ cup
30g (1 oz)	sesame seeds	1/6 cup

Topping

1½ tbs	vegan margarine	1½ tbs
2 tbs	wholewheat flour	2 tbs
285ml (½ pt)	soya (soy) milk	1⅓ cups
55g (2 oz)	tomato purée (paste)	¼ cup
As required	sea salt	As required
As required	freshly ground black pepper	As required
1 tsp	dried basil	1 tsp
4 tbs	nutritional yeast	4 tbs

1 Chop the onions and sauté them in the vegetable oil in a large saucepan for a few minutes until tenderized.

2 Grate the carrots finely. Set aside. Toast the sesame seeds until lightly browned, cool slightly, and grind in a blender. Set aside.

3 Remove the pan from the heat and add the beans (drained) to the pan, mashing them coarsely.

4 Put the water in a small cup and beat in the gram (chick pea) flour with a fork. Add this to the bean mixture. Stir in the tahini, carrots, marjoram and ground sesame seeds.

5 Turn the mixture into an oiled pan and bake at 350°F/180°C (Gas Mark 4).

6 Meanwhile, make the topping. Melt the margarine in a small pan and stir in the flour. Gradually stir in the milk and the tomato purée (paste), stirring constantly until thickened. Stir in the basil and seasoning. Remove from the heat and stir in the yeast.

7 When the roast has been in the oven for about half an hour take it out and spoon the topping over it. Return it to the oven and bake for about 15 minutes longer.

Note: Serve this roast with seasonal vegetables and potatoes.

Italian Macaroni and Beans

340g (¾ lb)	wholewheat macaroni	3 cups
455g (1 lb)	cooked drained chick	2½ cups
or 2 tins	peas (garbanzo beans)	or 2 cans
(c.400g each)		(c.14-16 oz each)
4 tbs	olive oil	4 tbs
2-3 cloves	garlic	2-3 cloves
As required	freshly ground black pepper	As required
As required	nutritional yeast	As required

1 Cook the macaroni until just tender and drain. Drain the chick peas (garbanzo beans).
2 Heat the olive oil in a saucepan. Crush the garlic and add it to the pan, stirring for a minute or two. Add the chick peas (garbanzo beans) and macaroni, and continue stirring. Season with pepper (if the beans and pasta were cooked in salted water additional salt should not be needed).
3 Spoon the mixture into serving dishes, sprinkled with lots of yeast.

Note: This is a vegan version of a traditional Italian dish. It is practically vegan in its natural state, but the yeast adds a lovely flavour. Serve it with a green salad. Quick and Easy. Suitable for One.

'Hummus' Patties

2 cloves	garlic	2 cloves
455g (1 lb)	cooked drained chick	2½ cups
or 2 tins	peas (garbanzo beans)	or 2 cans
(c.400g each)		(c.14-16 oz each)
115g (4 oz)	wholewheat breadcrumbs	2 cups
3 tbs	tahini	3 tbs
2 tsp	ground cumin seeds	2 tsp
Juice of ½	lemon (optional)	Juice of ½
As required	vegetable oil	As required

1 Put the drained beans in a large mixing bowl and mash them well. Crush the garlic and add it to the bowl.
2 Add the breadcrumbs, tahini, cumin seeds, and lemon juice if using (the taste and texture will be fine without it). Add seasoning if desired. Mix well and form into eight large or 16 small patties.
3 Heat some oil in a frying pan, and shallow-fry the patties until lightly browned on both sides.

Note: Having always loved the flavour of hummus I translated it from a spread to rissoles. Serve them with a green salad for a light lunch or dinner, or with potatoes and vegetables for a more filling meal. Quick and Easy. Suitable for One.

Chick Pea and Mushroom Flan

	Wholewheat pastry made from 6 oz (175g/1½ cups) flour etc. (see p.41)	
1	onion	1
3 tbs	vegetable oil	3 tbs
2-3 cloves	garlic	2-3 cloves
115g (4 oz)	mushrooms	2 cups
455g (1 lb)	cooked drained chick	2½ cups
or 2 tins	peas (garbanzo beans)	or 2 cans
(c.400g each)		(c.14-16 oz each)
As required	sea salt	As required
As required	freshly ground black pepper	As required
170g (6 oz)	tofu	¾ cup
1 tbs	soya (soy) sauce	1 tbs
5 tbs	nutritional yeast	5 tbs
5 tbs	water	5 tbs

1 Roll out the pastry and put it in a flan tin (pie dish). Prick the bottom, then bake the shell at 425°F/220°C (Gas Mark 7) for 10 minutes. Remove from oven and lower heat to 350°F/180°C (Gas Mark 4).
2 Slice the onion thinly. Sauté it in 2 tbs oil in a saucepan for 2-3 minutes. Crush the garlic and add it to the pan; cook for a minute or two longer. Clean and slice the mushrooms and stir them; cook for another 3-4 minutes.
3 Stir the drained chick peas (garbanzo beans) into the pan. Season to taste. Put the mixture into the flan case (pie crust).
4 Put the tofu, remaining tbs oil, soya (soy) sauce, nutritional yeast and water in a liquidizer and blend thoroughly. Season well. Spoon this mixture over the top of the beans and smooth it out evenly.
5 Bake the flan for about half an hour until set on top.

Note: Serve with seasonal vegetables or salad.

Lentil Curry

225g (½ lb)	red lentils	1½ cups
1 tsp	sea salt	1 tsp
As required	freshly ground black pepper	As required
1	bay leaf	1
2	onions	2
1 clove	garlic	1 clove
2 tbs	vegetable oil	2 tbs
1	sweet apple	1
1 tbs	curry powder	1 tbs
1 tsp	lemon juice	1 tsp
1 small tin (c.225g)	vegan baked beans	1 8 oz can
5cm (4-inch) piece	cucumber	4-inch piece

1 Cover the lentils with water, add the salt, pepper and bay leaf, and simmer until tender (15-20 minutes).
2 Finely chop the onions and garlic. Peel, core and chop the apple and chop the cucumber finely.
3 Heat the oil gently; add the onions, garlic and apple and fry gently until soft and lightly brown. Stir in the curry powder and fry for 2 minutes.
4 Add the lemon juice, baked beans, lentils and chopped cucumber and heat thoroughly. (If desired, add more sea salt and/or freshly ground black pepper at this stage.)

Note: This is a very 'British' curry, originally adapted from a recipe in a woman's magazine. Do read the ingredients on the can of baked beans if not Heinz as some brands contain dairy ingredients. Serve the 'curry' over rice.

Italian Lentils and Spaghetti

2	onions	2
1 large	carrot	1 large
1	green pepper	1
2 cloves	garlic	2 cloves
2 tbs	olive oil	2 tbs
1 tin (c.400g)	tomatoes	1 can (c.14-16 oz)
2	bay leaves	2
2 tsp	thyme	2 tsp
1 tbs	oregano	1 tbs
1 tbs	basil	1 tbs
340g (¾ lb)	red lentils	2 cups
340g (¾ lb)	wholewheat spaghetti	¾ lb
2 tbs	Smokey Snaps (soy bakon bits)	2 tbs

1 Chop the onion, carrots and green pepper coarsely and the garlic very finely. Sauté them in the olive oil until tender.
2 Add the tomatoes and the herbs and then the lentils.

Add enough water to cover and simmer for 15-20 minutes.
3 Add the pasta and enough additional water to just cover. Cook all the ingredients together until the spaghetti is cooked al dente (approximately 10 minutes).
4 Sprinkle with the Smokey Snaps (soy bakon bits) and serve.

Note: This is an unusual dish because the pasta is cooked with the lentil mixture.

Lentil and Rice Loaf

170g (6 oz)	red lentils	1 cup
225g (½ lb)	brown rice	1⅓ cups
1 small	onion	1 small
1 tbs	vegetable oil	1 tbs
1 tbs	wholewheat flour	1 tbs
3 tbs	soya (soy) milk	3 tbs
½ tsp	dried sage	½ tsp
55g (2 oz)	walnuts	½ cup
As required	sea salt	As required

1 Cook the rice until very tender.
2 Cover the lentils with salted water and cook until very tender. Mash well.
3 Chop the onion finely and sauté it in the oil until tender. Add the flour and stir well. Then pour in the milk, stirring constantly.
4 Chop the walnuts and add these to the saucepan together with the cooked rice, cooked lentils and sage. Mix together well.
5 Pack into an oiled bread tin, and bake in a moderate oven at 350°F/180°C (Gas Mark 4) for 30-40 miinutes until slightly browned on top.

Note: Serve this with seasonal vegetables.

Masoor Dahl

255g (9 oz)	red lentils	1½ cups
2 tsp	cumin seeds	2 tsp
As required	sea salt	As required
½ tsp	turmeric	½ tsp
Pinch	cayenne pepper	Pinch
225g (½ lb)	tomatoes	½ lb
340g (¾ lb)	potatoes	¾ lb
1135ml (1 litre)	water	4 cups
2	onions	2
4 cloves	garlic	4 cloves
55g (2 oz)	vegan margarine	¼ cup

1 Rinse the lentils and place them in a saucepan. Grind the cumin seeds and add them to the pan, as well as the salt, turmeric and cayenne.
2 Chop the tomatoes and potatoes into fairly small pieces. Add them to the pan. Pour the water over everything, cover, bring to the boil, then lower the heat and simmer for about half an hour.
3 Slice the onions thinly. Chop the garlic finely. Heat the margarine in a frying pan, and add the onions and garlic. Fry until golden brown.
4 Stir the contents of the frying pan into the lentil mixture and serve.

Note: Dahl is the generic term for pulse dishes in Indian cooking. Red lentils are the easiest kind to find and cook. Dahl is usually served as a side dish, and this could certainly be served as just part of an Indian meal, but if served over rice it is substantial enough as a meal in itself. Quick and Easy.

Lentil Loaf with Tofu Topping

225g (½ lb)	red lentils	1¼ cup
240ml (8 fl oz)	water	1 cup
1	onion	1
4 tsp	miso	4 tsp
1 tbs	tahini	1 tbs
2 tsp	lemon juice	2 tsp
170g (6 oz)	tofu	⅔ cup
2 tbs	soya (soy) milk	2 tbs
1 tbs	vegetable oil	1 tbs

1 Wash the lentils well, cover them with the water, bring to the boil, lower the heat and simmer for about 15 minutes until tender and the water has been absorbed.
2 Chop the onion very finely.
3 When the lentils are cooked, beat in the miso, then add the tahini, lemon juice, and onion. Turn into a greased loaf tin or baking dish.
4 Put the tofu, milk and oil in a liquidizer and blend thoroughly.
5 Spread the tofu mixture on top of the lentil mixture as

evenly as possible. Bake at 375°F/190°C (Gas Mark 5) for about 45 minutes, until lightly browned and firm.

Note: Serve this loaf with potatoes, grilled tomatoes or a tomato sauce, and a green vegetable.

Lentil Burgers

225g (½ lb)	brown lentils	1⅓ cups
1135ml (2 pints)	water	5 cups
115g (4 oz)	bulgur wheat	⅔ cup
As required	sea salt	As required
2 tsp	yeast extract	2 tsp
2 tsp	tomato purée (paste)	2 tsp
2	onions	2
225g (½ lb)	mushrooms	4 cups
As required	wholewheat flour	As required
3 tbs	vegetable oil plus additional as required	3 tbs

1 Cover the lentils with boiling water and leave to soak for several hours. Drain.
2 Put the lentils into a small saucepan, cover with the water, bring to the boil, lower the heat, cover and leave to simmer for about 15 minutes.
3 Add the bulgur wheat and a little salt, and continue cooking for a further 10 minutes or so, until the lentils and wheat are tender and all the water has been absorbed.
4 Stir in the yeast extract and tomato purée (paste).
5 Chop the onion and mushrooms finely. Sauté in the oil until tender. Stir into the lentil mixture.
6 Leave the mixture to cool, then form into four burgers. Coat each side in a little wholewheat flour, then fry in vegetable oil until browned on both sides.

Note: These are nice 'meaty' burgers which can be served in a bun with the usual burger trimmings or with gravy and vegetables as a main course.

Megedarra

285g (10 oz)	brown rice	1¾ cups
285g (10 oz)	brown lentils	1¾ cups
As required	sea salt	As required
As required	vegetable oil	As required
3 large	onions	3 large
As required	freshly ground black pepper	As required
As required	soya (soy) yogurt	As required

1 Put the rice and lentils in a large saucepan, pour boiling water over them, cover the pan and leave to soak for several hours.

2 Chop one of the onions finely and fry in a little oil until tenderized and turning golden.

3 Drain the rice and lentils then return them to the saucepan, cover with fresh water, add a little sea salt, and bring to the boil. Add a little salt, lower the heat and leave to cook until tender for about 25 minutes. Taste for salt and add a little more if necessary. Grind in pepper to taste.

4 A few minutes before the rice and lentils are ready slice the other two onions thinly and fry them in very hot oil, stirring constantly so they don't burn but turn very dark brown.

5 Put the sliced fried onions on top of the rice and lentil mixture. Spoon yogurt over the dish while eating it.

Note: This is my version of a traditional Middle-Eastern dish. It would be vegan in its native habitat were it not for the yogurt topping, but in my opinion the yogurt really *makes* the dish.
Suitable for One.

Lentil Pastichio

225g (½ lb)	brown lentils	1⅓ cups
4 tbs	vegan margarine	4 tbs
1 large	onion	1 large
2 cloves	garlic	2 cloves
1 small	green pepper	1 small
115g (4 oz)	mushrooms	2 cups
1 tin	tomatoes	1 can
(c.400g)		(c.14 oz)
2 tsp	dried oregano	2 tsp
2 tsp	cinnamon	2 tsp
30g (1 oz)	wholewheat flour	¼ cup
285ml (½ pt)	soya (soy) milk	1⅓ cups
As required	sea salt	As required
As required	freshly ground black pepper	As required
30g (1 oz)	nutritional yeast	¼ cup
225g (½ lb)	wholewheat macaroni	2 cups

1 Rinse the lentils, cover with water and a little salt, bring to the boil, then lower the heat and simmer, covered.

2 Melt 2 tbs of the margarine in a large saucepan. Chop the onion and sauté it for a few minutes until it begins to soften. Meanwhile, crush the garlic and chop the pepper and mushrooms. Add these ingredients to the saucepan, together with the tomatoes, oregano and cinnamon. Bring to the boil, then lower the heat and leave to simmer.

3 Cook the macaroni until just tender.

4 Grease a large casserole dish. Put the cooked and drained macaroni on the bottom. Then make a layer of the lentil mixture. Finally, spoon the sauce over the top. Bake at 400°F/200°C (Gas Mark 6) for about half an hour.

5 After the tomato mixture has been simmering for about 10 minutes (by which time the lentils should have been simmering for about 20 minutes) spoon the lentils into the larger pan and let the whole lot simmer together for a few more minutes.

6 Melt the remaining 2 tbs margarine in another saucepan. Sprinkle in the flour, then slowly stir in the milk to make a white sauce. Season well, remove from the heat and stir in the yeast.

Note: Pastichio is a Greek dish of macaroni and minced meat. This is a vegan version using brown lentils instead.

Aduki-vegetable Pie

1	onion	1
2	leeks	2
2	carrots	2
2 small	swedes (rutabagas)	2 small
1	cooking (sour) apple	1
225g (½ lb)	aduki beans	1 cup
85g (3 oz)	currants	½ cup
85g (3 oz)	walnuts	⅔ cup
2 tbs	vegetable oil	2 tbs
As required	sea salt	As required
Pinch	cinnamon	Pinch
	Wholewheat pastry made from 225g (½ lb/1½ cups) flour etc. (see p.41)	

1 Cover the aduki beans with boiling water and leave to soak for several hours or overnight. Drain, cover with fresh water and cook until tender.

2 Chop the onion, leeks, carrots, swedes (rutabagas) and apple. Chop the walnuts separately.

3 Sauté the vegetables in the oil until tender.

4 Combine the cooked aduki beans, sautéed vegetables, currants, chopped walnuts, salt and cinnamon.

5 Line a pie dish with the pastry (all of it or, if preferred, save some to make strips across the top). Fill with the bean and vegetable mixture.

6 Bake in a moderately hot oven at 375°F/190°C (Gas Mark 5) for about half an hour, until the pastry is golden brown.

Note: Aduki beans do not take too long to cook and are combined here with other interesting ingredients in a pie.

Virginian Black-eyed Beans with Southern Corn Bread

340g (¾ lb)	black-eyed beans	1½ cups
1	onion	1
1	bay leaf	1
½ tsp	thyme	½ tsp
3 whole	cloves	3 whole
As required	sea salt	As required
As required	freshly ground black pepper	As required

1 Cover the beans with boiling water, leave to soak for several hours or overnight, then drain.
2 Chop the onion coarsely and combine it with the beans in a saucepan. Cover with water and add the bay leaf, thyme and cloves.
3 Cook over a low heat until the beans are tender (about 45 minutes). If necessary, add additional water to prevent drying out. Season to taste.
4 Serve with Southern Corn Bread (see below).

Note: This is an unusual and delicious combination of ingredients which benefits greatly from being served with corn bread.

Southern Corn Bread

115g (4 oz)	wholewheat flour	1 cup
115g (4 oz)	cornmeal	¾ cup
2 tbs	raw cane sugar	2 tbs
4 tsp	baking powder	4 tsp
1 tsp	sea salt	1 tsp
200ml (⅓ pt)	soya (soy) milk	¾ cup
85g (3 oz)	vegan margarine	⅓ cup

1 Mix the flour, cornmeal, sugar, baking powder and salt in a bowl.
2 Melt the margarine and add it with the milk to the dry mixture. Stir just until this is moistened, then immediately pour the batter into a greased baking pan.
3 Bake in a hot oven at 425°F/220°C (Gas Mark 7) for about an hour, until the top is golden and firm and drawing away from the edges of the pan.

Armenian Black-eyed Beans and Nuts

225g (½ lb)	black-eyed beans	1¼ cups
2	onions	2
100ml (4 fl oz)	olive oil	½ cup
1 tsp	raw cane sugar	1 tsp
1 tsp	sea salt	1 tsp
1 tin (c.225g)	tomatoes	1 can (c.8 oz)
2 tsp	tomato purée (paste)	2 tsp
140g (5 oz)	mixed nuts	1 cup
1 tbs	chopped parsley	1 tbs

1 Cover the black-eyed beans with boiling water and leave to soak for several hours or overnight. Cook until tender and drain.
2 Chop the onions and sauté them in the olive oil until soft. Chop the nuts coarsely.
3 Liquidize the tomatoes and add them to the saucepan with the rest of the ingredients.
4 Simmer for 10-15 minutes before serving.

Note: This is a black-eyed bean dish from the East.

Quick and Easy Chilli

225g (½ lb)	bulgur wheat	½ lb
4 tbs	vegetable oil	4 tbs
1 large	onion	1 large
2 tins (c.395-455g)	tomatoes	2 cans (c.14-16 oz)
As required	sea salt	As required
1 tsp (or more to taste)	chilli seasoning	1 tsp (or more to taste)
455g (1 lb) or 2 tins (c.400g each)	cooked, drained kidney beans	2½ cups or 2 cans (c.14-16 oz each)

1 Chop the onion and sauté it in the oil until it begins to soften.
2 Add the bulgur wheat and cook for 2-3 minutes more, stirring constantly.
3 Add the cans of tomatoes and some more water if needed (the liquid should be about three times the volume of the bulgur wheat). Add the seasoning and the cooked beans.
4 Simmer until tender (about 15 minutes).

Note: Bulgur wheat – in place of the minced meat normally found in chilli – now appears in vegan chillies as served by various restaurants, but I think I was the first person in the UK to provide a recipe for this combination (in *Vegan Cooking* 1982). The chilli seasoning called for is not chilli powder as used in Indian dishes, but the mixture of Mexican chilli spices by McCormicks and others, available at many supermarkets.
Quick and Easy. Suitable for One.

Kidney Bean Burgers

455g (1 lb) or 2 tins (c.400g each)	cooked drained kidney beans	2½ cups or 2 cans (c.14-16 oz each)
55g (2 oz)	rolled oats	½ cup
2 tbs	soya (soy) sauce	2 tbs
2 tbs	vegetable oil	2 tbs

1 Drain and mash the beans in a bowl (a potato masher or pastry blender is useful for this).
2 Add the oats and soya (soy) sauce, and knead well with the hands. Form into four large burgers.
3 Sauté them in the oil on each side, starting out with a high heat to brown, then lowering the heat so that they are cooked right through.

Note: Serve these burgers in a bun with the usual burger trimmings, or, if preferred, they can be served with gravy and vegetables.
Quick and Easy. Suitable for One.

Chili con Elote

2	onions	2
2 cloves	garlic	2 cloves
3 tbs	vegetable oil	3 tbs
2 small or 1 large	green pepper	2 small or 1 large
285ml (½ pt)	vegetable stock	1⅓ cups
2½ tbs	tomato purée (paste)	2½ tbs
285g (10 oz)	cooked sweetcorn (corn) (fresh, frozen or tinned/ canned	1⅔ cups
455g (1 lb) or 2 tins (c.400g each)	cooked drained kidney beans	2½ cups or 2 cans (c.14-16 oz each)
3 tsp	Mexican chili seasoning	3 tsp

1 Chop the onion and garlic. Sauté in the oil until lightly browned.
2 Chop the green pepper, add to the saucepan and cook for a further 2-3 minutes.
3 Add the stock and tomato purée (paste) to the saucepan and bring to the boil. Add the corn. Lower heat to simmer point.
4 Mash half the beans in a bowl. Add both the mashed beans and whole beans to the saucepan together with the seasoning. Stir well.
5 Simmer, uncovered, for about 15 minutes, by which time all the liquid should have been absorbed.
6 Serve immediately.

Note: 'Elote' means maize in Spanish, and the combination of beans and maize is a traditional Mexican one. This is good with flour tortillas.

Chilli Bean Roast with Tomato Sauce

2	onions	2
1 small	green pepper	1 small
3 cloves	garlic	3 cloves
4 tbs	vegetable oil	4 tbs
2 tsp	ground cumin	2 tsp
1 tsp	dried oregano	1 tsp
½ tsp (or to taste)	chilli powder	½ tsp (or to taste)
225g (1 lb) or 2 tins (c.400g each)	cooked drained Borlotti (pinto) beans	2½ cups or 28-32 oz canned
115g (4 oz)	wholewheat breadcrumbs	2 cups
30g (1 oz)	wholewheat flour	¼ cup
425ml (¾ pt)	water	2 cups
3 tbs	tomato purée (paste)	3 tbs
Few drops	Tabasco sauce	Few drops
As required	sea salt	As required
As required	freshly ground black pepper	As required

1 Chop the onions and green pepper finely. Crush the garlic. Heat 2 tbs of the oil in a frying pan and sauté these ingredients until they begin to brown. Stir in the cumin, oregano and chilli powder and cook for a minute or two longer. Remove from heat.
2 Mash the drained beans in a bowl. Add the breadcrumbs and the contents of the frying pan and mix well. Turn the mixture into a baking dish and bake at 350°F/180°C (Gas Mark 4) for about half an hour.
3 To make the sauce, heat the remaining 2 tbs oil and stir in the flour. Add the water slowly, stirring constantly to avoid lumps. Stir in the tomato purée (paste) and Tabasco sauce. When the mixture is thick and boiling season to taste.

Note: Serve with a seasonal green vegetable and boiled or baked potatoes.

9
Vegetables

Mushroom and Tomato Pie

3	onions	3
2 tbs	vegetable oil	2 tbs
55g (2 oz)	vegan margarine	¼ cup
1 stick (optional)	celery	1 stick (optional)
6	tomatoes	6
455g (1 lb)	mushrooms	1 lb
1 tsp or 1 tbs fresh	dried basil or marjoram	1 tsp or 1 tbs fresh
680g (1½ lbs)	mashed potatoes	3 cups

1 Chop the onions finely and sauté them in the oil and margarine for 3-4 minutes.
2 Chop the celery finely (if used), chop the tomatoes and slice the mushrooms. Add these to the onions.
3 Stir well over a moderate heat for 2-3 minutes. Add the herb. Lower the heat, cover the saucepan, and simmer for about 10 minutes.
4 Place the mixture in a baking dish and cover with mashed potatoes. Bake for about half an hour in a moderately hot oven at 375°F/190°C (Gas Mark 5) until golden brown on top. Alternatively, if the ingredients have all been kept hot, place under the grill (broiler) until browned.

Note: This dish can be accompanied by a salad if desired, or a cooked vegetable, but is also sufficient on its own.

Potato Yahni

1125g (2½ lb)	potatoes	2½ lb
455g (1 lb)	onions	1 lb
455g (1 lb)	tomatoes	1 lb
1 tbs	raw cane sugar	1 tbs
140ml (¼ pt)	olive oil	⅔ cup
1	bay leaf	1 bay leaf
As required	sea salt	As required
As required	freshly ground black pepper	As required

1 Peel the potatoes thinly and cut into uniform size. Chop the onions finely and peel and chop the tomatoes.
2 Heat the oil and fry the onions until golden brown.
3 Add the tomatoes and simmer with the sugar and bay leaf until soft.
4 Add the potatoes, seasoning, and enough water to half cover them.
5 Cook until the potatoes are soft and the sauce is thick. Serve immediately.

Note: In Britain a main dish based on potatoes seems strange, but this Eastern European stew is nutritious and delicious. Serve with thick slices of crusty wholewheat bread.

Potato Kephtides

2	spring onions (scallions)	2
2 large	tomatoes	2 large
1 tbs	vegan margarine	1 tbs
455g (1 lb)	cold boiled potatoes	1 lb
55g (2 oz)	wholewheat flour	½ cup
As required	sea salt	As required
As required	freshly ground black pepper	As required
As required	vegetable oil	As required

1 Chop the spring onions (scallions) finely. Skin and chop the tomatoes. Melt the margarine.
2 Sieve the potatoes and mix them with all the other ingredients except the oil. Knead slightly and roll out to 2cm (¾ inch) thick. Cut into rounds about 7cm (2½ inches) thick. Cut into rounds about 7cm (2½ inches) across.
3 Heat the oil until smoking hot and fry the round kephtides quickly. Alternatively, they can be baked on a greased baking sheet in a hot oven at 425°F/220°C (Gas Mark 7) until golden brown. They should be crisp outside but very soft inside.

Note: This is another potato-based dish, this time from Greece. Serve with a mixed salad.
Quick and Easy.

Potato-paprika

4 tbs	vegetable oil	4 tbs
3	onions	3
1	green pepper	1
1	red pepper	1
8 large	cooked potatoes	8 large
200ml (⅓ pt)	soya (soy) yogurt	¾ cup
2 tsp	paprika	2 tsp
As required	sea salt	As required
Sprinkling	caraway seeds	Sprinkling

1 Chop the onions and slice the peppers into thin slivers.
2 Sauté the onions in the oil until they start to turn brown, then add the peppers.
3 Cube the cooked potatoes and add these to the pan. Sprinkle with paprika, salt and seeds. Fry lightly, stirring well.
4 Pour on the yogurt, heat through without bringing to the boil, and serve.

Note: This potato dish is self-contained.
Quick and Easy. Suitable for One.

Potato Gnocchi

1350g (3 lb)	potatoes	3 lb
225g (½ lb)	wholewheat flour	2 cups
55g (2 oz)	vegan margarine	¼ cup
8 tbs	water	8 tbs
8 tbs	gram (chick pea) flour	8 tbs
As required	sea salt	As required
As required	freshly ground black pepper	As required
As required	tomato sauce	As required
As required	nutritional yeast (optional)	As required

1 Cook the potatoes. Drain them and place them back in the pan and over the heat again. Shake them around the pan so that they are well dried out. Remove the skins and mash the potatoes in a large bowl.
2 Add the flour and margarine to the potatoes. Stir the gram (chick pea) flour into the water with a fork and add this to the potatoes. Mix well and season to taste. (This can all be done well in advance and the mixture left in the refrigerator until meal time.)
3 Heat the water to boiling point in a large saucepan and sprinkle in a little sea salt. Tear off walnut-sized balls from the potato mixture and drop them into the water. (If making the full amount this will probably have to be done in three or four stages.) When the water has returned to the boil, lower the heat and simmer the gnocchi for a few minutes. (They will rise to the surface.) Either remove them individually with a slotted spoon or carefully drain the pan into a colander.
4 Serve the gnocchi topped with a well-flavoured tomato sauce – sprinkled with nutritional yeast if desired.

Note: This is my version of an Italian classic potato dish. The tomato sauce can be a homemade one or a good quality bottled variety.
Suitable for One.

Cabbage and Potato Casserole

455g (1 lb)	cooked potatoes	1 lb
455g (1 lb)	cooked cabbage	1 lb
2 tbs	Smokey Snaps (soy bakon bits)	2 tbs
30g (1 oz)	vegan magarine	1 oz
As required	soya (soy) milk	As required

1 Slice the potatoes and put a layer in the bottom of an oiled baking dish.
2 Sprinkle with Smokey Snaps (soy bakon bits).
3 Chop the cabbage and place a layer in the baking dish.
4 Repeat the layers until the ingredients have all been used up, finishing with the potato.
5 Pour over enough milk to moisten and dot with margarine.
6 Bake in a moderately hot oven at 375°F/190°C (Gas Mark 5) for about half an hour.

Note: This is a great way to use up leftover cabbage and potatoes. It is simple and inexpensive but tasty, nutritious and filling, needing no accompaniments.

Smokey Leek Pasties

15g (½ oz)	vegan margarine	1 tbs
15g (½ oz)	wholewheat flour	¼ cup
140ml (¼ pt)	soya (soy) milk	⅔ cup
3	leeks	3
	wholewheat pastry made from 225g (½ lb/2 cups) flour and 115g (4 oz/½ cup) vegan margarine (see p.41)	
½ tsp	dried sage	½ tsp
As required	sea salt	As required
As required	freshly ground black pepper	As required
1-2 tbs	Smokey Snaps (soy bakon bits)	1-2 tbs
As required	sea salt	As required

1 Heat the margarine in a small saucepan and add the flour. Add the milk carefully, stirring constantly to avoid lumps.
2 Chop the leeks and blanch them in boiling water for 3 minutes then drain well.
3 Roll out the pastry and cut into 4 rounds with a saucer.
4 Mix the leeks, Smokey Snaps (soy bakon bits) and sage with the white sauce. Season to taste.
5 Spoon the mixture on to the centre of the pastry circles. Bring the edges up to meet on top and pinch well together all round.
6 Bake in a hot oven at 425°F/220°C (Gas Mark 7) for

10 minutes, then lower the heat to moderate 350°F/180°C (Gas Mark 4) and cook for a further 20-30 minutes until the pastry is well cooked.

Note: Serve with a mixed salad.

Aubergine 'Au Gratin'

680-900g (1½-2 lb)	aubergines (eggplants)	1½-2 lb
4 squares	Shredded Wheat	4 squares
2	onions	2
As required	sea salt	As required
4 tbs	vegetable oil	4 tbs
1 tin (c.400g)	tomatoes	1 can (c.14-16 oz)
2 tbs	tomato purée (paste)	2 tbs
2 tsp or 2 tbs fresh	dried basil or marjoram	2 tsp or 2 tbs fresh

1 Chop the onion and sauté it for 2-3 minutes in the oil, adding the crushed Shredded Wheat. Sauté, stirring well, until slightly browned. Season with salt.
2 Slice the aubergines (eggplants). Place alternate layers of aubergine (eggplant) and browned mixture in a greased baking dish.
3 Blend the tomatoes, tomato purée (paste) and herbs in a liquidizer and pour this over the layers.
4 Bake in a moderately hot oven at 375°F/190°C (Gas Mark 5) for 45 minutes-1 hour, until the aubergine (eggplant) is tender when tested with a fork.

Note: The idea for this dish came from America. Shredded Wheat is one of the few breakfast cereals that are vegan, and it does not contain sugar. Serve the savoury with boiled or baked potatoes and a salad.

Creole-style Aubergine

455-680g (1-1½ lb)	aubergines (eggplants)	1-1½ lb
85g (3 oz)	vegan margarine	⅓ cup
55g (2 oz)	wholewheat flour	½ cup
680g (1½ lb)	ripe tomatoes	1½ lb
2 small	green peppers	2 small
2 small	onions	2 small
1 tsp	sea salt	1 tsp
2 tsp	raw cane sugar	2 tsp
1	bay leaf	1
3	cloves	3
55g (2 oz)	wholewheat breadcrumbs	1 cup

1 Peel and dice the aubergines (eggplants). Cook for 10 minutes in boiling water then drain well and place in an oiled baking dish.

2 Melt 55g (2 oz/¼ cup) of the margarine and stir in the flour.

3 Skin and slice the tomatoes, chop the green peppers and onions and add these to the saucepan, stirring well.

4 Add the salt, sugar, bay leaf and cloves and cook for 5 minutes.

5 Pour the mixture over the aubergines (eggplants). Cover with the breadcrumbs and top with the rest of the margarine.

6 Bake in a moderate oven at 350°F/180°C (Gas Mark 4) for about half an hour.

Note: This is another aubergine (eggplant) dish, also best accompanied by boiled or baked potatoes.

Stuffed Green Peppers

4	green peppers	4
1	onion	1
2 large	tomatoes	2 large
3 tbs	vegan margarine	3 tbs
2 tins	creamed-style sweetcorn	About 1½ lb
(c.340g each)	(corn)	canned
1 tsp	sea salt	1 tsp
55g (2 oz)	wholewheat breadcrumbs	1 cup

1 Cut a slice from the stem end of the green pepper and scoop out the seeds and dividing membranes. Parboil for about 2 minutes in boiling water then drain thoroughly.

2 Chop the onion, peel and chop the tomatoes and sauté both in 2 tbs of the margarine until softened.

3 Add the creamed sweetcorn (corn) and salt, and heat to bubbling.

4 Stuff the mixture into the parboiled pepper cases.

5 Melt the remaining tablespoons of margarine and toss the breadcrumbs in this.

6 Sprinkle the breadcrumbs over the peppers and place them in an oiled shallow baking dish.

7 Bake in a fairly hot oven at 400°F/200°C (Gas Mark 6) for about half an hour, until the peppers are tender.

Note: Rice-filled green peppers are not uncommon, but here is a very different stuffing. Serve the peppers with boiled or baked potatoes.

Tomato and Sweetcorn Savoury

1	onion	1
2 tbs	vegetable oil	2 tbs
1 small	green pepper	1 small
1 tin	sweetcorn (corn)	1 can
(c.400g)		(c.14-16 oz)
4 large	tomatoes	4 large
2 tbs	cornflour (cornstarch)	2 tbs
285ml (½ pt)	water	1⅓ cups
½ tsp	garlic salt	½ tsp
3 tbs	Smokey Snaps (soy bakon bits)	3 tbs

1 Chop the onion and green pepper finely.

2 Sauté them in the vegetable oil until they begin to soften.

3 Chop the tomatoes and add them to the saucepan. Add the corn and sauté for a few more minutes, stirring well.

4 Dissolve the cornflour (cornstarch) in a little water, add the rest of the water, mix well and add to the saucepan. Bring to the boil, stirring constantly.

5 Add the garlic salt and Smokey Snaps (soy bakon bits) and simmer for a few more minutes.

Note: This simple dish is always appreciated. Serve over brown rice.
Quick and Easy.

Lebanese-style Green Bean Stew

1	onion	1
3 tbs	vegetable oil	3 tbs
225g (½ lb)	potatoes	½ lb
340g (¾ lb)	fresh or frozen green beans	¾ lb
2 tsp	ground cumin	2 tsp
Pinch	cayenne pepper	Pinch
1 tin	tomatoes	1 can
(c.400g)		(14-16 oz)
As required	sea salt	As required
As required	freshly ground black pepper	As required

1 Chop the onion and sauté in the oil for 2-3 minutes.
2 Peel the potatoes and chop into small pieces. Add to the saucepan and continue cooking for a further 3-4 minutes, stirring often.
3 If using fresh beans, top and tail them (long ones can be snapped in half). Add to the saucepan. Sprinkle in the cumin and cayenne and stir well.
4 Put the tomatoes into a liquidizer and blend. Add to the saucepan. Stir, bring to the boil, then lower the heat (but not too much), cover and leave to cook for 12-15 minutes, stirring occasionally. By this time the beans and potato should be tender and the tomatoes reduced to a thick paste. Taste for seasoning and add salt and pepper.
5 Serve immediately.

Note: In the Middle East (at least where Western eating habits have not entirely taken over) vegetables are far more likely to form the basis of a main meal than in the West. Serve this stew with crusty wholewheat bread or pitta bread.

Potato and Pea Curry

455g (1 lb)	potatoes	1 lb
2	onions	2
2 tbs	vegan margarine	2 tbs
2.5cm	fresh ginger	1 inch
(1 inch) piece		piece
2 tsp	cumin seeds	2 tsp
2 tsp	coriander seeds	2 tsp
2 tsp	turmeric powder	2 tsp
1 tsp	chilli powder	1 tsp
225g (½ lb)	fresh (shelled) or frozen peas	½ lb
As required	sea salt	As required
1 tsp	lemon juice	1 tsp
2 tsp	garam masala	2 tsp

1 Cook the potatoes until nearly tender. Drain, peel if desired, and cut into small chunks.

2 Chop the onions. Melt the margarine and sauté the onions for 2-3 minutes. Peel and chop the ginger finely and add to the saucepan. Continue frying until the onion is tender.
3 Grind the cumin and coriander until fine. Add to the onions with the turmeric and chilli powder. Lower the heat and cook for a further 2-3 minutes.
4 Stir the potatoes and peas into the saucepan. Add the salt. Sprinkle in the lemon juice. Cover and cook over a very low heat until the peas and potatoes are just tender.
5 Turn off the heat. Sprinkle the garam masala over the mixture and stir gently.

Note: Vegetarianism is so prevalent in India that it is no surprise to discover that many of the finest vegetable-based main dishes come from that part of the world. Serve this one over plain or pilau rice, accompanied by chapatis or papadums, and chutney if desired.

Spiced Potato and Cauliflower

680g (1½ lb)	potatoes	1½ lb
2	onions	2
3 tbs	vegetable oil	3 tbs
2.5cm	fresh ginger	1 inch
(1 inch) piece		piece
2 cloves	garlic	2 cloves
½ tsp	mustard seeds	½ tsp
1 tbs	coriander seeds	1 tbs
1 tsp	cumin seeds	1 tsp
¼ tsp	fenugreek seeds	¼ tsp
1 tsp	ground turmeric	1 tsp
2	bay leaves	2
Juice of 1	lemon	Juice of 1
1 small	cauliflower	1 small
As required	sea salt	As required

1 Scrub (and peel if desired) the potatoes. Cut into cubes and set aside.
2 Chop the onions. Sauté over a low heat for 3-4 minutes. Meanwhile, peel and finely chop the ginger and crush the garlic. Add to the saucepan.
3 Put all the seeds into a coffee grinder or liquidizer and grind to a powder. Add to the saucepan with the turmeric and stir well.
4 Stir in the potatoes and bay leaf. Add 140ml (¼ pt/⅔ cup) water and the lemon juice. Bring to the boil, then lower the heat and leave to simmer for 10-15 minutes until the potatoes are beginning to soften.
5 Cut the cauliflower into small florets and add to the saucepan with another 140ml (¼ pt/⅔ cup) water. Cook for a further 10-15 minutes until all the vegetables are tender. Add salt if required.

Note: This dish can be served over rice or with chapatis (and chutney if desired).

Baked Vegetable Curry and Coconut Rice Casserole

285g (10 oz)	long grain brown rice	1¾ cups
55g (2 oz)	vegan margarine	¼ cup
2	cinnamon sticks	2
4	cloves	4
2 large or 4 small	onions	2 large or 4 small
1 tin (c.400ml)	coconut milk	1 can (c.14 oz)
As required	sea salt	As required
As required	water	As required
900g (2 lb)	mixed vegetables (e.g. carrots, peas, Jerusalem artichokes, broccoli)	2 lb
3	tomatoes	3
2-3 cloves	garlic	2-3 cloves
½ tsp	turmeric	½ tsp
½ tsp	powdered ginger	½ tsp
2 tsp	ground coriander	2 tsp
1-2 tsp	chilli powder	1-2 tsp
2 tsp	garam masala	2 tsp
170-225ml (6-8 fl oz)	soya (soy) milk	¾-1 cup

1 Cover the rice with boiling water and leave to soak for several hours. Drain.
2 Slice one large (or two small) onions. Melt half the margarine in a saucepan. Fry the sliced onion in it for a minute or two. Add the cinnamon and cloves and fry for 3-4 minutes longer.
3 Empty the tin of coconut milk into a liquidizer and blend thoroughly.
4 Add the drained rice to the saucepan and cover with the coconut milk. Add enough water for the fluid to be about an inch above the rice. (If necessary more can be added during cooking time.) Add a little salt to taste, cover and bring to the boil, then lower the heat and simmer until tender for about 25 minutes.
5 Meanwhile, chop the vegetables and cook them until just tender. Drain and set aside.
6 Skin and chop the tomatoes.
7 Grate the remaining onion(s). Heat the remaining margarine in a large frying pan or saucepan, add the grated onion and cook for 3-4 minutes. Crush the garlic and add it to the pan and fry for another minute. Stir in the chopped tomatoes and the turmeric, ginger, coriander, chilli powder and garam masala and a little salt to taste. Fry for 3-4 minutes. Add the cooked vegetables and soya (soy) milk and cook for a few minutes longer.
8 Layer the rice and vegetables in a greased casserole dish, beginning and ending with the rice. Cover and bake at 425°F/220°C (Gas Mark 7) for 20 minutes.

Note: Serve hot with chapatis or papadums prepared under the grill.
Suitable for a dinner party.

Curried Vegetable Ring

85g (3 oz)	vegan margarine	⅓ cup
8	onions	8
1	cooking apple	1
3 tsp	curry powder	3 tsp
2 tsp	wholewheat flour	2 tsp
570ml (1 pt)	vegetable stock	2½ cups
1 tbs	mango chutney	1 tbs
2 tsp	tomato ketchup	2 tsp
1 tbs	raisins	1 tbs
340g (¾ lb)	carrots	¾ lb
55g (2 oz)	turnips	2 oz
¼	cucumber	¼
170g (6 oz)	mushrooms	3 cups
900g (2 lb)	mashed potatoes	4 cups

1 Chop the onions finely and peel and chop the apple.
2 Melt 30g (1 oz) of the vegan margarine and fry the onions and apple until soft.
3 Add the curry powder and fry for a further minute. Add the flour and stir well. Add the vegetable stock, stirring constantly to avoid lumps. Bring to the boil, and boil for 1 minute, stirring.
4 Add the chutney, ketchup and raisins. Cover and simmer while preparing the vegetables.
5 Chop the carrots, turnips, cucumber and mushrooms. Melt the remaining margarine and fry the vegetables until golden.
6 Add the vegetables to the curry sauce and simmer gently for about 20-30 minutes.
7 Make a mashed potato border on a hot dish and pour the curried vegetables into the centre.

Note: This dish is a strictly *British* version of 'curry'. However, the combination of the sweet curry and creamy mashed potatoes works well.

San Clemente Curry

1 large	onion	1 large
1 tbs	vegan margarine	1 tbs
455g (1 lb)	button mushrooms	1 lb
2 tsp	curry powder	2 tsp
(or more to taste)		(or more to taste)
2	tomatoes	2
Pinch	sea salt	Pinch
4 tsp	lemon juice	4 tsp
285ml (½ pt)	soya (soy) yogurt	1⅓ cups
4	avocados	4

1 Chop the onion. Sauté in the margarine along with the mushrooms until tender.
2 Stir in the curry powder and cook for a few moments longer.
3 Chop the tomato and add to the saucepan, with the salt. Heat through.
4 Add the lemon juice and yogurt. Stir well and heat until just below boiling point.
5 Peel and halve the avocados. Place on the rice and fill with the mushroom mixture.

Note: This dish owes much more to California than to the Indian sub-continent.
Quick and Easy.

Avocado à la King

55g (2 oz)	vegan margarine	¼ cup
30g (1 oz)	wholewheat flour	¼ cup
285ml (½ pt)	soya (soy) milk	1⅓ cups
225g (½ lb)	mushrooms	4 cups
2 tinned	red pimentos	2 canned
2 large	avocados	2 large
As required	sea salt	As required
As required	freshly ground black pepper	As required

1 Heat half the margarine, add the flour and cook gently for a minute and then gradually add the milk, stirring constantly, to make a white sauce. Set aside.
2 Slice the mushrooms and sauté in the remaining margarine until tender.
3 Chop the pimentos coarsely. Add to the white sauce along with the mushrooms.
4 Peel and dice the avocados. Add to the white sauce just before serving. Season to taste.

Note: This is a rich luncheon dish. Serve over wholewheat toast.
Quick and Easy.

Vegetable Pancakes

	Crepe batter made from 225g (½ lb/2 cups) wholewheat flour (see p.15)	
2	onions	2
45g (1½ oz)	vegan margarine	3 tbs
4 sticks	celery	4 sticks
340g (¾ lb)	courgettes (zucchini)	¾ lb
225g (½ lb)	fresh (shelled) or frozen peas	½ lb
1 tsp	dried marjoram	1 tsp
½ tsp	garlic salt	½ tsp
3-4 tbs	nutritional yeast	3-4 tbs

1 Chop the onions finely. Heat the margarine in a frying pan and sauté them for 2-3 minutes. Chop the celery finely and add it to the pan; sauté the mixture for another 2-3 minutes. Dice the courgettes (zucchini) finely and add them to the pan; sauté the mixture for 2-3 minutes more.
2 Add the peas to the pan (if frozen then raise the heat briefly). Stir in the marjoram and garlic salt. Lower the heat, cover and cook for about 3 minutes more. Uncover the pan and remove from heat.
3 Fry the pancakes and fill each one with some of the vegetable mixture; fold over and place on a baking sheet. (Or transfer each pancake as it is done to the sheet and fill it on the sheet.) When all the pancakes have been filled, sprinkle the top with nutritional yeast and bake in a moderate oven at 350°F/180°C (Gas Mark 4) for about 15 minutes.

Vegetable Gratin

680g (1½ lb)	vegetable(s)	1½ lb
55g (2 oz)	vegan margarine	¼ cup
55g (2 oz)	wholewheat flour	½ cup
570ml (1 pt)	soya (soy) milk	2½ cups
2 jars (c.35g each)	vegan cheese spread	2 jars
As required	sea salt	As required
As required	freshly ground black pepper	As required
55-85g (2-3 oz)	wholewheat breadcrumbs	1-1½ cups

1 Cook the vegetable(s) and drain.
2 Melt the margarine in a saucepan and stir in the flour. Add the milk slowly, stirring constantly to avoid lumps. When it has thickened and boiled, lower the heat and stir in the spread. When that has melted season to taste.
3 Mix the vegetable(s) and sauce and put in a greased oven dish (or, alternatively, put the vegetable(s) in the dish and pour the sauce over). Sprinkle the breadcrumbs on top and bake at 400°F/200°C (Gas Mark 6) for 15-20 minutes.

Note: British health food stores now stock vegan 'cheese' spreads under various brand names, such as *Plamil Veeze, Fromsoya* spread or *Marigold Soyacheese.* In this recipe such a spread is used to make a 'cheese' sauce.

You can make this with just one kind of vegetable, like cauliflower, or a mixture. It is a good way of using leftover vegetables. Serve with boiled, baked or fried potatoes.

10
Nuts

Introduction

Lacto-vegetarians already know that nuts are not just for nibbling. As a high-protein food they can play an important part in a vegan diet. They may be high in calories, but nobody should be put off using them for that reason: used in main dishes rather than as a snack between meals there is no way they will lead to obesity. Nuts can be used in a wide variety of dishes and are a favourite ingredient in 'centrepiece' dishes like roasts. The following nuts all appear in recipes in this chapter.

Almonds – one of my favourites and one of the most versatile. Unblanched almonds have the more interesting flavour although blanched ones are more useful for cooking. Really fresh ones will be crunchy and have a hint of sweetness but the flavour of almonds is best brought out by toasting them under the grill (broiler). They can either be toasted whole or chopped first and then toasted. Blanched almonds can be bought flaked (slivered). In this form they are very lightweight so a small amount goes a surprisingly long way. Blanched almonds are also sold as ground almonds.

Brazil nuts – the richest nuts. One problem, however, is that individual nuts can often be 'off' and taste really awful. Nevertheless, I have never had a nut roast or similar dish spoiled by bad nuts, so it seems safe enough to give recipes for them. Grinding them in a liquidizer can be difficult as they tend to go gummy with large chunks left unground; the solution is to grind them together with slices of bread to be used as breadcrumbs in the recipe.

Hazelnuts – I do not like these raw, but they are very good in cooked dishes.

Walnuts – fresh walnuts out of the shell can be absolutely delicious, but bought shelled they are often quite bitter. If they are *really* bitter then return them to the shop as it means they are rancid. Buying halves rather than pieces can mean fresher nuts, and the lighter they are, the better the flavour is likely to be. As with Brazil nuts, the best way to grind them is together with bread.

Pecans – more expensive than any of the preceding nuts but worth it for their exquisite flavour. They are similar to walnuts but have a very sweet taste. Lightly toasting them brings out that flavour.

Peanuts – botanically speaking these are legumes and not nuts at all but they have the same high-protein food value as 'true' nuts. I personally do not like raw peanuts so the recipes in this chapter use roasted nuts. The ones in shells are best, otherwise it is worth trying to find unsalted dry roasted peanuts at a wholefood shop. Failing that, roasted salted peanuts can be rinsed and dried. Of course, there is also peanut butter, a marvellous food. British peanut butters sold at wholefood shops are often made with the skins still on them although this gives a bitter taste and no extra food value. Commercial peanut butters in Britain unfortunately have salt and/or sugar added, so I have long since made my own.

Cashews – again, a botanic legume but a nut in every other sense of the word. They make a lovely milk or cream (see Chapter 2) and with their light, delicate, slightly sweet taste they are unique. Toasting gives them quite a different flavour, though equally delicious. They can be bought more cheaply as broken rather than whole cashews, and for many dishes (certainly for liquidizing or grinding) cashew pieces are fine, though whole cashews have a better flavour.

Chestnuts – not really a nut at all but a starch. These are much lower in calories than real nuts but also lack the protein content of true nuts. The important thing is that they are delicious and add extra variety to vegan meals. As far as I am concerned, fresh chestnuts take far too long to prepare and canned ones are too soft, so I always buy dried chestnuts. They can be soaked and cooked until soft, but the best way of preparing them is to soak them in boiling water in a wide-rimmed thermos flask. Pour water in first as dropping them into an empty flask can break it; leave for at least 12 hours and preferably longer, and they should come out ready for use.

Recipes

Savoury Nut Roast

1	onion	1
3 tbs	vegetable oil	3 tbs
2 small	tomatoes	2 small
30g (1 oz)	wholewheat flour	¼ cup
140ml (¼ pt)	water	⅔ cup
1 tbs	soya (soy) sauce	1 tbs
115g (4 oz)	hazelnuts	¾ cup
115g (4 oz)	broken cashew nuts	¾ cup
85g (3 oz)	wholewheat breadcrumbs	1½ cups
1 tsp	dried mixed herbs	1 tsp
30g (1 oz)	soya (soy) flour	¼ cup

1 Chop the onion finely and sauté it in the oil until tender.
2 Skin and chop the tomatoes and add them to the pan. Cook for 5 minutes.
3 Stir in the flour and slowly add the water, stirring constantly to avoid lumps. Remove from the heat.
4 Grind the hazelnuts and add them to the sauce together with all the other ingredients. Mix very thoroughly and place in a bread tin or pie dish.
5 Bake in a moderate oven at 350°F/180°C (Gas Mark 4) for 45 minutes-1 hour.

Note: I make this nut roast nearly every Christmas. The flavour of ground hazelnuts together with the texture of cashews is an unbeatable combination. Serve it with gravy and seasonal vegetables.

Shepherd's Pie

3 tbs	vegetable oil	3 tbs
2	onions	2
2	tomatoes	2
1 large	carrot	1 large
225g (½ lb)	mushrooms	4 cups
55g (2 oz)	hazelnuts	½ cup
2 tbs	rissole mix (from health food shops)	2 tbs
30g (1 oz)	wholewheat flour	¼ cup
	water	
2 tsp	yeast extract	2 tsp
340-455g (¾-1 lb)	mashed potato	1½-2 cups

1 Chop the onions and sauté them until tender.
2 Grate the carrot and chop the tomatoes and mushrooms. Add them to the saucepan and sauté until the mushrooms are tender.
3 Stir in the yeast extract and flour for a minute or two. Add the water slowly, stirring constantly to avoid lumps.
4 Grind the hazelnuts and add them to the saucepan together with the rissole mix.
5 Place the mixture in a casserole, cover with the mashed potato, and brown under the grill.

Note: In this dish ground hazelnuts are also the key ingredient. Serve with a green vegetable.

Hazelnut Savoury

170g (6 oz)	hazelnuts	1⅓ cups
2 sticks	celery	2 sticks
3	spring onions (scallions)	3
1 tsp	garlic salt	1 tsp
340g (¾ lb)	mashed potatoes	1½ cups
30g (1 oz)	vegan margarine	2 tbs
30g (1 oz)	wholewheat flour	¼ cup
140ml (¼ pt)	soya (soy) milk	⅔ cup

1 Grind the nuts and chop the celery and spring onions (scallions) finely.
2 Combine these ingredients with the mashed potatoes and garlic salt.
3 Melt the margarine in a small saucepan and stir in the flour. Slowly add the milk, stirring constantly to avoid lumps. When boiling and thickened, combine this sauce with the mashed potato and nut mixture.
4 Place the mixture in a baking dish and bake in a moderate oven at 350°F/180°C (Gas Mark 4) for about half an hour.

Note: This recipe also contains hazelnuts and mashed potatoes, but it is completely different from the previous dish. It too should be served with a green vegetable.

Hazelnut and Potato Patties

2	onions	2
2 tbs	vegetable oil plus additional for frying	2 tbs
2 tsp	yeast extract	2 tsp
680g (1½ lb)	cooked, peeled potatoes	1½ lb
170g (6 oz)	hazelnuts	1½ cups

1 Chop the onions and fry them in the oil for a few minutes until they begin to brown.
2 Remove from the heat and add the yeast extract. Mash the potatoes and add them to the pan.
3 Grind the nuts (if they are lightly roasted and blanched beforehand the flavour will be better). Add them to the potato mixture and knead well with your hands.
4 Form into patties (about 16) and shallow-fry them until browned on both sides.

Note: If you have leftover cooked potatoes nothing could be quicker or simpler than these patties. Serve with a mixed salad.
Quick and Easy. Suitable for One.

Curried Cashews

285g (10 oz)	whole cashews	2 cups
1 small	onion	1 small
1 clove	garlic	1 clove
Small piece	fresh ginger	Small piece
1	fresh chilli	1
1 tsp	turmeric	1 tsp
1	cinnamon stick	1
2	cardamom pods	2
Grated rind of ½	lemon	Grated rind of ½
As required	sea salt	As required
200ml (⅓ pt)	water	¾ cup
30g (1 oz)	creamed coconut	2 tbs

1 Chop the onion and chilli finely, making certain the chilli seeds have been discarded. Crush the garlic and grate the ginger.
2 Combine these ingredients with all of the spices and cover them with the water. Simmer for a few minutes.
3 Add the cashews and creamed coconut, and simmer for a further 20-30 minutes.

Note: Nuts are not normally considered in connection with curries, but this recipe is delicious. Serve with plain or pilau rice.

Cashew Rice Roast

115g (4 oz)	brown rice	¾ cup
225g (½ lb)	cashews	1⅔ cups
115g (4 oz)	wholewheat breadcrumbs	2 cups
1	onion	1
2 cloves	garlic	2 cloves
4 tbs	vegetable oil	4 tbs
2 tsp	yeast extract	2 tsp
1 tsp	dried mixed herbs	1 tsp
As required	sea salt	As required
As required	freshly ground black pepper	As required

1 Cook the rice until tender (or use leftover cooked rice) and grind the cashew nuts.
2 Chop the onion and garlic finely and sauté them in the vegetable oil until browned.
3 Combine all the ingredients and press the mixture into a loaf tin.
4 Bake for about half an hour in a moderate oven at 350°F/180°C (Gas Mark 4).

Note: This is a simple, effective main dish, which should be served with vegetable accompaniments.

Cashew-stuffed Aubergines

2 large or 4 small	aubergines (eggplants)	2 large or 4 small
455g (1 lb)	onions	1 lb
225g (½ lb)	cashews	1⅔ cups
2 tsp	yeast extract	2 tsp

1 Cut the tops off the aubergines (eggplants) and simmer them in boiling water for half an hour. Set them aside to drain and cool.
2 Chop the onions finely and cook them in enough water to cover, along with the yeast extract, until tender. Drain the surplus liquid.
3 Grind the cashews and mix them with the cooked onion.
4 Slice the aubergines (eggplants) in half, remove the centres and, when finely chopped, add them to the cashew-onion mixture.
5 Pile the mixture on to the aubergine (eggplant) halves and bake for 20 minutes in a fairly hot oven at 400°F/200°C (Gas Mark 6) for 20 minutes.

Note: This is an unusual filling for aubergines (eggplants) but a very pleasing one. Serve with seasonal vegetables and potatoes.

Savoury Stuffed Aubergines

2 large or 4 small	aubergines (eggplants)	2 large or 4 small
1	onion	1
2 large	tomatoes	2
85g (3 oz)	almonds, Brazils or hazelnuts	⅔ cup
1 clove	garlic	1 clove
4 tbs	rolled oats	4 tbs
4 tbs	vegetable oil	4 tbs
2 tbs	wholewheat flour	2 tbs
1 tin (c.400g)	tomatoes	1 can (14-16 oz)
1 tsp	dried basil or marjoram	1 tsp
As required	sea salt	As required
As required	freshly ground black pepper	As required

1 Cut the tops off and place the aubergines (eggplants) in boiling water for 5-10 minutes.
2 Set aside to drain, then slice them in half and remove the flesh, leaving the skins intact.
3 Chop the garlic finely. Chop the onion, the 2 large tomatoes, and the aubergine (eggplant) flesh.
4 Sauté the above ingredients in half the oil for a few minutes.
5 Grind the nuts and add them to the saucepan together with the oats, stirring well.
6 Fill the aubergine (eggplant) skins with this mixture and bake them in a moderately hot oven 375°F/190°C (Gas Mark 5) for about half an hour.
7 Meanwhile, heat the rest of the oil in a small saucepan and stir in the flour. Remove from the heat.
8 Pour the whole tin of tomatoes into the liquidizer and blend them thoroughly. Add this to the saucepan, mixing well. Return to the heat, stirring constantly to avoid lumps. When thickened and boiling, add the herbs and seasoning to taste.
9 Pour this tomato sauce over the aubergines (eggplants) when ready to serve.

Note: This is a more elaborate stuffed aubergine (eggplant) dish with a Mediterranean flavour.

Nut Croquettes

225g (½ lb)	mixed nuts	1⅔ cups
30g (1 oz)	vegetable fat or vegan margarine	2 tbs
55g (2 oz)	wholewheat flour	½ cup
285ml (½ pt)	soya (soy) milk	1⅓ cups
1 small	onion	1 small
1 tsp	lemon juice	1 tsp
1 tsp	dried mixed herbs	1 tsp
As required	sea salt	As required
As required	freshly ground black pepper	As required
As required	vegetable oil for frying	As required

1 Chop the nuts very finely and grate the onion.
2 Melt the fat, stir in the flour, then add the milk, stirring constantly to avoid lumps.
3 When thickened, add all the other ingredients, seasoning to taste.
4 Leave the mixture to cool, then form into croquette shapes.
5 Deep fry them in hot oil until brown.

Note: I sometimes make small versions of these and serve them (either hot or cold) at parties; they are always very popular.

Steamed Nut Savoury

2	onions	2
2 tbs	vegetable oil	2 tbs
2 tbs	wholewheat flour	2 tbs
1 tsp or 1 tbs fresh	dried thyme	1 tsp or 1 tbs fresh
3 tbs	soya (soy) flour	3 tbs
2 tsp	yeast extract	2 tsp
140ml (¼ pt)	water	⅔ cup
170g (6 oz)	Brazil nuts	1⅓ cups
55g (2 oz)	broken cashews	½ cup
115g (4 oz)	wholewheat breadcrumbs	2 cups

1 Chop the onions finely and sauté them in the oil until brown.
2 Add the flour. Slowly add the water, stirring constantly to avoid lumps, and then add the yeast extract. When the sauce has boiled and thickened, remove the pan from the heat.
3 Grind the Brazils, and add them to the mixture together with the broken cashews, flour, breadcrumbs and thyme. Mix well.
4 Turn into a pudding basin, cover with tin foil and steam for 1½-2 hours.

Note: This makes a pleasant change from a nut roast, with a similar flavour but a completely different texture. Serve with seasonal vegetables (and gravy if desired).

Nut Crunch with Mushroom Cream

115g (4 oz)	wholewheat breadcrumbs	1 cup
55g (2 oz)	ground almonds	½ cup
1-2 cloves	garlic	1-2 cloves
115g (4 oz)	vegan margarine	½ cup
1 tsp	dried mixed herbs	1 tsp
115g (4 oz)	chopped or flaked almonds	1 cup
340g (12 oz)	mushrooms	6 cups
30g (1 oz)	wholewheat flour	¼ cup
140ml (½ pt)	soya (soy) milk	⅔ cup
2	tomatoes	2
As required	sea salt	As required
As required	freshly ground black pepper	As required
As required	grated nutmeg	As required

1 Combine the crumbs and ground almonds. Rub half the margarine into this mixture, then stir in the mixed herbs, chopped almonds, and garlic, crushed.
2 Turn the mixture into a greased ovenproof dish. Press down firmly and bake in a hot oven at 425°F/220°C (Gas Mark 7) until lightly browned and crisp.
3 Slice the mushrooms and sauté them in the remainder of the margarine until tender.
4 Add the flour and stir well. Then add the milk slowly, stirring constantly to avoid lumps. Bring to the boil and simmer for 2 minutes. Season to taste.
5 Spoon the mixture on top of the breadcrumbs and nut base and spread evenly.
6 Slice the tomatoes and arrange them on the top.
7 Return dish to the oven for 10-15 minutes and serve hot.

Note: This kind of dish, sometimes called a 'croustade' is always popular. Serve it with seasonal vegetables and potatoes.
Suitable for a dinner party.

Spinach and Almond Roast

340-455g (¾-1 lb)	spinach	¾-1 lb
1	onion	1
1 clove	garlic	1 clove
2 tbs	vegetable oil	2 tbs
225g (½ lb)	ground almonds	2 cups
85g (3 oz)	wholewheat breadcrumbs	1½ cups
2 tbs	tomato purée (paste)	2 tbs
1 tbs	soy sauce	1 tbs
1 tsp	dried marjoram	1 tsp
As required	sea salt	As required
As required	freshly ground black pepper	As required

1 Wash and chop the spinach. Steam it for a few minutes until just tender.
2 Chop the onion and garlic finely. Fry them in the oil for a few minutes until just beginning to brown.
3 Combine all the ingredients and place them in a baking dish (or loaf pan if preferred). Bake at 350°F/180°C (Gas Mark 4) for about half an hour.

Note: Serve this roast with vegetables – a mixture of cauliflower, carrot and peas goes well.

Almond and Vegetable Curry

55g (2 oz)	flaked (slivered) almonds	½ cup
2	onions	2
1 clove	garlic	1 clove
30g (1 oz)	vegan margarine	2 tbs
2 tsp	cumin seeds	2 tsp
2 tsp	coriander seeds	2 tsp
8	cloves	8
½ tsp	cinnamon	½ tsp
½ tsp	turmeric	½ tsp
¼ tsp (or to taste)	chilli powder	¼ tsp (or to taste)
As required	sea salt	As required
As required	freshly ground black pepper	As required
570ml (1 pt)	water	2½ cups
1 tbs	tomato purée (paste)	1 tbs
680g (1½ lb)	mixed vegetables (fresh or frozen)	1½ lb
115g (4 oz)	ground almonds	1 cup

1 Toast the flaked (slivered) almonds under the grill (broiler) until very lightly browned and set aside.
2 Chop the onions. Crush the garlic. Heat the margarine in a large saucepan and fry the onions and garlic for a few minutes until they begin to change colour.
3 If using fresh vegetables, chop them quite small, grading them in size so that whatever takes longest to cook is the smallest. (Frozen vegetables can be used straight from the freezer.)
4 Grind the cumin and coriander seeds and the cloves. Add to the saucepan, together with the other spices and seasonings. Continue frying for a minute or two longer, then pour in the water and add the tomato purée (paste).
5 Add the vegetables to the saucepan. When the mixture is boiling, lower the heat, cover, and simmer for a few minutes until the vegetables are nearly done.
6 Stir in the ground almonds and cook for a few minutes longer. Sprinkle the toasted flaked (slivered) almonds over the top before serving.

Note: A friend mentioned using ground almonds in various dishes, and it occurred to me that they ought to work well in a curry, as indeed they do, making it rich and creamy. To make it quicker you could use ground spices instead of grinding whole ones, or even use curry powder, but it won't taste as nice. Serve the curry over brown rice, with mango chutney.

Brazil Nut Moussaka

680g (1½ lb)	aubergines (eggplants)	1½ lb
As required	sea salt	As required
2	onions	2
115g (4 oz)	vegetable oil	8 tbs
225g (½ lb)	Brazil nuts	1½ cups
115g (4 oz)	breadcrumbs	2 cups
3 tbs	tomato purée (paste)	3 tbs
285ml (½ pt)	water	1⅓ cups
2 tsp	yeast extract	2 tsp
1 tsp	cinnamon	1 tsp
30g (1 oz)	vegan margarine	2 tbs
2 tbs	wholewheat flour	2 tbs
710ml (1¼ pt)	soya (soy) milk	3 cups
As required	sea salt	As required
As required	freshly ground black pepper	As required
Grating	nutmeg	Grating

1 Slice the aubergines (eggplants) thinly, salt them, put them in a colander with a weight on them, and leave them for at least half an hour.
2 Chop the onions. Heat half the oil in a saucepan and sauté the onions for a few minutes.
3 Grind the nuts. Add them to the saucepan, along with the breadcrumbs, water, yeast extract and cinnamon. Bring to the boil, then lower the heat and simmer for a few minutes.
4 Rinse the aubergine (eggplant) slices, drain on kitchen (paper) towels and squeeze gently. Heat the other half of the oil in a frying pan and fry the slices gently (it may be necessary to do them in batches), turning them once. Drain well.
5 Heat the margarine in a saucepan, and stir in the flour. Add the milk very gradually, stirring constantly, and bring to the boil. Season with salt, pepper and nutmeg.
6 Place the aubergine (eggplant) slices and the nutmeg mixture in layers in a casserole, starting and ending with aubergine. Pour the sauce over the top.
7 Bake at 375°F/190°C (Gas Mark 5) for about half an hour.

Note: Using Brazil nuts in place of 'mince' in moussaka gives an unusual and pleasing result. Serve this dish with a green salad.

Curried Rice and Walnut Roast

285-340g (10-12 oz)	brown rice	1½-2 cups
2	onions	2
2 cloves	garlic	2 cloves
2 tbs	vegetable oil	2 tbs
225g (½ lb)	walnuts	½ lb
85g (3 oz)	wholewheat breadcrumbs	1½ cups
2 tsp	curry powder	2 tsp
As required	sea salt	As required
As required	freshly ground black pepper	As required
285ml (½ pt)	soya (soy) yogurt	1⅓ cups

1 Cook the rice (or remove previously cooked rice from the refrigerator).
2 Chop the onions and garlic finely. Sauté them in the oil for a few minutes in a large saucepan. Remove from heat.
3 Grind the walnuts. Add them to the pan together with the breadcrumbs, curry powder, seasoning and yogurt. Stir well and turn into a casserole dish.
4 Bake at 350°F/180°C (Gas Mark 4) for about half an hour.

Note: This recipe is a way of using leftover rice in a roast instead of stir-frying it.

Cornmeal and Walnut Squares with Soya Gravy

For the squares:

2	onions	2
2 tbs	vegetable oil plus additional for frying	2 tbs
170g (6 oz)	cornmeal	1⅓ cups
170g (6 oz)	wholewheat flour	1⅓ cups
170g (6 oz)	chopped walnuts	1⅓ cups
850ml (1½ pt)	hot water	3¾ cups
2-3 tbs	soy (soya) sauce	2-3 tbs

For the gravy:

570ml (1 pt)	water	2½ cups
55g (2 oz)	wholewheat flour	½ cup
2-3 tbs	soy sauce	2-3 tbs

1 Chop the onions finely. Heat the oil in a heavy-bottomed saucepan and fry the onions until they begin to brown. Stir in the cornmeal and flour and stir over a medium heat for several minutes.
2 Add the hot water, nuts and soy sauce, stirring constantly. Lower the heat, and continue stirring until it is thick and smooth. Transfer the mixture to a greased baking sheet and smooth to about an inch thick. Leave to cool then refrigerate.
3 To make the gravy put the water, flour and soya (soy) sauce in a liquidizer and blend. Pour the mixture into a saucepan and heat gently, stirring constantly to avoid lumps. When the mixture is boiling lower the heat to minimum and let it simmer for a few minutes until it no longer has any 'raw' taste.
4 Cut the nut mixture into squares and shallow-fry the squares until they are well browned on both sides.

Note: This requires advance preparation but takes only minutes at meal time. Serve the squares with the gravy and seasonal vegetables.

Pecan Roast

1 small	onion	1 small
170g (6 oz)	pecans	1 cup
170g (6 oz)	wholewheat breadcrumbs	3 cups
2 tbs	minced parsley	2 tbs
140g (5 oz)	tomato purée (paste)	5 oz
230ml (8 fl oz)	water	1 cup
As required	sea salt	As required
As required	freshly ground black pepper	As required

1 Grate the onion. Chop the nuts.
2 Combine all the ingredients in a large mixing bowl and

mix well. Transfer to a baking dish, and bake at 375°F/190°C (Gas Mark 5) for about 40 minutes.

Note: This is a nice 'meaty' roast. Serve it with seasonal vegetables and potatoes.

Chestnut Stew

2	onions	2
4	tomatoes	4
170g (6 oz)	mushrooms	3 cups
2 tbs	vegetable oil	2 tbs
As required	freshly ground black pepper	As required
140ml (¼ pt)	water	⅔ cup
170g (6 oz)	dried chestnuts soaked in a wide-rimmed thermos flask until tender (see p.77)	6 oz
2 tsp	yeast extract	2 tsp
2 tbs	chopped parsley	2 tbs

1 Chop the onions. Skin the tomatoes; set two aside and chop the other two. Chop the mushrooms.
2 Heat the oil in a large saucepan. Sauté the onions, chopped tomatoes and mushrooms for a few minutes. Grind pepper into the mixture. Add the water and chestnuts. Bring to the boil, then lower the heat and simmer, uncovered, for 10-15 minutes.
3 Check the stew and if it is dry then add a little more water; if there is too much liquid then raise the heat (this will depend on size and juiciness of the tomatoes).
4 Slice the remaining tomatoes and place them under a grill (broiler) until tender.
5 Stir the yeast extract into the stew. Serve it topped with the slices of grilled (broiled) tomato and parsley.

Note: I serve this stew over brown rice, but it could be served with potatoes or bread instead.

Chestnut and Mushroom Pie

2	onions	2
3 tbs	vegetable oil	3 tbs
340g (¾ lb)	mushrooms	2 cups
55g (2 oz)	wholewheat flour	½ cup
425ml (¾ pt)	vegetable stock or water	2 cups
2 tbs	soya (soy) sauce	2 tbs
As required	sea salt	As required
As required	freshly ground black pepper	As required
¼ tsp	freshly ground nutmeg	¼ tsp
225g (½ lb)	dried chestnuts soaked in a wide-rimmed thermos flask until tender (see p.77) Pastry made from 225-340g (½-¾ lb/2-3 cups) wholewheat flour and 115g (4 oz/¼ cup) vegan margarine (see p.41)	½ lb

1 Chop the onions and sauté them in the oil in a saucepan for a few minutes until they begin to brown. Slice the mushrooms, add them to the pan and cook for a few minutes longer until they are tenderized.
2 Sprinkle the flour over the vegetables and stir well. Slowly pour over the stock or water, stirring constantly. Bring to the boil, lower the heat and simmer. Season with soya (soy) sauce, salt, pepper and nutmeg. Stir in the nutmeg and let the mixture cool a little.
3 Roll out the pastry and line the bottom and sides of a pie dish with about two-thirds of it. Put in the chestnut and mushroom mixture and top with the rest of the pastry. Prick with a fork, then bake at 400°F/200°C (Gas Mark 6) for about half an hour.

Note: This is a delicious combination of tastes and textures. Serve it with seasonal vegetables for a special occasion.
Suitable for a dinner party.

Chestnut Roast

225g (½ lb)	dried chestnuts which have been soaked in a Thermos flask (see p.77)	½ lb
2	onions	2
3 tbs	vegetable oil	3 tbs
115g (4 oz)	wholewheat breadcrumbs	4 oz
2 tbs	soya (soy) sauce	2 tbs
2 tbs	soya (soy) flour	2 tbs
225ml (8 fl oz)	water	1 cup
1 tsp	dried sage	1 tsp
½ tsp	dried thyme	½ tsp
As required	sea salt	As required
As required	freshly ground black pepper	As required

1 Drain the chestnuts and mash them in a large bowl (there is no need to make them particularly smooth).
2 Chop the onions and sauté them in the oil for a few minutes until tenderized. Add them to the bowl.
3 Add all the remaining ingredients and stir well. Transfer the mixture to a baking dish and bake in a moderate oven 350°F/180°C (Gas Mark 4) for about half an hour.

Note: This would be a good Christmas dish, particularly with a miso gravy over it.

Chestnut Burgers

225g (½ lb)	dried chestnuts which have been soaked in a Thermos flask (see p.77)	½ lb
1	onion	1
1 tbs	vegetable oil plus additional for frying burgers	1 tbs
1 tsp	yeast extract	1 tsp
115g (4 oz)	wholewheat breadcrumbs	2 cups
30g (1 oz)	soya (soy) flour	¼ cup
½ tsp	dried sage	½ tsp
As required	sea salt	As required
As required	freshly ground black pepper	As required
285ml (½ pt)	hot water	1⅓ cups

1 Drain the chestnuts and mash them in a bowl.
2 Chop the onion finely. Sauté it in the oil until tender and beginning to brown. Add it to the mashed chestnuts.
3 Stir in the yeast extract, breadcrumbs, soya (soy) flour, sage and seasoning, then pour in the hot water. Mix with a spoon, then cool slightly and form into eight burgers.
4 Fry the burgers until browned on both sides.

Note: Serve this either with salad or with gravy, a green vegetable (Brussels sprouts have a particular affinity with chestnuts), and potatoes.
Quick and Easy.

Tofu and other Soya Foods

11

Introduction

Known in the Far East for centuries, it is only in the past two or three decades that tofu – also called 'soya (soy) bean curd' – has appeared in the west. Soya (soy) beans are known to be a very high protein food, but they are not at all easy to digest. By extracting the milk and curdling it the protein is retained in a very easily digested form. Not only is tofu highly nutritious, it is also highly versatile. On the first tasting, people complain it is bland, but it is this blandness that is its greatest strength since it can absorb any flavour, savoury or sweet. Its texture can also change depending on the way it is cooked.

Tofu is usually classified in three forms: firm, medium or soft. Most of the vacuum-packed tofu sold in the UK is firm, and so most of the recipes in this chapter are geared to firm tofu. Medium tofu can be found in some wholefood shops which make their own tofu; it can be used interchangeably with firm tofu in any recipe. (Tofu sold in Chinese shops is medium in texture but has a distinctive flavour that makes it unsuitable for some dishes.) Silken tofu is very soft and suitable only for dishes requiring puréed tofu. (There is also a 'firm silken tofu' available which is similar to ordinary medium tofu in texture, but as silken tofu contains more moisture than ordinary tofu I would not recommend it for dishes requiring deep-fried tofu.)

Freezing tofu alters its texture, making it 'spongy'. There are recipes specifically for frozen tofu in this chapter. I recommend freezing tofu in slices rather than in a full block. It can then be quickly defrosted (about 10 minutes) by pouring boiling water over the slices. It is important after defrosting frozen tofu to squeeze it gently to get rid of excess water. Dried tofu is also available at some wholefood shops and is very similar in texture to frozen tofu.

An appealing product readily available in the UK (but not, to the best of my knowledge, available yet in the USA) is smoked tofu. It can be sliced and eaten 'raw' in sandwiches, and for parties I often put out cocktails sticks with diced smoked tofu and pineapple chunks; they are always very popular. Recipes using smoked tofu will be found in this chapter. Another product available in Britain is marinated tofu: the tofu is packed in a marinade of soy sauce and ginger. I tend to use this mainly in vegetable stir-fries or, alternatively, freeze and deep-fry it; I have not, therefore, included recipes for marinated tofu in this book.

Another soya (soy) food which deserves to be better known is tempeh. In this product the whole bean, rather than just the milk, is used, but because it is fermented it is easy to digest while at the same time providing fibre. A special kind of spore links the beans together into a solid block that can be sliced and then steamed or fried. Because it is a 'live' food it is usually bought frozen, and it needs to be used fairly quickly after defrosting. A light-coloured block will have a milder flavour than one with a lot of black in it. It is best to try lighter ones first to see how you like the taste.

After thawing, which takes two to three hours at room temperature or about twelve hours in the refrigerator, tempeh should be steamed; it should never be eaten raw. Instructions about the time needed to steam tempeh range from five minutes to half an hour; 15 to 20 minutes is clearly sufficient. If you do not have a steamer it is quite easy to improvise one: all you need is a large saucepan with a tight-fitting lid and the lid of a small saucepan that will fit inside. Fill the large saucepan with about an inch or two of water, place the smaller lid on it, then place the tempeh cubes on it; cover the large saucepan, bring to the boil, then lower the heat to simmer, and you will be steaming the tempeh. At the time of writing, the newest soya (soy) product available in the UK is smoked tempeh 'rashers'.

One final soya (soy) food forms the basis of much Chinese Buddhist vegetarian cookery. It is available in Chinese speciality shops as 'bean curd skin', though in fact the skin is skimmed off the soya (soy) milk before tofu is made. It is then dried and sold in large sheets. Its popularity stems from its texture which, after steaming, is remarkably 'meaty'.

Recipes

To make tofu at home the following are required: a large saucepan (holding at least 3½ litres (6 pints/9 cups), a liquidizer, a colander, a small box (about 150mm× 100mm (6in×4in) with small holes punched in the bottom and sides (the holes can be punched into an ordinary plastic sandwich box, and the sides cut off the lid so it fits in on top), a large piece of muslin (about 75cm (2 ft)) and a small piece of muslin (to fit inside the box). If the tofu is to be mashed or puréed rather than sliced or cubed, the box can be omitted and the colander lined with muslin.

Home-made Tofu

225g (½ lb)	soya (soy) beans	1 cup
As required	boiling water	As required
As required	cold water	As required
1 heaped tsp	nigari, lemon juice or Epsom salts	1 heaped tsp

1 The night before, cover the beans with boiling water and leave them to soak. In the morning drain and rinse. Place a cup of the soaked beans in the liquidizer, add a cup of cold water and blend. Then add about 2 cups of boiling water to the liquidizer and blend again. *Note:* if your liquidizer is not large enough then a smaller quantity can be done each time as long as the proportions are kept more or less the same – it is *not* necessary to measure with any great precision when making tofu.
2 Place the large piece of muslin over the saucepan and carefully pour the contents of the liquidizer into it. Pull up the sides to make it into a sack so that the soya (soy) milk runs through, and squeeze gently to get all of the liquid into the saucepan. (The pulp left in the muslin is called 'okara' and can be used in savouries; it is high in protein but, unlike tofu, is not very easy to digest.)
3 Once all of the beans have been used up put the saucepan on to a medium to high heat and bring to the boil, stirring the bottom from time to time. Keep a careful eye on it because it can boil over very suddenly and dramatically. As soon as it starts to boil turn the

heat right down very low so it is still simmering but no longer threatening to erupt. Leave to simmer for about three minutes.
4 Meanwhile, put the heaped teaspoon of nigari, lemon juice or Epsom salts into a teacup. Fill it half full of boiling water and stir well. Remove the soya (soy) milk from the heat, then gently stir in the dissolved coagulant, trying to make certain it has been stirred through all of the liquid. Leave for about three minutes, by which time curds should have formed.
5 Place the muslin-lined box (if used) in the colander, then gradually pour the contents of the saucepan into it, so that the whey runs through and the curds settle in the box. Then put the colander over the empty saucepan to continue to drain, and place something heavy (about 900g (2 lb)) on top. Leave for an hour or so before unmoulding. 225g (half a pound) of soya (soy) beans will make about 340g (¾ lb/1½ cups) of tofu (though it can vary by 55g (2 oz/¼ cup) either way).
6 If the tofu is not to be used immediately it should be stored in the refrigerator in an airtight container of water, where it will keep for about a week. (Most instructions tell you to change the water every day, but if the container is left undisturbed then this really is not necessary.)

Tofu and Onions

455g (1 lb)	tofu	2 cups
3	onions	3
3 tbs	vegetable oil	3 tbs
140ml (¼ pt)	water	⅔ cup
2 tsp	cornflour (cornstarch)	2 tsp
2 tsp	soya (soy) sauce	2 tsp

1 Slice the onions thinly and sauté them in oil until tender.
2 Cut the tofu into small cubes and add them to the onions. Stir well.
3 Combine the cornflour (cornstarch) with the water and soya (soy) sauce. Pour the mixture over the tofu and onions. Bring to the boil, stirring constantly until thickened.
4 Simmer for 2-3 minutes before serving.

Note: This is a very simple dish which is best served over brown rice.
Quick and Easy.

Sweet and Sour Tofu and Vegetables

455g (1 lb)	tofu	2 cups
1 tin	pineapple chunks	1 can
(c.400g)		(14-16 oz)
455g (1 lb)	tomatoes	1 lb
1 bunch	spring onions (scallions)	1 bunch
85g (3 oz)	almonds	¾ cup
4 tbs	vegetable oil	4 tbs
4 tbs	soya (soy) sauce	4 tbs
2 tsp	cornflour (cornstarch)	2 tsp

1 Cut the tofu into small cubes. Finely chop the spring onions (scallions). Sauté them both in the oil for 3 minutes.
2 Chop the tomatoes and add them to the pan. Cook for 5 minutes.
3 Drain the pineapple and add to the pan together with the whole almonds. Cook for 2-3 minutes.
4 Dissolve the cornflour (cornstarch) in the soy sauce and pour the mixture over the vegetables and tofu. Stir well until thickened and simmer for a minute or two.

Note: This dish can now be found in some Chinese restaurants. Serve it over brown rice.
Quick and Easy.

Sea-flavoured Crisp Tofu Slices

565-680g	tofu	2½-3 cups
(1¼-1½ lbs)		
2 tbs	gram (chick pea) flour	2 tbs
4 tsp	kelp powder	4 tsp
4 tbs	water	4 tbs
85g (3 oz)	wholewheat flour	¾ cup
55g (2 oz)	cornmeal	½ cup
1½ tbs	soy sauce	1½ tbs

1 Slice the tofu fairly thinly (there should be 4 or 5 slices per person).
2 Put the flour on one plate and the cornmeal on another. Add 2 tsp kelp powder to each plate and mix well.
3 In a shallow bowl mix the gram (chick pea) flour, water and soy (soya) sauce with a fork.
4 Dredge each slice of tofu with the flour mixture, then dip it into the gram (chick pea) flour mixture, and finally dredge it in the cornmeal mixture. Place the slices on an oiled baking sheet. Bake them for about 10 minutes at 375°F/180°C (Gas Mark 5), then turn them over and bake for a further 10 minutes.

Note: In this recipe the tofu is baked. The kelp gives it an oceanic tang. Serve it with slices of lemon and/or vegan tartare sauce, with fried potatoes and peas or salad.

Mushroom Stroganoff

455g (1 lb)	mushrooms	1 lb
4 tbs	vegetable oil	4 tbs
55g (2 oz)	wholewheat flour	½ cup
425ml (¾ pt)	vegetable stock	2 cups
1 clove	garlic	1 clove
1	onion	1
340g (¾ lb)	tofu	1½ cups
As required	sea salt	As required
As required	freshly ground black pepper	As required
As required	mustard powder	As required

1 Slice the mushrooms and sauté them in the oil until tender.
2 Chop the onion and garlic finely and add them to the saucepan. Sauté for a further 5 minutes.
3 Add the flour, stirring well. Slowly add the vegetable stock, stirring constantly to avoid lumps. Cook for a minute or two.
4 Put the tofu in the liquidizer and add enough water to make aobut 570ml (1 pint) of tofu cream. Blend thoroughly.
5 Add the tofu cream to the mushroom mixture, stirring well. Season and cook until well heated.

Note: In this recipe the tofu is liquified into a rich cream. Serve it over cooked noodles.
Quick and Easy.

Tofu Kebabs

455g (1 lb)	firm tofu	2 cups
2 tbs	olive oil	2 tbs
2 tbs	cider vinegar or wine vinegar	2 tbs
3 tbs	mustard	3 tbs
2 tsp	dried rosemary	2 tsp
1 tsp	dried sage	1 tsp
2 tsp	sea salt	2 tsp
1 tsp	freshly ground black pepper	1 tsp
115g (4 oz)	mushrooms	2 cups
1	green pepper	1

1 Drain the tofu and wrap it in a tea towel (dish towel) for a few minutes to get rid of excess moisture. Cut it into cubes.
2 In a large bowl combine the oil, vinegar, mustard, herbs and seasonings. (*Note:* Dried rosemary can be rather coarse; with a mortar and pestle it is easy to grind it to a powder.)
3 Put the tofu cubes into the bowl and stir them well so that the mustard mixture adheres to them.
4 Cover the bowl and put it into the refrigerator. Leave it to marinate for 2-3 hours, turning the tofu cubes once or twice.
5 Clean the mushrooms and remove the stalks. Chop the green pepper into chunks large enough to be threaded on to a skewer.
6 Thread the tofu cubes onto skewers, alternating with the green pepper and mushrooms. Place them on a grill pan under a hot grill (broiler). Grill (broil), turning the skewers from time to time, until they are nicely browned all over. Serve immediately.

Note: This is a different way of cooking tofu. Serve it in pitta bread or over rice.

Tofu Casserole

455g (1 lb)	tofu	2 cups
As required	vegetable oil for deep frying	As required
2 small or 1 large	onion	2 small or 1 large
2 cloves	garlic	2 cloves
45g (1½ oz)	vegan margarine	3 tbs
30g (1 oz)	wholewheat flour	¼ cup
285ml (½ pt)	soya (soy) milk	1⅓ cups
2 tbs	miso	2 tbs
As required	freshly ground black pepper	As required
55g (2 oz)	wholewheat breadcrumbs	1 cup

1 Cube the tofu and deep fry until golden. (This may be done in advance, and the cubes kept in the refrigerator until cooking time.)

2 Slice the onions thinly. Crush the garlic. Sauté in 30g (1 oz/2 tablespoons) of the margarine for 4-5 minutes, until softened and lightly browned.
3 Stir the flour into the onions. Gradually add the milk, stirring constantly to avoid lumps. Bring to the boil and, when thickened, remove from the heat. Immediately stir in the miso, and continue stirring well until smooth. Add pepper to taste, then stir in the tofu cubes.
4 Turn the mixture into an oiled baking dish, sprinkle with the breadcrumbs, dot with the remaining margarine, and bake in the oven at 350°F/180°C (Gas Mark 4) for about 20 minutes.

Note: Deep frying tofu gives it a light chewy texture which, in this recipe, forms a contrast to a creamy white sauce. Serve the casserole with seasonal vegetables and potatoes.

Warming Winter Stew

455g (1 lb)	tofu	2 cups
2 tbs	vegetable oil plus additional for deep frying	2 tbs
2	onions	2
225g (½ lb)	carrots	½ lb
225g (½ lb)	Savoy cabbage	½ lb
1 tbs	sesame oil	1 tbs
570ml (1 pt)	vegetable stock or water	2½ cups
2-3 tbs	miso	2-3 tbs
1 tsp	arrowroot	1 tsp
1 tbs	water	1 tbs

1 Cube the tofu and deep fry until golden brown. Drain and set aside.
2 Slice the onions thinly. Chop the carrots and cabbage. Sauté the vegetables in the oil for a minute or two. Add the deep-fried tofu cubes and the stock or water. Bring to the boil, cover and reduce the heat. Leave to simmer for about 10 minutes.
3 Remove a little of the hot liquid and use it to cream the miso before stirring it into the saucepan. Dissolve the arrowroot in the tablespoon of water and stir into the saucepan until thickened.

Note: Deep-fried tofu also works well in a stew. This is good over brown rice or, alternatively, on its own, accompanied by potatoes or bread.

Korean-style Kebabs

340-455g (¾-1 lb)	tofu	1-1½ cups
As required	oil for deep frying	As required
2	spring onions (scallions)	2
2 cloves	garlic	2 cloves
4 tbs	miso	4 tbs
1 tbs	raw cane sugar	1 tbs
2 tsp	sesame oil	2 tsp
1 tbs	tahini	1 tbs
Few drops	Tabasco sauce	Few drops
140ml (¼ pt)	water	⅔ cup
A dozen	mushrooms	A dozen
1	green pepper	1
1 small	apple	1 small
¼	cucumber	¼
4 small	tomatoes	4 small
115g (4 oz)	fresh or tinned (canned) pineapple chunks	¼ lb

1 Drain the tofu well. Cut into cubes and deep fry until golden. Drain and set aside.
2 Chop the spring onions (scallions) finely. Crush the garlic.
3 Combine the miso, sugar, sesame oil, tahini, spring onions (scallions), garlic and Tabasco sauce in a large bowl and mix well. Add the water and stir until smooth.
4 Remove the stalks from the mushrooms. Cut the green pepper and apple into bite-sized chunks. Slice the cucumber. Halve the tomatoes.
5 Add the vegetables and fruit to the miso mixture together with the tofu cubes. Mix thoroughly. Leave to marinate for at least an hour, turning occasionally.
6 Thread everything on to skewers and place under a hot grill (broiler). Grill (broil) for about 5 minutes on one side, turn over, pour a little of the marinade over everything and grill (broil) the other side for about 5 minutes.
7 Serve with the remainder of the marinade poured over as a sauce.

Note: This is another recipe for kebabs, in which the tofu is deep fried.

Tofu and Green Pea Bhajia

455g (1 lb)	tofu	2 cups
2	onions	2
2 tbs	vegetable oil	2 tbs
3	tomatoes	3
2 cloves	garlic	2 cloves
2	fresh chillies	2
1.5cm (½ in)	fresh ginger	½ inch
2 tsp	coriander seeds	2 tsp
2 tsp	turmeric	2 tsp
¼ tsp	chilli powder	¼ tsp
A little	sea salt	A little
225g (½ lb)	fresh or frozen peas	1⅓ cups

1 Cut the tofu into small cubes. Deep fry them in a deep-fat fryer or in a pan of oil heated to 350°F/180°C (Gas Mark 4) until lightly golden. Drain well.
2 Chop the onions. Fry in the vegetable oil for about 3 minutes.
3 Chop the tomatoes. Crush the garlic. De-seed and finely chop the chillies. Peel and finely chop the ginger. Add the ingredients with the coriander, turmeric and chilli powder to the onion and stir well. Cook for about 5 minutes.
4 Add the fried tofu cubes to the saucepan. Sprinkle a little salt over them, and stir well. Cover the pan and cook for 2-3 minutes.
5 Add the peas to the saucepan (if they are frozen the heat may need to be turned up briefly). Cover and cook until they are tender (3-4 minutes).

Note: Indian cookery uses a bland cheese called panir which is often cubed and fried. Tofu works beautifully in its place. Serve this with Basmati rice, and with chutney and pappadums or chapatis.

Tofu 'Scrambled Eggs'

455g (1 lb)	tofu	2 cups
2 tbs	vegetable oil	2 tbs
½ tsp	onion salt	½ tsp
1 tbs	soy sauce	1 tbs
½ tsp	turmeric	½ tsp
As required	Smokey Snaps (soy bakon bits) (optional)	As required

1 Mash the tofu and combine with the rest of the ingredients, except the oil.
2 Heat the oil and add the tofu mixture. Stir well over a high heat until well heated.

Note: Mashed tofu has a consistency remarkably like scrambled eggs. Here is a basic version. Serve on wholewheat toast.
Quick and Easy. Suitable for One.

Scrambled Tofu and Mushrooms

225g (½ lb)	mushrooms	4 cups
3 tbs	vegetable oil	3 tbs
455g (1 lb)	tofu	2 cups
3 tsp	turmeric	3 tsp
4 tsp	made mustard	4 tsp
2 tsp	garlic salt	2 tsp
As required	freshly ground black pepper	As required
4	spring onions (scallions)	4

1 Chop the mushrooms finely. Sauté in the oil until tender.
2 Mash the tofu in a bowl. Add the turmeric, mustard, garlic salt and pepper and mix well.
3 Add the tofu mixture to the mushrooms and stir over a medium heat until well heated.
4 Chop the spring onions (scallions) finely.
5 Stir the spring onions (scallions) into the tofu and serve everything piping hot.

Note: This is another simple tofu scramble. Serve on toast.
Quick and Easy. Suitable for One.

Tofu Piperade

4 tbs	olive oil	4 tbs
1 large	onion	1 large
2 cloves	garlic	2 cloves
1	green pepper	1
1	red pepper	1
4 large	tomatoes	4
½ tsp	dried thyme	½ tsp
½ tsp	dried oregano	½ tsp
As required	sea salt	As required
As required	freshly ground black pepper	As required
340g (¾ lb)	tofu	1½ cups
½ tsp	turmeric	½ tsp

1 Slice the onion thinly, crush the garlic cloves and thinly slice the peppers.
2 Sauté the above in the oil until tender but not brown.
3 Skin and chop the tomatoes. Add them to the pan along with the herbs and seasoning.
4 Cook, stirring occasionally, for about 10 more minutes.
5 Mash the tofu with the turmeric and add to the pan. Cook for several minutes more, stirring constantly, until the mixture is well heated.

Note: Serve on toast or on brown rice or with potatoes or – for an easy savoury flan – in a pre-baked flan case (pie shell).

Spicy Tofu Scramble with Red Pepper and Tomato

1	onion	1
1-2 cloves	garlic	1-2 cloves
2 tbs	vegetable margarine	2 tbs
2	red peppers	2
455g (1 lb)	tomatoes	1 lb
565-680g (1¼-1½ lb)	tofu	2-3 cups
2-3 tbs	soya (soy) sauce	2-3 tbs
1-2 tsp	Tabasco sauce	1-2 tsp

1 Slice the onion thinly. Chop the garlic finely. Sauté in the margarine for about 3 minutes.
2 Chop the red peppers finely. Add to the frying pan, lower the heat from medium to low, cover the pan, and leave to simmer for 3-5 minutes.
3 Skin and chop the tomatoes. Put the tofu into a tea towel (dish towel) and squeeze the moisture out. Add the tomatoes and tofu to the frying pan, with the soy (soya) sauce and Tabasco sauce; raise the heat and stir until everything is piping hot.

Note: This is another 'scrambled' tofu dish: in this one the tofu is made drier by squeezing out excess moisture. Serve on toast.

Tofu Knishes

225g (½ lb)	wholewheat flour	2 cups
2 tsp	baking powder	2 tsp
Pinch	sea salt	Pinch
1 tbs	soya (soy) flour	1 tbs
140g (5 oz)	vegetable margarine	5 oz
120ml (4 fl oz)	soya (soy) milk	½ cup
4 large or 6-8 small	spring onions (scallions)	4 large or 6-8 small
340g (¾ lb)	tofu	1½ cups
4 tbs	soya (soy) yogurt	4 tbs
As required	sea salt	As required

1 Combine the flour, baking powder, salt and soya (soy) flour in a large bowl. Cut in 115g (4 oz/½ cup) margarine then add the milk and mix well. Chill the dough for an hour or more.
2 Chop the spring onions (scallions) finely. Sauté in the remainder of the margarine in a frying pan until beginning to brown.
3 Put the tofu into a tea towel (dish towel) and squeeze the moisture out of it. Transfer it to a mixing bowl, and stir in the yogurt and a little salt. Add the sautéed spring onions (scallions).
4 Roll the dough about 3mm (⅛ inch) thick on a lightly floured surface. Cut into 7.5cm (3-inch) circles. Place about a tablespoon of the tofu mixture on each; fold

the dough over and pinch the edges together. Place on a greased baking tin and bake at 350°F/180°C (Gas Mark 4) for about half an hour.

Note: The same technique of squeezing the tofu is used in this recipe where, combined with soya (soy) yogurt, it resembles cottage cheese rather than eggs. Serve with salad or cooked vegetables.

Tofu and Pea Curry

1	onion	1
1 inch piece	fresh ginger	1 inch piece
2 cloves	garlic	2 cloves
3 tbs	vegetable oil	3 tbs
2 tsp	ground coriander	2 tsp
2 tsp	ground cumin	2 tsp
1 tsp	turmeric	1 tsp
¼ tsp (or to taste)	chilli powder	¼ tsp (or to taste)
455-680g (1-1½ lb)	firm tofu	2-3 cups
455g (1 lb)	fresh (shelled) or frozen peas	1 lb
As required	sea salt	As required
As required	freshly ground black pepper	As required
140ml (¼ pt)	water	⅔ cup
1 tbs	lemon juice	1 tbs

1 Grate the onion and ginger. Crush the garlic. Heat the oil in a pan and cook these ingredients for 3-4 minutes over a low heat. Stir in the spices and cook for a few minutes longer.
2 Crumble the tofu into the pan. Add the peas and seasoning and stir well. Pour in the water and bring to the boil. Lower the heat, cover and simmer for 3-4 minutes until the peas are just tender. Add the lemon juice and serve immediately.

Note: Mashed tofu can also be used in Indian dishes in place of panir. Serve with rice and the usual Indian trimmings.
Quick and Easy.

Tofu Burgers

340g (¾ lb)	tofu	1½ cups
55g (2 oz)	wholewheat flour	½ cup
55g (2 oz)	soya (soy) flour	½ cup
3 tsp	miso	3 tsp
1	onion	1
2 tbs	vegetable oil plus additional for shallow-frying burgers	2 tbs

Optional accompaniments: lettuce or alfalfa sprouts and sliced tomatoes or ketchup.

1 Drain the tofu well. Mash in a bowl. Add the flours and the miso.
2 Chop the onion finely. Sauté in the 2 tablespoons oil until lightly browned.
3 Add the onions to the tofu mixture in the flour, mixing thoroughly (and particularly making sure that the miso is well spread through the mixture). Form into four burgers.
4 Shallow fry in a little more oil, turning once, until well-browned on both sides.

Note: Another use for mashed tofu is to make burgers. Serve them in wholewheat buns with any desired accompaniments.
Quick and Easy. Suitable for One.

Swiss Steak

565g (1¼ lb)	frozen tofu	2½ cups
2 tsp	yeast extract	2 tsp
285ml (½ pt)	water	1⅓ cups
plus 2 tbs		plus 2 tbs
55g (2 oz)	wholewheat flour	½ cup
plus 2 tbs		plus 2 tbs
1 tsp	paprika	1 tsp
1 tsp	oregano	1 tsp
1 tsp	freshly ground black pepper (plus additional to taste)	1 tsp
4 tbs	vegetable oil	4 tbs
2	onions	2
225g (8 oz)	tomatoes	½ lb
2 sticks	celery	2 sticks
1	green pepper	1
115g (4 oz)	mushrooms	2 cups

1 For this dish it is easiest if the tofu has been frozen in slices 8-12mm (⅓-½ inch) thick. Defrost the slices and squeeze excess liquid from them.
2 Dissolve the yeast extract in 285ml (½ pt/1⅓ cups) warm water.
3 Place the tofu slices in a shallow bowl, and pour the yeast extract liquid over them. Leave to marinate for an hour or two, turning the slices occasionally if possible.
4 Combine the 55g (2 oz/½ cup) flour with the paprika, oregano, and teaspoon pepper and spread out on a plate.
5 Lift each tofu slice from the marinade, gently squeezing the marinade from it back into the bowl, and coat both sides with the flour. Sauté in 2 tablespoons of the vegetable oil in a frying pan (skillet), turning once, until lightly browned on both sides. Set aside.
6 Chop the onions and sauté in the remaining oil for 2-3 minutes. Peel and chop the tomatoes. Chop the celery and mushrooms finely. Add to the saucepan.
7 Add the yeast extract marinade to the saucepan, bring to the boil, cover and simmer for about 3 minutes.
8 Combine the 2 tablespoons flour with the 2 tablespoons water in a cup. Stir this into the vegetable mixture until thickened.
9 Place the tofu slices at the bottom of an oiled casserole. Pour the vegetable mixture over them. Bake at 350°F/180°C (Gas Mark 4) for about half an hour.

Note: Frozen tofu is particularly useful for 'meaty' dishes like this one. It is nice with baked or fried potatoes.

Savoury Tofu 'Mince'

455g (1 lb)	frozen tofu	2 cups
1 large	onion	1 large
3 sticks	celery	3 sticks
2	carrots	2
425ml (¾ pt)	water	2 cups
2-3 tsp	yeast extract	2-3 tsp
3-4 tsp	curry powder	3-4 tsp
30g (1 oz)	raisins	1/6 cup

1 Defrost the tofu and squeeze out as much moisture as possible.
2 Chop the onion, celery and carrot finely. Place in a saucepan.
3 Crumble the tofu into the saucepan. Add the water and bring to the boil. Stir in the yeast extract, curry powder and raisins. Lower the heat and simmer for about 15 minutes.

Note: Serve over brown rice or pasta, or with mashed potatoes.

Crispy Fried Sea-flavoured Frozen Tofu

455-650g (1-1½ lbs)	frozen tofu which has been sliced into 12-16 slices before freezing	2-3 cups
1 oz	kombu	1 oz
85g (3 oz)	cornmeal	¾ cup
2 tsp	kelp powder	2 tsp
570ml (1 pt)	boiling water	2½ cups
As required	vegetable oil	As required
4 tbs	soy sauce	4 tbs

1 Put the frozen tofu slices in a large container. Pour in the boiling water; add the soy (soya) sauce and kombu. Cover the container and leave it for about 10 minutes, then put it in a cool room or refrigerator to marinate for at least an hour or two (this can be done in the morning and the marinade left in the refrigerator all day).
2 Spread the cornmeal out on a plate and mix in the kelp powder.
3 Remove the tofu slices from the marinade. (The kombu itself is not used in this dish but can be added to any other dish that requires pre-soaked kombu; the marinade itself can also be used in a soup, stew or gravy.) Squeeze them very gently, then place on the plate with the cornmeal mixture and coat them thoroughly on both sides.
4 Shallow fry the slices in oil on each side until lightly browned.

Note: Frozen tofu can also be used to make a 'fishy' dish like this one, flavoured with a sea vegetable. If desired,

serve with slices of lemon and vegan tartare sauce, and seasonal vegetables or salad (or chips . . .).
Quick and Easy.

Tofu Goulash

140g (5 oz)	dried-frozen tofu	5 oz
2	onions	2
1 large or 2 small	green peppers	1 large or 2 small
3 tbs	vegetable oil	3 tbs
2 tbs	wholewheat flour plus additional for coating	2 tbs
3 tsp	paprika	3 tsp
225g (½ lb)	tomatoes	½ lb
570ml (1 pt)	water	2½ cups
3 tsp	yeast extract	3 tsp
3 tbs	tomato purée (paste)	3 tbs
As required	freshly ground black pepper	As required
As required	wholewheat noodles	As required

1 Rehydrate the tofu.
2 Chop the onions and green pepper. Sauté in the oil for 3-4 minutes.
3 Squeeze excess liquid from the tofu and cut into cubes approximately 2.5cm×2.5cm×1cm (1 inch by 1 inch by ½ inch). Spread some flour on to a plate and roll the cubes in this. Add to the saucepan and stir well for about 2 minutes.
4 Sprinkle in the paprika and the flour and stir for another 2 minutes.
5 Chop the tomatoes coarsely (skinned if desired). Add them to the saucepan together with the water, yeast extract, tomato purée (paste) and pepper. Bring to the boil, lower the heat, cover and simmer for about 15 minutes, stirring occasionally. Serve over cooked noodles.

Note: This recipe was formulated specifically for dried tofu. Serve it over noodles.

Smoked Tofu Stew

1	onion	1
2 sticks	celery	2 sticks
1 large or 2 small	carrots	1 large or 2 small
170g (6 oz)	mushrooms	3 cups
340-455g (¾-1 lb)	potatoes	¾-1 lb
3 tbs	vegetable oil	3 tbs
225g (½ lb)	smoked tofu	1 cup
425ml (¾ pt)	vegetable stock or water	2 cups
2 tsp	yeast extract	2 tsp
2-3	bay leaves	2-3
2 tbs	water	2 tbs
2 tbs	wholewheat flour	2 tbs
As required	sea salt	As required
As required	freshly ground black pepper	As required

1 Chop the onion, celery, carrot, mushrooms and potatoes. Dice the tofu. Heat the oil in a large saucepan and sauté the vegetables and tofu for a few minutes.
2 Pour in the stock, stir in the yeast extract and add the bay leaves. Bring to the boil, then lower the heat, cover and cook for about 45 minutes.
3 Stir the flour into the water, then stir this into the saucepan. Season to taste and serve.

Note: Smoked tofu adds a lovely flavour to a traditional stew. Serve it with warm, crusty bread.

Smoked Tofu, Courgette and Sweetcorn Risotto

285-340g (10-12 oz)	brown rice	1 cup
2	onions	2
2 cloves	garlic	2 cloves
2 tbs	vegetable oil	2 tbs
225g (½ lb)	courgettes (zucchini)	½ lb
455g (1 lb)	smoked tofu	2 cups
225g (½ lb)	frozen sweetcorn (corn)	½ lb
285ml (½ pt)	water	1⅓ cups
4 tbs	tomato purée (paste)	4 tbs
2 tsp dried or 2 tbs fresh	marjoram	2tsp dried or 2 tbs fresh
As required	freshly ground black pepper	As required

1 Cook the rice if it is not already cooked.
2 Chop the onions and garlic and sauté them in the oil in a large saucepan for 3-4 minutes.
3 Dice the courgettes (zucchini) and tofu. Add them to the pan and continue sautéing over a low to medium heat for a few more minutes, stirring frequently.
4 Add the rice and frozen sweetcorn (corn) to the pan together with the tomato purée (paste). Stir in the water, then turn the heat up to high and bring to the boil. Sprinkle in the marjoram and pepper, lower the heat, cover, and leave to cook for 3-4 minutes longer. Serve immediately.

Note: Using leftover rice makes this a very fast dish. Quick and Easy.

Smokey Duvec

140-170g (5-6 oz)	brown rice	1 cup
455-680g (1-1½ lbs)	potatoes	1-1½ lbs
1 large	onion	1 large
2 cloves	garlic	2 cloves
2 tbs	vegetable oil	2 tbs
4	green or red peppers (or a mixture)	4
4	tomatoes	4
455g (1 lb)	smoked tofu	2 cups
140ml (¼ pt)	water or vegetable stock	⅔ cup
115g (4 oz)	fresh (shelled) or frozen peas	¾ cup
As required	freshly ground black pepper	As required
4 tbs	chopped parsley	4 tbs

1 Cook the rice and potatoes if not already cooked.
2 Chop the onion and garlic and sauté them in the oil in a large saucepan for 3-4 minutes.
3 Chop the peppers and add them to the pan. Chop the tomatoes (skinned if preferred) and add them too, stirring well. Chop the potatoes (peeled if preferred) and dice the tofu; add to the pan and continue sautéing for a few minutes, stirring well.
4 Cover the mixture with water, bring to the boil, lower the heat, cover and leave to cook for a few minutes, stirring once or twice.
5 Stir in the rice, peas and black pepper, raise the heat briefly, then lower it again and cover the pan, leaving it to cook for a few minutes longer over a very low heat.
6 Serve immediately, sprinkled with parsley.

Note: Duvec (pronounced dyuvetch) is a Balkan stew. If leftover rice and potatoes are used it takes no time at all to make.
Quick and Easy.

Pease Pudding and Smoked Tofu Bake

2 tins (400g each)	pease pudding	2 cans
1 tsp	dried mixed herbs	1 tsp
455g (1 lb)	smoked tofu	2 cups
2 tbs	vegetable oil	2 tbs
55-85g (2-3 oz)	wholewheat breadcrumbs	1-1½ cups
2-3 tbs	nutritional yeast	2-3 tbs
30g (1 oz)	vegan margarine	2 tbs

1 Put the pease pudding in a bowl. Mash it and add the herbs.
2 Dice the tofu. Heat the oil in a frying pan and fry the tofu cubes, turning frequently, until nicely browned. Add the cubes to the pease pudding.
3 Turn the mixture into a baking dish. Sprinkle with breadcrumbs and yeast and dot with margarine. Bake at 350°F/180°C (Gas Mark 4) for about 20 minutes.

Note: Cans of pease pudding are available in most British health food stores (under the Plamil brand) and supermarkets (under the 'Foresight' brand). I got the idea for this recipe from a non-vegetarian one by Derek Jarman in *The Observer*. Serve it with steamed cabbage or another green vegetable.

Sweet and Sour Smoked Tofu

Sauce

2	onions	2
2	carrots	2
2 tbs	vegetable oil plus additional for deep frying	2 tbs
1 tin (c.430g)	pineapple pieces in juice	1 lb can
2 tbs	soy (soya) sauce	2 tbs
2 tsp	raw cane sugar	1 tsp
2 tbs	cider vinegar or wine vinegar	2 tbs
570ml (1 pt)	pineapple juice (made up with water if necessary)	2½ cups
1 tbs	cornflour (cornstarch)	1 tbs
3 tbs	water	3 tbs
As required	sea salt	As required
As required	freshly ground black pepper	As required

Tofu

455g (1 lb)	smoked tofu	2 cups
115g (4 oz)	wholewheat flour	1 cup
30g (1 oz)	cornflour (cornstarch)	¼ cup
425ml (¾ pt)	water	2 cups

1 Chop the onions and carrots. Fry them in the oil in a saucepan for a few minutes until they begin to brown.
2 Add the pineapple chunks, soy sauce, sugar, vinegar and pineapple juice. Bring to the boil, then lower the heat and simmer for 10-15 minutes.
3 Meanwhile, dice the tofu. Mix the flour, cornflour (cornstarch) and water in a bowl. Dip the tofu chunks into the batter and deep fry them until lightly browned. Drain well.
4 Mix the cornflour (cornstarch) and water for the sauce in a cup, and pour into the pineapple mixture. Stir constantly until thickened, simmer for a minute or two and serve over the deep-fried tofu.

Note: Something deep fried in a light batter and served with a Chinese-style sweet and sour sauce is always appealing. Here, smoked tofu combines really well with such a sauce. Serve over brown rice.

Smoked Tofu Pasties

225g (½ lb)	smoked tofu	1 cup
225g (½ lb)	tomatoes	½ lb
3	onions	3
1 tsp	mixed herbs	1 tsp
As required	sea salt	As required
As required	freshly ground black pepper	As required
340g (¾ lb)	wholewheat pastry	¾ lb

1 Chop the smoked tofu into small cubes. Peel and chop the tomatoes. Peel and chop the onions. Mix together in a bowl, along with the herbs, and salt and pepper to taste.
2 Divide the pastry into 8 portions. Roll each one out, and spoon some of the tofu mixture on to half; fold over and place on a baking sheet.
3 When all the pasties have been filled and folded, score the tops lightly with a knife or prick them with a fork. Bake at 425°F/220°C (Gas Mark 7) for 20 minutes, then lower the heat and bake for a further half hour at 350°F/180°C (Gas Mark 4).

Note: Smoked tofu makes a good filling for pasties. Serve them with cooked vegetables or salad.

Steamed Savoury Smoked Tofu Pudding

225g (½ lb)	wholewheat flour	2 cups
3 tsp	baking powder	3 tsp
1 tsp	sea salt	1 tsp
115g (4 oz)	hard vegetable fat	½ cup
225g (½ lb)	smoked tofu	1 cup
2	onions	2
1 tin (c.225g)	tomatoes	1 can (c.8 oz)
1 tsp	dried sage	1 tsp
As required	tomato sauce	As required

1 Mix the flour, baking powder and salt in a large bowl. Grate the fat and mix it in. Add enough water to make a dough, and roll out about two-thirds of it, then transfer it to a large greased pudding bowl.
2 Dice the smoked tofu. Chop the onions. Remove the tomatoes from the tin (can) (the juice can be kept for the sauce if desired) and chop them coarsely. Combine these ingredients in a bowl and stir in the sage. Spoon this mixture into the pastry-lined pudding bowl.
3 Roll out the remaining third of pastry to make a lid and fit it over the tofu mixture. Cover the bowl with tin foil,

and place in a large saucepan of boiling water. Lower the heat and leave it to steam for about 2 hours.
4 Serve the pudding with tomato sauce – a good quality proprietary brand or homemade (the quickest homemade sauce is simply a tin (can) of tomatoes liquidized with herbs and seasoning to taste).

Note: A savoury steamed pudding is a perfect dish for a cold winter night. Serve with seasonal vegetables.

Smoked Tofu Charlotte

225g (½ lb)	mushrooms	4 cups
5 sticks	celery	5 sticks
70g (2½ oz)	vegetable margarine	¼ cup plus 1 tbs
170g (6 oz)	smoked tofu	¾ cup
2 tbs	vegetable oil	2 tbs
55g (2 oz)	wholewheat flour	½ cup
425ml (¾ pt)	soya (soy) milk	2 cups
As required	sea salt	As required
As required	freshly ground black pepper	As required
115g (4 oz)	wholewheat breadcrumbs	2 cups

1 Chop the mushrooms and celery. Sauté them in 55g (2 oz/¼ cup) margarine for a few minutes.
2 Dice the smoked tofu and sauté in the oil in a frying pan at the same time.
3 Stir the flour into the mushrooms and celery, cook for about a minute, then gradually stir in the milk. Stir until thickened, then season. Stir in the tofu.
4 Transfer to a greased baking dish and top with breadcrumbs. Sprinkle shavings of the remaining margarine on top, and bake at 375°F/175°C (Gas Mark 5) for 15-20 minutes.

Note: This is quite a light dish, so serve it with baked or roast potatoes.

Leek and Smoked Tofu Au Gratin

	Soya (soy) flour 'cheese' made from 115g (4 oz) margarine etc. (see p.13)	
8	leeks	8
225g (½ lb)	smoked tofu	1 cup
55g (2 oz)	vegan margarine	¼ cup
2 tbs	vegetable oil	2 tbs
45g (1½ oz)	wholewheat flour	⅓ cup
570ml (1 pt)	soya (soy) milk	2½ cups
As required	sea salt	As required
As required	freshly ground black pepper	As required
55g (2 oz)	fresh breadcrumbs	1 cup

1 Trim and wash the leeks and chop them coarsely. Cook in a small amount of lightly salted boiling water until tender. Drain.
2 Meanwhile, dice the tofu and sauté in the oil until lightly browned.
3 Melt the margarine in a saucepan and stir in the flour. Cook for a minute and then gradually stir in the milk. Bring to the boil, stirring constantly. Then stir in about three-quarters of the 'cheese'. Taste and add additional seasoning if required.
4 Place the cooked leeks and sautéed tofu in a shallow ovenproof dish and pour the sauce over them. Top with the breadcrumbs and the remainder of the 'cheese', finely chopped or grated. Place under a moderate grill (broiler) until nicely browned. Serve immediately.

Note: This recipe, ideal for a light lunch, is best with boiled new potatoes.

Smoked Tofu and Mashed Potato Cakes

455g (1 lb)	potatoes	1 lb
455g (1 lb)	smoked tofu	2 cups
2 tbs	finely chopped parsley	2 tbs
1-2 tbs	grated onion	1-2 tbs
As required	freshly ground black pepper	As required
As required	wholewheat flour	As required
As required	vegetable oil for frying	As required

1 Cook the potatoes until tender, then cool, peel and mash.
2 Mash the tofu or put it through a mincer.
3 Combine the mashed potato, tofu, parsley, onion and pepper, and form into patties. Dip them lightly, on both sides, in the flour.
4 Shallow fry the cakes on both sides until nicely browned.

Note: If you still have an old-fashioned meat mincer then use it for this dish. With leftover potatoes it takes no time at all to make. Serve with salad or cooked seasonal vegetables.
Quick and Easy.

Tempeh Croquettes with Mushroom Sauce

455g (1 lb)	tempeh	2 cups
55g (2 oz)	vegetable margarine	¼ cup
55g (2 oz)	wholewheat flour	½ cup
285ml (½ pt)	soya (soy) milk	1⅓ cups
2	spring onions (scallions)	2
2 tbs	soya (soy) flour	2 tbs
1 tbs	soya (soy) sauce	1 tbs
3 tsp	lemon juice	3 tsp
As required	sea salt	As required
As required	freshly ground black pepper	As required
2 tbs	gram (chick pea) flour	2 tbs
4 tbs	water	4 tbs
115g (4 oz)	fresh breadcrumbs	2 cups
As required	oil for deep frying	As required

For the sauce:

115g (4 oz)	mushrooms	2 cups
2 tbs	vegetable oil	2 tbs
3 tbs	wholewheat flour	3 tbs
230ml (8 fl oz)	water	1 cup
1-2 tsp	miso	1-2 tsp

1 Steam the tempeh for about 15 minutes. Set aside.
2 Heat the margarine, stir in the flour, then gradually stir in the milk, stirring constantly to avoid lumps. When it has thickened remove from the heat and mash the tempeh into this. Return to the heat and stir well for a further minute. Remove from heat.
3 Chop the spring onions (scallions) finely and add to the mixture. Stir in the soya (soy) flour, soya (soy) sauce, lemon juice and seasoning. Spread out on a plate to cool, then shape into croquettes.
4 Beat the gram (chick pea) flour into the water with a fork. Dip the croquettes into the breadcrumbs, then into the flour mixture, and then once again into the breadcrumbs. Leave the croquettes for two hours or longer, to allow them to dry out so that the breadcrumbs will adhere to them when deep fried.
5 When ready to serve, just heat up the oil and deep-fry the croquettes until nicely browned.
6 To make the sauce, chop the mushrooms and sauté them in the oil until tender. Stir in the flour, then gradually add the water, stirring constantly to avoid lumps. When boiling and thickened, lower the heat and stir in the miso (softened, if necessary in a little hot water).

Note: This dish elicited greater praise from my partner than just about anything I have made before or since. Serve it with some of the side dish vegetables in Chapter 14.

Suitable for a dinner party.

Tempeh Hash with Potatoes

455g (1 lb)	potatoes	2 cups
455g (1 lb)	tempeh	1 lb
570ml (1 pt)	water	2½ cups
4 tsp	yeast extract	4 tsp
1	onion	1
1	green pepper	1
4 tbs	vegetable oil	4 tbs
2 tbs	wholewheat flour	2 tbs
2 tbs	tomato purée (paste)	2 tbs
As required	freshly ground black pepper	As required

1 Cook the potatoes.
2 Heat 285ml (½ pt/1⅓ cups) water and dissolve 2 teaspoons yeast extract in it. Place the tempeh in the saucepan, lower the heat, and simmer for 5-7 minutes before turning over and simmering for a further 5-7 minutes on the other side. The liquid should have mostly been absorbed by now, but if there is any left, drain it. Chop the tempeh finely and set aside.
3 Chop the onion and green pepper finely. Fry in the oil for 3-4 minutes until they begin to brown.
4 Dice the tempeh and potato and add them to the saucepan. Cook for a minute or two longer, stirring constantly. Add the flour and stir well, then slowly pour in the remaining water, stirring constantly. Stir in the remaining yeast extract, the tomato purée (paste) and pepper. Heat thoroughly and serve.

If desired, steps 1-2 can be carried out in advance, and the tempeh and potato kept refrigerated until ready to prepare the dish.

Note: 'Hash' is an all-American favourite. I adapted a 'meaty' recipe and came up with this.

Indonesian-style Tempeh

340g (¾ lb)	tempeh	1½ cups
225g (½ lb)	potatoes	½ lb
2 tsp	coriander seeds	2 tsp
1	onion	1
1 clove	garlic	1 clove
2 tbs	vegetable oil	2 tbs
1 tsp	turmeric	1 tsp
1 tsp	sea salt	1 tsp
1 tsp	raw cane sugar	1 tsp
1 tsp	lemon juice	1 tsp
1 tsp	finely grated fresh ginger	1 tsp
570ml (1 pt)	water	2½ cups
115g (4 oz)	cabbage	1 cup
30g (1 oz)	creamed coconut	1 oz
As required	brown rice	As required

1 Cube the tempeh. Cut the potatoes into small pieces and set aside.
2 Grind the coriander. Grate the onion. Crush the garlic.
3 Heat the vegetable oil in a large saucepan. Add the coriander, turmeric, onion, garlic, salt, sugar, lemon juice and ginger. Stir for a minute. Add the tempeh and potatoes, and stir for another minute or two. Add the water, bring to the boil, lower the heat, cover and simmer for about 10 minutes.
4 Shred the cabbage. Grate or finely chop the creamed coconut. Add these ingredients to the saucepan. Cover and cook for a further 5-10 minutes until the potatoes are thoroughly cooked.

Note: Tempeh has its origins in Indonesia, and this recipe incorporates some traditional flavours from that part of the world. Serve it over brown rice. (Lovers of spicy food could serve Sambal Oelek with this, an Indonesian chilli relish found at many delicatessens.)

Tempeh Stroganoff

2 cloves	garlic	2 cloves
4 tbs	vegetable oil	4 tbs
3 tbs	soya (soy) sauce	3 tbs
140ml (¼ pt)	apple juice	⅔ cup
½ tsp	ground ginger	½ tsp
½ tsp	paprika	½ tsp
As required	freshly ground black pepper	As required
455g (1 lb)	tempeh	2 cups
340g (¾ lb)	mushrooms	6 cups
2 tbs	vegetable margarine	2 tbs
½ tsp	dried basil	½ tsp
A little	freshly grated nutmeg	A little
225g (½ lb)	tofu	1 cup
Juice of	lemon	Juice of
1 small		1 small

1 Crush the garlic. Combine in a large saucepan 2 tablespoons oil, the soya (soy) sauce, apple juice, ginger, paprika, pepper and the garlic. Cube the tempeh. Add to the mixture in the saucepan and cook over a low heat for about 5 minutes, stirring occasionally.

2 Slice the mushrooms. Melt the margarine in a frying pan and add the mushrooms. Sprinkle in the basil, and grate a little nutmeg. Stir over a medium to low heat for about 5 mintues until tender. Add the mushrooms to the tempeh and stir well.

3 Put the tofu, remaining 2 tablespoons oil, and lemon juice in a liquidizer and blend thoroughly. Add the mixture to the tempeh and mushroom mixture, and heat over a low heat until it is warmed through.

Note: In this dish tempeh is the 'meat' and tofu provides the 'cream'. Serve it over noodles.

Japanese-style Tempeh Kebabs

340g (¾ lb)	tempeh	1½ cups
4 tbs	soya (soy) sauce	4 tbs
2 tbs	cider vinegar or wine vinegar	2 tbs
3 tbs	water	3 tbs
Juice of ½	lemon	Juice of ½
2 tsp	sesame oil	2 tsp
2cm (¾ inch)	fresh ginger	¾ inch
2 cloves	garlic	2 cloves
1 tsp	mustard powder	1 tsp
225g (½ lb)	courgettes (zucchini)	½ lb
115g (4 oz)	mushrooms	2 cups
6-8 small	tomatoes	6-8 small

1 Dice the tempeh into small cubes, then steam it for about a quarter of an hour (if you do not have a steamer, improvise one – see p.85). Cool the tempeh.

2 In a mixing bowl combine the soya (soy) sauce, vinegar, water, lemon juice and sesame oil.

3 Grate the ginger finely. Crush the garlic. Add to the above mixture, together with the mustard powder. Mix well, then transfer to a shallow dish.

4 After the tempeh has cooled place the cubes in the marinade and turn well. Cover and leave in refrigerator for an hour or more to marinate, turning the cubes from time to time.

5 Slice the courgettes (zucchini). Clean the mushrooms and remove the stalks. Remove stalks, if necessary, from tomatoes.

6 Thread the tempeh and vegetables alternately on skewers. Place under a hot grill (broiler), and grill (broil) until well browned, turning from time to time, and pouring any remaining marinade over the cubes.

Note: This is a Japanese-style marinade which I found works very well for kebabs.

Tempeh Burgers

455g (1 lb)	tempeh	2 cups
340ml (12 fl oz)	tomato ketchup	1½ cups
4 tbs	cider vinegar or wine vinegar	4 tbs
8 tbs	water	8 tbs
1 tbs	soya (soy) sauce	1 tbs
Good pinch	black pepper	Good pinch
Good pinch	cayenne pepper	Good pinch
Optional	lettuce	Optional
Optional	sliced raw onion	Optional

1 If the tempeh is frozen then defrost it. Cut it into 4 pieces.

2 Put the ketchup, vinegar, water, soya (soy) sauce and seasoning into a saucepan. Bring to the boil.

3 Place the tempeh in the saucepan, cover and lower to simmer. Cook on one side for 5-7 minutes, then turn over and cook on the other side for 5-7 minutes.

4 Leave to cool. (If desired, this may be left in the refrigerator until meal-time.)

5 Heat a grill (broiler) to moderately hot and place the tempeh under it. Cook on one side for 5-10 minutes until well cooked, then turn over, spreading any remaining sauce over the top half of the tempeh, and grill (broil) the other half for the same amount of time.

Note: Steaming tempeh in a flavoured sauce can give it a 'burgery' flavour with no great effort. Serve with lettuce and/or onion if desired.

Quick and Easy. Suitable for One.

Tempeh Chilli

340g (¾ lb)	tempeh	1½ cups
2	onions	2
3 tbs	vegetable oil	3 tbs
170g (6 oz)	mushrooms	3 cups
3 tbs	Mexican chilli seasoning	3 tbs
2	tomatoes	2
4 tbs	tomato purée (paste)	4 tbs
140ml (¼ pt)	water	⅔ cup
1½ tbs	soya (soy) sauce	1½ tbs

1 Chop the onions and sauté in the oil for 2-3 minutes.
2 Chop the mushrooms, add to the saucepan and continue sautéeing for a further 2-3 minutes.
3 Mash or crumble the tempeh and add to the saucepan. Continue cooking for about 2 more minutes.
4 Stir in the chilli seasoning. Peel and chop the tomatoes. Add to the saucepan with the water and tomato purée (paste). Stir well. Add the soya (soy) sauce. Bring to the boil, then lower the heat and simmer for 10-15 minutes.

Note: The tempeh does not need to be steamed before use for this dish as it is cooked in the sauce. Serve it with corn chips or over rice or in tacos (with shredded lettuce if desired).

Mock 'Ham'

225g (½ lb)	dried bean milk sheets	½ lb
200ml (⅓ pt)	water	¾ cup
4 tbs	soya (soy) sauce	4 tbs
1 tbs	cider vinegar or wine vinegar	1 tbs
1 tsp	raw cane sugar	1 tsp
1 tbs	sesame oil	1 tbs

1 Break the sheets into small pieces.
2 Combine the water, soya (soy) sauce, vinegar and sugar in a large saucepan. Add the pieces of milk skin sheets and turn them in the sauce. Bring to the boil, then lower the heat and simmer for about 20 minutes until the sauce has been absorbed. Add the sesame oil.
3 Turn out on to a large piece of muslin and roll up the cloth into a sausage shape. Tie it up securely with lots of string. Steam it over hot water for 2 hours.
4 Remove from the heat and leave it to cool, then chill it thoroughly in the refrigerator before unwrapping and slicing it.

Note: This is an example of a Buddhist vegetarian dish. It goes down very well at a buffet as an open sandwich on bread spread with vegan margarine.

Mock 'Chicken'

3 tbs	soya (soy) sauce	3 tbs
1 tbs	raw cane sugar	1 tbs
1 tbs	sesame oil	1 tbs
225g (½ lb)	dried bean milk sheets	½ lb
As required	vegetable oil for deep frying	As required

1 Heat the soya (soy) sauce, sugar and sesame oil in a small saucepan until boiling, then remove from the heat and leave to cool.
2 Cover the bean milk sheets with hot water and leave for 2-3 minutes until soft. Drain.
3 Lay a single sheet out on a large piece of muslin and sprinkle with a little of the sauce mixture. Cover with another sheet and more sauce until all have been used up, finishing with a layer of bean milk sheet. If the sheets are not whole but fragmented – as will very likely be the case – it does not matter; just make up a whole sheet of pieces without worrying at this stage about them cohering. If any pieces are tough rather than tender then discard those.
4 When the layers are complete, roll them up in a sausage shape inside a large piece of muslin and tie up the sausage with strong twine. Steam over hot water for 2 hours.
5 Remove from the heat and leave it to cool. Deep-fry in hot oil for 3-4 minutes (if it is not completely immersed in the oil, then it is a good idea to turn it over after 2 minutes).
6 Drain thoroughly, then slice and serve hot or as an ingredient in another dish. (See below.)

Note: This is another example of a Buddhist vegetarian dish.

Mock 'Chicken' Cooked Indonesian Style

1	*onion*	*1*
2 cloves	*garlic*	*2 cloves*
2.5cm	*fresh ginger*	*1 inch*
(1 inch) piece		*piece*
6	*blanched almonds*	*6*
2 tbs	*soya (soy) sauce*	*2 tbs*
2 tbs	*vegetable oil*	*2 tbs*
2 tsp	*ground cumin*	*2 tsp*
2 tsp	*ground coriander*	*2 tsp*
1 tsp	*turmeric*	*1 tsp*
½ tsp	*chilli powder*	*½ tsp*
(or more to		*(or more to*
taste)		*taste)*
285ml (½ pt)	*water*	*1⅓ cups*
30g (1 oz)	*creamed coconut*	*2 tbs*
1 tbs	*cider vinegar or wine vinegar*	*1 tbs*
2 tsp	*dark brown raw cane sugar*	*2 tsp*
	mock 'chicken' made from 225g (½ lb) soya (soy) milk skin (see recipe above)	

1 Chop the onion, garlic and ginger. Put them into a liquidizer, food processor or pestle and mortar, along with the almonds and soy sauce, and blend into a paste. (If you are using a liquidizer some of the water will probably be necessary as well.)

2 Heat the oil in a saucepan and add the paste, along with the cumin, coriander, turmeric and chilli. Stir over a low to medium heat for about 2 minutes. Add the water, creamed coconut, vinegar and sugar and stir well. Bring to the boil. Slice the 'chicken' and add to the saucepan. Cover the pan and simmer over low heat for 15-20 minutes.

Note: This uses a 'mock chicken' above as an ingredient in a tasty dish. Serve it over brown rice.

12
Ready-made Health Food Products

Introduction

Most of the recipes in this chapter are based on canned vegetarian savouries which have been available in British health food shops for decades. They are based on peanuts and other nuts and without tasting at all like meat they have served the same function in meals. Different combinations of nuts and flavourings taste different, and no particular version is suggested for any one dish; it is very much a matter of individual preference.

Other recipes are based on the only meat analogue which I happen to like – vegan 'sausages'. There are many different kinds: dried mixes based on t.v.p. (textured vegetable protein), ready-made canned soft ones, refrigerated ones based on beans, frozen t.v.p. ones. Again, the kind to use for any of the recipes is a matter of personal preference (but do read the ingredients as some vegetarian 'sausages' contain eggs).

Vegan pâtés are used for two recipes in this chapter. There is undoubtedly scope for this product to be used in more dishes, but it is expensive when used in that way.

Finally, dried 'veggieburger' mixes (there are at least two British brands and one American one) are used in traditional favourites.

Recipes

Potato and Nutmeat Casserole

900g (2 lb)	potatoes	2 lb
2 small or 1 large tin (c.565-680g)	nut savoury	1¼-1½ lbs
200ml (⅓ pt)	soya (soy) milk	¾ cup
1 small	onion	1 small
2 tbs	vegetable oil	2 tbs
½ tsp	dried sage or marjoram	½ tsp
2 tbs	wholewheat flour	2 tbs
As required	sea salt	As required

1 Cook the potatoes until tender (or use leftover cooked potatoes), drain, cool and dice them and set aside.
2 Chop the onion finely and sauté it in the oil until tender.
3 Add the flour and stir well for 1-2 minutes. Slowly add the milk, stirring constantly to prevent lumps. Bring to the boil and add the herbs and salt.
4 Dice the nut savoury and add it to the milk mixture together with the potatoes.
5 Place the whole mixture in an oiled casserole and bake for about half an hour at 350°F/180°C (Gas Mark 4).

Note: Serve with a seasonal green vegetable.

Nutmeat Stew

2	onions	2
225g (½ lb)	mushrooms	4 cups
2 tins (c.400g each)	tomatoes	28-32 oz canned
1	bay leaf	1
2 small or 1 large tin (c.565-680g)	nut savoury	1¼-1½ lbs
1 tsp	garlic salt	1 tsp
1 tbs	vegan margarine	1 tbs

1 Chop the onion, slice the mushrooms, and sauté them gently in the margarine with the bay leaf for 10 minutes.
2 Dice the nut savoury, and add it to the pan with the tomatoes and garlic salt and cook for several minutes more on a gentle heat. Remove the bay leaf before serving.

Note: This can be served with rice, with boiled or baked potatoes, or with fresh, crusty bread.
Quick and Easy.

Sweet and Sour Nutmeat

2 small or 1 large tin (c.565-680g)	nut savoury	1¼-1½ lbs
2 tbs (or more if required)	vegetable oil	2 tbs (or more if required)
4 tsp	cornflour (cornstarch)	4 tsp
1 tbs	soya (soy) sauce	1 tbs
1 tbs	cider vinegar or wine vinegar	1 tbs
1 tbs	raw cane sugar	1 tbs
1 tin (c.225g)	pineapple chunks	1 can (c.8 oz)
1 small	onion	1 small
285ml (½ pt)	vegetable stock or water	1⅓ cups
½ tsp	powdered ginger	½ tsp

1 Dice the nut savoury and fry the cubes in the oil until browned and crisp.
2 Grate the onion, combine it with the soya (soy) sauce, vinegar, sugar and stock and heat gently.
3 Mix the cornflour (cornstarch) with a little water and add it to the saucepan. Stir until the mixture thickens.
4 Drain the pineapple and add this to the saucepan. Stir until heated, then pour the mixture over the nut savoury cubes.

Note: Serve over brown rice.

Lasagne Bolognese

225g (½ lb)	wholewheat lasagne	½ lb
1	onion	1
1	carrot	1
1 stick	celery	1 stick
2 tbs	vegetable oil	2 tbs
2 small or 1 large tin (c.565-680g)	nut savoury	1¼-1½ lbs
1 tin	tomato purée (paste)	1 can
1 tin (c.400g)	tomatoes	1 can (14-16 oz)
	soya (soy) flour 'cheese' (see p.13) made up from 115g (4 oz/½ cup) vegan margarine etc.	
570ml (1 pt)	soya (soy) milk	2½ cups
55g (2 oz)	vegan margarine	¼ cup
30g (1 oz)	cornflour (cornstarch)	¼ cup
Pinch	dry mustard	Pinch
As required	sea salt	As required
As required	freshly ground black pepper	As required

1 Cook the lasagne in boiling salted water for about 15-20 minutes until tender. Set aside to drain.

2 Chop the onion, carrot and celery and fry them in the vegetable oil until tender.

3 Mash the nut savoury and add it to the saucepan together with the tomato purée (paste) and tomatoes. Cover the pan and simmer for a few minutes.

4 Heat the margarine in a small saucepan. Add the cornflour (cornstarch), then slowly add the milk, stirring constantly to avoid lumps. When thickened, add mustard, salt and pepper as well as about three-quarters of the 'cheese'. Continue stirring over a gentle heat until well blended.

5 In an oiled casserole, layer a third of the lasagne, top with half the nutmeat sauce and a third of the 'cheese' sauce. Repeat and top the third layer of lasagne with the remainder of the 'cheese' sauce and cover with the remainder of the 'cheese', grated or cut into small pieces.

6 Bake in a fairly hot oven at 400°F/200°C (Gas Mark 6) for about half an hour.

Note: This is a great alternative for anyone who craves traditional 'meaty' lasagne.

Nutmeat Hash

2	onions	2
2 tbs	vegetable oil	2 tbs
2 tsp	yeast extract	2 tsp
2 small or 1 large tin (c.565-680g)	nut savoury	1¼-1½ lbs
680g (1½ lb)	potatoes	1½ lb
1	green pepper	1
1 clove	garlic	1 clove
285ml (½ pt)	vegetable stock	1⅓ cups
As required	sea salt	As required
As required	freshly ground black pepper	As required

1 Chop the onions. Sauté them in the oil until tenderized. Add the yeast extract.

2 Mash the nutmeat. Grate the potatoes coarsely. Chop the green pepper finely. Crush the garlic. Combine those ingredients with the onion and stir in the stock. Season to taste.

3 Turn the mixture on to a greased tray or trays and pat it down to a thickness of ¾-1 inch. Cover the top with foil.

4 Bake at 350°F/180°C (Gas Mark 4) for about 15 minutes, then lower the heat to 300°F/160°C (Gas Mark 2) and cook for a further half hour. Serve with a spatula.

Note: 'Hash' is about as American as steak and kidney pie is British. Here is a meat-free version.

Nutmeat Goulash

2	onions	2
1	green pepper	1
455-680g (1-1½ lbs)	potatoes	1-1½ lbs
1 clove	garlic	1 clove
2 tbs	vegetable oil	2 tbs
225g (½ lb)	tomatoes	½ lb
2 small or 1 large tin (c.565-680g)	nut savoury	1¼-1½ lbs
285ml (½ pt)	water	1⅓ cups
2 tbs	soya (soy) sauce	2 tbs

1 Chop the onions and green pepper. Dice the potatoes. Crush the garlic. Heat the oil in a large saucepan and sauté these ingredients for a few minutes, stirring frequently.

2 Chop the tomatoes. Add them to the pan and cook for a couple of minutes longer. Dice the nutmeat and add it to the pan with the water and soy sauce. Bring to the boil, then lower the heat, cover the pan, and simmer for 20-30 minutes, until the potatoes are cooked and most of the liquid is absorbed.

Note: Serve with warm, crusty wholemeal bread.

Savoury Stuffed Pancakes

	Crepe batter 170g (6 oz/1½ cups) wholewheat flour (see p.15)	
340-455g 14-16 oz	vegetable pâté	14-16 oz
1 tbs	soya (soy) milk	1 tbs
4 large	tomatoes	4 large
As required	vegan margarine or vegetable oil for frying	As required

1 Beat the pâté with the milk.

2 Chop the tomatoes roughly.

3 Heat the margarine or oil, pour in a little batter at a time and fry on both sides.

4 Fill each pancake with a little pâté and some of the chopped tomato.

Note: This is simple and delicious. Serve the pancakes with a green salad.

Cauliflower à la Crème

1 very large	cauliflower	1 very large
As required	sea salt	As required
340-455g (14-16 oz)	vegetable pâté	14-16 oz
200ml (⅓ pt)	soya (soy) milk	¾ cup
Sprinkling	paprika	Sprinkling

1 Remove the outside leaves from the cauliflower, leaving the tender ones round the sides, and wash it thoroughly.
2 Place the cauliflower, stalk side down, in a large saucepan of boiling salted water. Cover and simmer gently until tender.
3 Heat the milk and pâté together, stirring well to avoid lumps.
4 Drain the cauliflower, pour the sauce over it and dust with paprika.

Note: To make a full meal out of this dish serve it with baked or sautéed potatoes.

Quick 'Sausage' Pie

2 tbs	vegetable oil	2 tbs
4 large	onions	4 large
455-570g (1-1½ lb)	vegan 'sausages'	1-1½ lb
½ tsp	thyme	½ tsp
900g (2 lb)	mashed potatoes	4 cups

1 Chop the onions and fry them in the oil until tender. Add the 'sausages' and fry them with the onions until everything is browned.
2 Place in an oiled pie dish, sprinkle with thyme and cover with mashed potatoes.
3 Bake in a moderate oven at 350°F/180°C (Gas Mark 4) until the top is golden brown, or if the ingredients have been kept warm, place under the grill (broiler) instead.

Note: Any kind of vegan 'sausages' are good in this dish, which should be served with a green salad.
Quick and Easy. Suitable for One.

'Sausage' and Macaroni Casserole

455-570g (1-1½ lb)	cooked vegan 'sausages'	1-1½ lb
2	onions	2
1 small	green pepper	1 small
2 tins (c.400g each)	tomatoes	28-32 oz canned
285ml (½ pt)	soya (soy) yogurt	1⅓ cups
2 tbs	vegetable oil	2 tbs
1 tsp	mixed herbs	1 tsp
1 tsp	raw cane sugar	1 tsp
As required	cayenne pepper	As required
225g (½ lb)	wholewheat macaroni	2 cups

1 Cook the macaroni until tender in boiling salted water. Set aside to drain.
2 Chop the onion and green pepper and sauté them in the vegetable oil until tender.
3 Mash the 'sausages' and add to the saucepan.
4 Empty the canned tomatoes into a liquidizer and blend; add this to the saucepan together with the mixed herbs, sugar, cayenne pepper, and yogurt. Cook for several minutes on a very low heat until thoroughly heated and cooked.
5 Add the macaroni, stir well, and cook for a further 2-3 minutes before serving.

Note: For this dish you need a soft 'sausage' like Granose Sausalatas or Goodlife Bean Bangers. It is a self-contained dish.

Toad in the Hole

85g (3 oz)	vegan margarine	⅓ cup
285g (10 oz)	wholewheat flour	2½ cups
Pinch	sea salt	Pinch
2 tsp	baking powder	2 tsp
570ml (1 pt)	soya (soy) milk	2½ cups
455-680g (1-1½ lb)	vegan 'sausages'	1-1½ lb

1 Melt the margarine.
2 In a bowl combine the flour, salt, baking powder, melted margarine and milk.
3 Place the sausages in a greased casserole dish. Pour the batter over them. Bake at 425°F/225°C (Gas Mark 7) for about 15 minutes, then at 350°F/180°C (Gas Mark 4) for a further 15-20 minutes.

Note: Anyone who becomes a vegan probably never expects to eat this traditional British dish again, since apart from the sausage it normally contains eggs. However, the latter are – quite obviously – not at all necessary. I like to serve it with steamed cabbage. Suitable for One.

Cornmeal 'Sausage' Bake

150g (5 oz)	wholewheat flour	1¼ cup
115g (4 oz)	cornmeal	1 cup
½ tsp	raw cane sugar	½ tsp
Pinch	sea salt	Pinch
2 tsp	baking powder	2 tsp
1 tsp	bicarbonate of soda (baking soda)	1 tsp
4 tbs	vegetable oil	4 tbs
285-425ml (½-¾ pt)	soya (soy) yogurt	1⅓-2 cups
455-680g (1-1½ lbs)	vegan 'sausages'	1-1½ lbs

1 Put the dry ingredients in a bowl and mix. Add the oil. Add enough water to the yogurt to make it up to 570ml (1 pint/2½ cups), and add it to the bowl. Mix with a large spoon.
2 Put the sausages into a greased casserole dish and cover with the batter. Bake at 425°F/220°C (Gas Mark 7) for 20-25 minutes until lightly browned and set.

Note: This is an American dish, similar to the one above.

Pease Pottage with 'Sausages'

2	onions	2
455g (1 lb)	potatoes	1 lb
225g (½ lb)	carrots	½ lb
570ml (1 pt)	water	2½ cups
2 tsp	yeast extract	2 tsp
2 tins (c.400g each)	pease pudding	2 cans
As required	sea salt	As required
As required	freshly ground black pepper	As required
455g (1 lb)	vegan 'sausages'	1 lb

1 Chop the onions, potatoes and carrots. Put them in a large saucepan with the water and yeast extract. Bring to the boil, then lower the heat, cover and leave to simmer for about 15 minutes until soft.
2 Turn the mixture into a liquidizer and add the pease pudding. (If the liquidizer is not large enough this can easily be done in two stages.) Blend thoroughly.
3 Pour the mixture back into the saucepan and heat gently. Season to taste.
4 Meanwhile, prepare the 'sausages' according to the instructions. Serve the pottage in large bowls topped with the 'sausages'.

Note: Cans of pease pudding are available in most British health food stores (under the Plamil brand) and supermarkets (under the 'Foresight' brand). Although eaten with a spoon rather than a fork, this dish is too substantial to be called a 'soup'. Serve it with crusty bread.

Bolognese Sauce for Spaghetti

1	onion	1
1 clove	garlic	1 clove
1 tbs	vegetable oil	1 tbs
115g (4 oz)	mushrooms	2 cups
2 sticks	celery	2 sticks
1 tin (c.400g)	chopped tomatoes	1 can (14-16 oz)
1 packet (c.125g)	dried veggie burger mix	1 cup
285ml (½ pt)	vegetable stock or water	1⅓ cups
As required	sea salt	As required
As required	freshly ground black pepper	As required

1 Chop the onion and garlic finely. Heat the oil and sauté them for 3-4 minutes. Chop the mushrooms and celery and add them to the pan. Continue cooking for a few minutes longer, stirring frequently.
2 Add the tomatoes, dried mix and stock or water. Bring to the boil, then lower the heat and simmer, uncovered, for 15-20 minutes. Season to taste.

Note: In this and the following recipe, dried veggie burger mix is used in place of meat for traditional favourites. Quick and Easy.

Cottage Pie

2	onions	2
3 tbs	vegetable oil	3 tbs
2 packets (c.125g each)	dried veggie burger mix	2 cups
570ml (1 pt)	water	2½ cups
900g (2 lb)	mashed potatoes	4 cups

1 Chop the onions. Heat the oil in a saucepan and fry the onions for a few minutes until just beginning to brown.
2 Stir in the burger mix and the water, bring to the boil, then lower the heat and simmer for a few minutes.
3 Transfer the mixture to a greased casserole, top with mashed potato, and bake at 375°F/190°C (Gas Mark 5) for 20-30 minutes until the top has begun to brown.

13
Sea Vegetables

Introduction

Sea vegetables – which are certainly not 'weeds' – are greatly under-used in vegan cooking. Very low in calories, fat free, loaded with vitamins and minerals, they add a whole new range of tastes to meals, a real 'tang of the sea'. Of course they don't have the texture of more familiar unvegan 'seafoods', but combine them with tofu or tempeh and you get both taste and texture.

Sea vegetables may seem expensive to buy, but a look at the recipes in this chapter will show how very small is the amount needed for any one dish, for most sea vegetables swell to many times their dry weight. And after a packet is opened, as long as it is stored in an airtight container or bag, it will keep for years. Perhaps the main reason sea vegetables are not used more is simply because people do not know what to do with them. This chapter aims to change that situation. The following sea vegetables appear in the recipes which follow.

Kombu – a type of kelp, a bit tough and chewy but full of flavour. Soak for at least 10 minutes before using.

Wakame (pronounced wa-ka-may) – a softer, greenish leaf with a hard stem (which should be discarded). Rinse well and soak for about 10 minutes before using.

Hijiki (sometimes spelled 'hiziki') – is generally liked by anyone who tries it. It comes in thin strips and should be soaked for about 20 minutes before cooking. It is good served cold in salads.

Arame (ar-a-may) – looks very like hijiki but it has been shredded after picking as in its natural form it is a wide leaf. It has a sweeter taste than hijiki and is one of my favourites.

Dulse – the only one in this chapter to be found on British shores. Dulse has quite a strong flavour and goes well in stews. It should not need pre-soaking (but check the instructions on the packet you buy).

Nori – quite different from any of the other sea vegetables, and one which more people are likely to have tried as it is used as the outer layer for Japanese rice sushi. I must admit it is my favourite, both for its flavour and convenience. It comes in sheets which you toast over a flame. This takes only a couple of minutes before the colour changes (be careful that it doesn't catch the flame), and it is ready to eat. When mixed with something moist it softens up.

Recipes

Arame and Peanut Stir-fry

30g (1 oz)	dried arame	1 oz
1 large	green pepper	1 large
2 large	carrots	2 large
225g (½ lb)	mushrooms	4 cups
10-12	spring onions (scallions)	10-12
1 or 2 cloves	garlic	1 or 2 cloves
2 tbs	vegetable oil	2 tbs
2 tsp	finely grated fresh ginger	2 tsp
2 tbs	soya (soy) sauce	2 tbs
115g (4 oz)	roasted peanuts	¾ cup
As required	brown rice	As required

1 Soak the arame in cold water for about 10 minutes.
2 Slice the green pepper, carrots and mushrooms thinly. Chop the spring onions (scallions) and garlic finely.
3 Heat the oil in a wok or frying pan. Add all the vegetables and stir-fry for 3-4 minutes.
4 Drain the arame and add it to the wok together with the soy sauce and fresh ginger. Mix in well and stir-fry for a further 2-3 minutes.

Note: This classic Oriental stir-fry is best served over brown rice. The best peanuts to use are the unsalted dry-roasted peanuts available at some wholefood stores and supermarkets. Second-best are whole peanuts which you have shelled. If neither of these alternatives is available, then the salted kind should be very well rinsed and dried. Some salt may adhere to them so it may be a good idea to add a little less soya (soy) sauce.
Quick and Easy.

Arame and Rice Casserole

285g (10 oz)	brown rice	1¾ cup
30g (1 oz)	arame	1 oz
1 large	onion	1 large
2 tbs	vegetable oil	2 tbs
3 tbs	wholewheat flour	3 tbs
200ml (⅓ pt)	soya (soy) milk	1½ cups
340g (¾ lb)	tofu	1½ cups
1 tbs	soy sauce	1 tbs
1 tsp	freshly ground nutmeg	1 tsp
As required	sea salt	As required
As required	freshly ground black pepper	As required

1 Cook the rice until tender (or use leftover cooked rice).
2 Rinse the arame well. Cover it with cold water in a saucepan, bring to the boil, lower the heat, cover and simmer for about 5 minutes. Drain and rinse again.
3 Chop the onion finely. Heat the oil in a large saucepan and sauté the onion for 3-4 minutes. Stir in the flour and then add the milk, stirring constantly to avoid lumps. When it has thickened remove from the heat.
4 Crumble the tofu into the mixture, and add the rice, soy sauce, nutmeg and seasoning. Mix well and turn into an oiled casserole.
5 Bake at 350°F/180°C (Gas Mark 4) for about half an hour, covering it for the first 15 minutes, then uncovering it for the final 15 minutes.

Note: This rich casserole is full of flavour. Serve with seasonal vegetables.

Arame and Tofu Pancakes

	Crepe batter made from 225g (½ lb/2 cups) wholewheat flour etc. (see p.15)	
30g (1 oz)	arame	1 oz
3 tbs	vegan margarine	3 tbs
25g (1½ oz)	wholewheat flour	⅓ cup
425ml (¾ pt)	soya (soy) milk	2 cups
2 tbs	soy sauce	2 tbs
As required	sea salt	As required
As required	freshly ground black pepper	As required
3 tbs	vegetarian Worcester sauce	3 tbs
225g (½ lb)	tofu	1 cup
140ml (¼ pt)	soya (soy) yogurt	⅔ cup
5 tbs	nutritional yeast	5 tbs

1 Cover the arame with cold water in a saucepan, bring to the boil, lower the heat and simmer for about 5 minutes. Drain and chop.
2 Heat the margarine in a saucepan and stir in the flour. Gradually add the milk, stirring constantly to avoid lumps. When it has thickened simmer for a minute or two, then season with the sauces, salt and pepper. Crumble in the tofu and stir in the chopped arame. Mix well.
3 Fry the pancakes (there should be 4-5 per person) and fill each with the arame/tofu mixture before folding them over or rolling them up.
4 In a small bowl mix together the soya (soy) yogurt and the yeast. When all the pancakes have been filled, spoon the yogurt mixture over the top. Place all the pancakes under a fairly hot grill (broiler) until the yogurt is well heated and serve immediately.

Millet and Arame Bake

225g (½ lb)	millet	1⅓ cup
710ml	water	3 cups
(1¼ pts)		
Pinch	sea salt	Pinch
30g (1 oz)	arame	1 oz
2 tbs	vegetable oil	2 tbs
2	onions	2
2	green peppers	2
225g (½ lb)	mushrooms	4 cups
2 tbs	wholewheat flour	2 tbs
170ml	soya (soy) milk	¾ cup
(6 fl oz)		
1 tsp	powdered ginger	1 tsp
2 tbs	soya (soy) sauce	2 tbs
55g (2 oz)	almonds	½ cup
As required	sea salt	As required
As required	freshly ground black pepper	As required

1 Dry roast the millet in a large heavy dry saucepan for a few minutes until it smells aromatic. Add the water and salt. Bring to the boil, lower the heat, cover the pan, and simmer until the water is absorbed (about 20 minutes).
2 Cover the arame with cold water in a saucepan, bring to the boil, and simmer for a few minutes. Drain and set aside. Chop the almonds in half and set aside.
3 Chop the onions and sauté them in the oil in a large saucepan. Chop the green peppers and mushrooms and add them to the pan. Cook for a few more minutes, then sprinkle in the flour. Stir well, then gradually add the milk, stirring constantly until thickened. Add the ginger and soya (soy) sauce.
4 Remove the saucepan from the heat. Stir in the cooked millet, arame, and almonds. Add seasoning to taste.
5 Turn the whole mixture into a large casserole dish and bake at 350°F/180°C (Gas Mark 4) for about half an hour.

Note: This dish combines a rarely used grain with a mild-flavoured sea vegetable and lots of other tasty ingredients.

Macaroni Arame

225-340g	wholewheat macaroni	2-3 cups
(½-¾ lb)		
30g (1 oz)	arame	1 oz
710ml	soya (soy) milk	3 cups
(1¼ pts)		
2 tbs	vegetable oil	2 tbs
2	onions	2
30g (1 oz)	wholewheat flour	¼ cup
2 tbs	soya (soy) sauce	2 tbs
As required	sea salt	As required
As required	freshly ground black pepper	As required
As required	wholewheat breadcrumbs or nutritional yeast	As required
30g (1 oz)	vegan margarine	2 tbs

1 Cook the macaroni until just tender and set aside.
2 Put the arame in a saucepan, cover with cold water, bring to the boil, then lower the heat and simmer for about 5 minutes. Drain the arame, cool it slightly (by pouring cold water over it if desired) and chop it.
3 Heat the milk in a saucepan. When it is boiling, lower the heat and add the arame. Let it simmer, uncovered, for a few minutes.
4 Chop the onions finely. Heat the oil in a large saucepan and sauté them for a few minutes until just beginning to turn brown. Stir in the flour, then add the milk and arame, stirring constantly to avoid lumps. When it is thick and smooth stir in the soya (soy) sauce and seasoning.
5 Turn the mixture into a casserole and sprinkle breadcrumbs or yeast on top. Add shavings of the margarine. Bake at 375°F/190°C (Gas Mark 5) for about 20 minutes.

Note: This recipe is simple and yet very effective.

Dulse and Vegetable Stew

115g (4 oz)	rolled oats	1 cup
1140ml	water	5 cups
(2 pts)		
2-3 tbs	vegetable oil	2-3 tbs
30g (1 oz)	dulse	1 oz
4 sticks	celery	4 sticks
225g (½ lb)	carrots	½ lb
225g (½ lb)	potatoes	½ lb
1 large or	onions	1 large or
2 small		2 small
225g (½ lb)	mushrooms	8 cups
2-3 tbs	soya (soy) sauce	2-3 tbs
As required	sea salt	As required
As required	freshly ground black pepper	As required

1 Put the oats and water in a saucepan and bring to the boil. Lower the heat, cover the pan and leave to simmer.
2 Chop the dulse and set aside.
3 Chop all the vegetables finely, and sauté them in the oil in a wok or frying pan for 3-4 minutes. Add them to the saucepan, together with the dulse, and continue to simmer for about half an hour longer, stirring occasionally.
4 Add the soya (soy) sauce and seasoning to taste, before serving.

Note: The dulse will almost dissolve in the oat and vegetable mixture, to give a lovely flavour to the stew. Serve it with thick slices of wholewheat bread.

Hijiki and Vegetables

30g (1 oz)	hijiki	1 oz
2 tbs	vegetable oil	2 tbs
225g (½ lb)	mushrooms	8 cups
3	spring onions (scallions)	3
225g (½ lb)	green beans	½ lb
2 small	white turnips	2 small
1 tbs	soya (soy) sauce	1 tbs
225g (½ lb)	mung bean sprouts	4 cups
1 tbs	arrowroot	1 tbs
200ml (⅓ pt)	water	¾ cup
As required	brown rice	As required
1 tbs	soya (soy) sauce	1 tbs

1 Rinse the hijiki well by covering with water and draining two or three times. Soak it in enough water to cover for about 20 minutes.
2 Slice the mushrooms and spring onions (scallions) and stir-fry in the oil in a wok or frying pan for about 3 minutes. Add the drained hijiki and stir well.
3 Peel and dice the turnips; slice the green beans. Add about three-quarters of the water to the pan, together with the turnip and beans. Bring to the boil, cover and leave to steam for a few minutes.
4 Remove the lid, add the bean sprouts and soya (soy) sauce and stir well. Mix the arrowroot with the remainder of the water and add to the mixture. Stir well until it thickens.

Note: This Far-Eastern dish should be served over brown rice.

Tempeh Fillets with Hijiki

30g (1 oz)	hijiki	1 oz
6 tsp	miso	6 tsp
455g (1 lb)	tempeh	1 lb
285ml (½ pt)	warm water	1⅓ cups

1 Rinse the hijiki under cold water. Cover it with warm water and leave to soak for about 30 minutes.
2 Combine the water and miso in a blender and blend well. Pour into a large saucepan. Slice each of the ½ lb tempeh blocks in half. Put them into the saucepan. Drain the hijiki and add to the saucepan.
3 Simmer, covered, over a very low heat for about 10 minutes. Turn the tempeh fillets over. Add a little additional water if it seems necessary. Cook for a further 10 minutes. Serve each tempeh fillet topped with hijiki.

Note: This is my attempt to replicate a vegan dish I enjoyed at a 'gourmet' vegetarian restaurant in Key West, Florida. Serve the fillets with seasonal vegetables.

Hijiki Sauce for Spaghetti

45g (1½ oz)	hijiki	1½ oz
1	onion	1
1	green pepper	1
2 tins	tomatoes	1½-2 lb
(c.400g each)		canned
1-2 cloves	garlic	1-2 cloves
2 tsp	dried oregano	2 tsp
2 tbs	olive oil	2 tbs
As required	black pepper	As required

1 Rinse the hijiki under cold water. Cover it with warm water and leave to soak for about 30 minutes.
2 Chop the onion, garlic and green pepper finely. Sauté them in the oil for 3-4 minutes.
3 Purée the tomatoes in a liquidizer. Add to the saucepan, with the oregano. Bring to the boil, then simmer, uncovered, for about 5 minutes. Add the soaked and drained hijiki and continue cooking for 15-20 minutes longer, stirring occasionally.
4 Grind in the pepper and serve over spaghetti.

Note: As non-vegan 'seafoods' are used in spaghetti sauces, I can see no reason why a vegan seafood should not feature in a pasta sauce.

Spaghetti and Hijiki Loaf

30g (1 oz)	hijiki	1 oz
170g (6 oz)	wholewheat spaghetti	6 oz
85g (3 oz)	wholewheat breadcrumbs	1½ cups
140ml (¼ pt) plus 3 tbs	soya (soy) milk	⅔ cup plus 3 tbs
1 tbs	vegan margarine	1 tbs
1 tbs	soya (soy) flour	1 tbs
As required	sea salt	As required
As required	freshly ground black pepper	As required

1 Soak the hijiki for about 20 minutes in cold water. Drain.
2 Break the spaghetti up into smallish pieces and cook until tender in boiling salted water. Drain and rinse.
3 Beat the soya (soy) flour into the 3 tbs milk.
4 Heat the 140ml (¼ pt/⅔ cup) milk together with the breadcrumbs and margarine in a large saucepan until the margarine has melted. Remove from the heat.
5 Add the hijiki, spaghetti, and soya (soy) flour mixture to the pan and mix thoroughly. Season to taste. Turn into a greased loaf tin (or casserole if preferred), cover with foil, and bake for about 30 minutes at 350°F/180°C (Gas Mark 4).

Note: This recipe combines pasta and hijiki in a very different style of dish.

Hijiki, Smoked Tofu and Sunflower Seed Pie

30g (1 oz)	hijiki	1 oz
455-680g (1-1½ lb)	smoked tofu	2-3 cups
55g (2 oz)	sunflower seeds	½ cup
680-900g (1½-2 lb)	mashed potato	3-4 cups

1 Soak the hijiki in cold water for about 20 minutes, then cook it for a few minutes until tender. Drain and cool it (by running cold water over it if desired to save time).
2 Put the smoked tofu into a bowl and mash it well.
3 Chop the hijiki and add it to the tofu together with the sunflower seeds. Mix well and transfer to an ovenproof dish.
4 Spoon the mashed potato on top. Bake at 375°F/190°C (Gas Mark 5) for 20-30 minutes.

Note: This is a very simple dish, with few ingredients, as the smoked tofu and hijiki have enough flavour of their own. The sunflower seeds add an interesting texture contrast. Serve with courgettes (zucchini) or any preferred vegetable.

Hijiki and Cashew Ragout

55g (2 oz)	hijiki	2 oz
225g (½ lb)	whole cashews	2 cups
4	onions	4
3 tbs	vegetable oil	3 tbs
4	tomatoes	4
3 tbs	wholewheat flour	3 tbs
3 tbs (or to taste)	soya (soy) sauce	3 tbs (or to taste)
As required	sea salt	As required
As required	freshly ground black pepper	As required

1 Clean, soak and cook the hijiki until tender. Drain well.
2 Place the cashews under a hot grill (broiler) and turn them frequently to brown evenly.
3 Chop the onions and sauté them in the oil in a saucepan until just transparent.
4 Chop the tomatoes and add them to the pan. Cook until tender.
5 Sprinkle the flour in and stir well. Slowly stir in enough water to make a thick sauce.
6 Add the cooked hijiki to the pan, then add the soya (soy) sauce and seasoning to taste. Stir in the cashews at the last minute. Serve with baked or boiled new potatoes.

Note: This takes no time at all. Serve with baked or boiled potatoes (sliced first if you want to save time).

Lentil and Kombu Stew

170g (6 oz)	brown lentils	1 cup
15g (½ oz)	kombu	½ oz
1	bay leaf	1
850ml (1½ pts)	water	3¾ cups
1	onion	1
1 large or 2 small	leeks	1 large or 2 small
2 tbs	vegetable oil	2 tbs
1 large or 2 small	carrots	1 large or 2 small
As required	sea salt	As required
As required	freshly ground black pepper	As required

1 Place the lentils and kombu in a large saucepan and cover with plenty of cold water. Leave to soak for a few hours.
2 Drain the lentils and kombu. Remove the kombu and chop it into bite-sized pieces. Return the lentils and kombu to the saucepan; add the bay leaf and 850ml (1½ pts/3¾ cups) water, cover and bring to the boil. Lower the heat and simmer for 15-20 minutes.
3 Chop the onion and leek. Heat the oil in a frying pan and sauté them for 2-3 minutes. Dice the carrot and

add to the pan; stir-fry for a minute or two longer.

4 Add the vegetables to the lentil/kombu mixture and stir well. Add the seasoning. Continue cooking for a further 10-20 minutes before serving.

Note: Kombu helps to tenderize lentils and speeds up the cooking process. Serve the stew with wedges of wholewheat bread.

Wakame and Vegetable Stew

30g (1 oz)	wakame	1 oz
2	onions	2
570ml (1 pt)	water	2½ cups
340g (¾ lb)	carrots	¾ lb
680g (1½ lb)	potatoes	1½ lb
340g (¾ lb)	Brussels sprouts	¾ lb
4 tbs	soya (soy) sauce	2 tbs

1 Soak the wakame for about 10 minutes, drain and chop.
2 Chop the onions coarsely. Put them in a large saucepan with the wakame and cover with the water. Bring to the boil, then lower the heat and simmer, uncovered for about 5 minutes.
3 Chop the carrots and potatoes into small pieces. Halve or quarter the Brussels sprouts. Add them to the saucepan, together with the soya (soy) sauce, and simmer for 15-20 minutes until the potato is tender.

Note: Serve this appealing stew with wholewheat bread.

Wakame and Potato Casserole with Tofu Topping

680g (1½ lb)	potatoes	1½ lb
30g (1 oz)	wakame	1 oz
565g (1¼ lb)	tofu	1¼ lb
6-8 tbs	soya (soy) milk	6-8 tbs
1 tbs	tahini	1 tbs
2 tsp	lemon juice	2 tsp
1 tbs	soya (soy) sauce	1 tbs
As required	sea salt	As required
As required	freshly ground black pepper	As required
4	spring onions (scallions)	4

1 Cook the potatoes until tender (or use leftover cooked potatoes).
2 Soak the wakame in cold water for about 10 minutes. Drain and chop it, discarding the central frond.
3 Put the tofu, soya milk, tahini, lemon juice and 1 tbs soya (soy) sauce (plus additional seasoning if desired) into a liquidizer or food processor and blend thoroughly.

4 Slice the cooked potatoes. Chop the spring onions (scallions) finely. In the bottom of a casserole put a layer of potatoes, then a layer of chopped wakame, a sprinkling of minced spring onion (scallion) and a little soya (soy) sauce. Repeat the layers until all the ingredients have been used.
5 Spoon the tofu mixture over the top, and bake at 375°F/190°C (Gas Mark 5) for about 40 minutes.

Note: Tofu combines well with a sea vegetable like wakame.

Vegetable Stir-fry with Nori

10-12	dried mushrooms	10-12
2	onions	2
2 tbs	vegetable oil	2 tbs
2 cloves	garlic	2 cloves
2 tsp	finely grated fresh ginger	2 tsp
225g (½ lb)	carrots	½ lb
225g (½ lb)	cabbage	½ lb
1 large	green pepper	1 large
2 tbs	soya (soy) sauce	2 tbs
1 tsp	cider vinegar or wine vinegar	1 tsp
2 sheets	nori	2 sheets

1 Soak the mushrooms in warm water for about half an hour.
2 Chop the onions. Heat the oil in a wok or frying pan and sauté the onions for a minute or two.
3 Crush the garlic. Add to the wok with the ginger. Continue stir-frying for a minute or two longer.
4 Chop the carrots, cabbage and pepper finely. Add to the wok and continue stir-frying for a further 2-3 minutes.
5 Drain the mushrooms, reserving some of the liquid. Chop them and add to the pan, with 4 tbs of the soaking liquid, the vinegar, and the soya (soy) sauce. Cook for a few minutes longer.
6 Toast the nori (see instructions on page 106). Crumble it into the vegetables and serve at once.

Note: Nori is certainly the easiest sea vegetable to use. Serve this over brown rice.

Creamy Rice and Nori Savoury

285-340g (10-12 oz)	brown rice	1½-2 cups
3 tbs	vegan margarine	3 tbs
3 tbs	wholewheat flour	3 tbs
710ml (1¼ pts)	soya (soy) milk	3 cups
2 tbs	soya (soy) sauce	2 tbs
1 tsp	mustard	1 tsp
2-3 sheets	nori	2-3 sheets
85g (3 oz)	wholewheat breadcrumbs	1½ cups

1 Cook the rice (or use rice which has already been cooked).
2 Melt the margarine in a saucepan. Stir in the flour, and then the milk, stirring constantly to avoid lumps until it has thickened. Season with soya (soy) sauce and mustard. Remove from the heat.
3 Stir the rice into the sauce. Toast the nori, crumble it, and stir it into the mixture. Spoon the mixture into a baking dish and cover with the breadcrumbs.
4 Bake at 400°F/200°C (Gas Mark 6) for 15-20 minutes.

Note: If you have leftover rice, this is a very speedy dish. Serve it with seasonal vegetables.

Kedgeree

285-340g (10-12 oz)	brown rice	1½-2 cups
115g (4 oz)	vegan margarine	½ cup
340-455g (¾-1 lb)	smoked tofu	1½-2 cups
2 sheets	nori	2 sheets
As required	sea salt	As required
As required	cayenne pepper	As required
4 tbs	minced parsley	4 tbs

1 Cook the rice until tender (or use leftover cooked rice).
2 Toast the nori and set aside.
3 Melt the margarine in a large saucepan. Dice the smoked tofu and add it to the pan; sauté until lightly browned. Add the cooked rice to the pan and continue to cook, stirring well. Shred the toasted nori into the mixture. Season with salt and cayenne. Sprinkle with the parsley and serve.

Note: Nori and smoked tofu make a lovely combination. Quick and Easy. Suitable for One.

Oriental-style Fried Rice with Tofu and Nori

285-340g (10-12 oz)	brown rice	1½-2 cups
2 sheets	nori	2 sheets
680g (1½ lb)	tofu	3 cups
4-6	spring onions (scallions)	4-6
2 cloves	garlic	2 cloves
½ inch piece	fresh ginger	½ inch piece
2 tbs	vegetable oil	2 tbs
As required	soya (soy) sauce	As required
As required	freshly ground black pepper	As required
1-2 tsp	sesame oil	1-2 tsp

1 Cook the rice until tender (or use leftover cooked rice). Toast the nori.
2 Dice half the tofu and deep-fry the diced tofu until golden. Mash the remainder of the tofu in a bowl.
3 Chop the spring onions, garlic and ginger very finely. Heat the vegetable oil in a wok and stir-fry these ingredients for 2-3 minutes.
4 Add the cooked rice and mashed tofu to the wok and continue stir-frying for about 2-3 minutes longer.
5 Add the deep-fried tofu cubes, soya (soy) sauce and pepper. Then tear the nori into pieces and add them to the mixture. Stir well for about a minute longer, then sprinkle in the sesame oil and serve piping hot.

Note: Mashed tofu adds a scrambled egg texture, deep-fried tofu a chewy texture, and nori gives a flavour of the sea to this dish.
Quick and Easy.

Tofu Nori Savoury

2 sheets	nori	2 sheets
565-680g (1¼-1½ lb)	tofu	2½-3 cups
55g (2 oz)	vegan margarine (plus extra as required)	½ cup
45g (1½ oz)	wholewheat flour	3 tbs
570ml (1 pt)	soya (soy) milk	2½ cups
As required	sea salt	As required
As required	freshly ground black pepper	As required
2 tsp	curry powder	2 tsp
4 tbs	wholewheat breadcrumbs	4 tbs

1 Toast the nori. Slice the tofu and place half the slices in a greased baking dish. Tear half the nori into pieces and place on top of the tofu; repeat with the second half of the tofu and nori.
2 Melt 55g (2 oz/½ cup) margarine in a saucepan and stir in the flour. Slowly add the milk, stirring constantly to

avoid lumps, until it comes to the boil. Season well and stir in the curry powder; cook for a minute or two longer.

3 Pour the sauce over the tofu/nori layers. Sprinkle with the breadcrumbs and top with shavings of margarine. Bake at 350°F/180°C (Gas Mark 4) for about half an hour.

Devilled Nori Tofu

455-680g (1¼-1½ lb)	tofu	2½-3 cups
570ml (1 pt)	water	2½ cups
2 tbs	soya (soy) sauce	2 tbs
2 sheets	nori	2 sheets
285ml (½ pt)	soya (soy) milk	1½ cups
2 tbs	vegetable oil	2 tbs
2 tsp	mustard	2 tsp
1 tbs	vegetarian Worcester sauce	1 tbs
Few drops	Tabasco sauce	Few drops

1 Slice the tofu. Bring the water to the boil; add the soya (soy) sauce; put the tofu slices into the pan; bring to the boil again; turn off heat and leave alone for 2-3 minutes. Drain.

2 Heat the nori slices over a gas flame or hot burner on one side until lightly coloured.

3 Put the milk, oil, mustard, Worcester sauce and Tabasco sauce into a liquidizer and blend thoroughly.

4 Place the tofu slices in a large, oiled casserole dish. Pour the sauce over them. Dip one side of each nori sheet into the sauce, then turn over so that the dry side is on top and lay on top of the casserole.

5 Bake at 425°F/220°C (Gas Mark 7) for about 20 minutes. Serve with a cooked vegetable like cauliflower or peas, and potatoes.

Nori and Potato Casserole

900g (2 lb)	potatoes	2 lb
1 small	onion	1 small
3 sheets	nori	3 sheets
30g (1 oz)	vegan margarine	2 tbs
570ml (1 pt)	soya (soy) milk	2½ cups
225g (½ lb)	tofu	1 cup
2 tbs	soya (soy) sauce	2 tbs
As required	sea salt	As required
As required	freshly ground black pepper	As required
30g (1 oz)	breadcrumbs	½ cup

1 Cook the potatoes (or use leftover potatoes). Slice them thickly (peeled if preferred). Chop the onion finely. Toast the nori and tear it into strips.

2 Layer the potato slices, onion and nori in a greased baking dish, ending with a layer of potato. Put dabs of the margarine on top.

3 Blend the milk, tofu and soya (soy) sauce in a liquidizer. Season to taste.

4 Pour the blended mixture over the potato casserole. Top with breadcrumbs. Bake at 350°F/180°C (Gas Mark 4) for 30-40 minutes (the longer time if the potatoes are leftovers from the refrigerator).

Note: The idea for this dish came from a Scandinavian 'fishy' recipe. Serve it with a seasonal green vegetable.

Smoked Tofu and Nori Crumble

55g (2 oz)	vegan margarine	¼ cup
55g (2 oz)	wholewheat flour	½ cup
570ml (1 pt)	soya (soy) milk	2½ cups
As required	sea salt	As required
As required	freshly ground black pepper	As required
2 sheets	nori	2 sheets
455-565g (1-1¼ lb)	smoked tofu	2-2½ cups

Crumble:

170g (6 oz)	wholewheat flour	1½ cups
55g (2 oz)	rolled oats	½ cup
115g (4 oz)	vegan margarine	½ cup

1 Melt the margarine in a saucepan and stir in the flour. Add the milk slowly, stirring constantly to avoid lumps. When the sauce has thickened and boiled season to taste. Remove from heat.

2 Toast the nori sheets and tear them into pieces. Dice the tofu. Combine these ingredients with the sauce, and transfer the mixture to a greased casserole dish.

3 Mix the flour and oats in a bowl and cut in the margarine with a pastry blender or fork. Put the crumble mixture on top of the tofu/nori mixture and bake at 400°F/200°C (Gas Mark 6) for about half an hour.

14
Vegetable Side Dishes

Introduction

This is a short chapter for two reasons. First, a large proportion of the recipes in this book are self-contained – vegetables with beans, nuts, soya (soy) foods etc combined with a grain – so that side dishes are not necessary, and when they are a simple mixed salad is often the best. Second, whereas in a meat-based diet the centre of a meal is usually a simple slab of something, needing, perhaps, the accompaniment of elaborately prepared and highly seasoned vegetables, a vegan centrepiece like a nut roast is already well flavoured and interesting, requiring only the simplest of vegetable accompaniments.

Everyone evolves their own way of cooking vegetables. I steam mine first in the barest minimum of water for just long enough for the vegetable in question to become tenderized. I then drain any water left in the pan. (After a cookery demonstration I was once asked if I used the water left over from cooking vegetables as stock; I looked really puzzled, because I so rarely have any usable quantity left. When I do have enough I freeze it for later use as vegetable stock.) I then put a little vegan margarine in the bottom of the pan and when it has melted I return the vegetables to it and continue cooking them very briefly in the margarine. I do this with every kind of vegetable from courgettes (zucchini), which need less than five minutes' cooking, to potatoes which need plenty of water and about half an hour's cooking.

So why include a chapter on vegetable side dishes at all? The answer is that there are always times when a special meal is called for, and for such occasions it is useful to have a repertoire of appealing vegan vegetable side dishes.

Recipes

Cabbage, Carrots and Apple

1	cabbage	1
2 large	carrots	2 large
2	dessert apples	2
30g (1 oz)	vegan margarine	2 tbs

1 Shred the cabbage, grate the carrots, and dice the apples.
2 Melt the margarine, add the cabbage and cook for 2-3 minutes, stirring well.
3 Add the carrots and apples, lower the heat, cover the pan tightly, and simmer until just tender.

Note: This has a pleasant sweet/savoury flavour.

Mushrooms and Celery

1-2 heads	celery	2
225g (½ lb)	mushrooms	4 cups
45g (1½ oz)	vegan margarine	3 tbs
2 tsp	wholewheat flour	2 tsp
140ml (¼ pt)	soya (soy) milk	⅔ cup
As required	sea salt	As required
As required	freshly ground black pepper	As required

1 Slice the celery into 2-inch pieces and cook until tender in salted water.
2 Prepare and slice the mushrooms into halves or quarters, depending on the size.
3 Melt the margarine, add the mushrooms and stir well.
4 Sprinkle the flour into the mixture, stirring again.
5 Add the drained celery pieces, stir in the milk carefully and mix well. Add seasoning to taste.
6 Cook gently for 4-5 minutes and serve.

Note: This side dish will complement any nut roast.

Savoury Fried Cabbage

455g (1 lb)	cabbage	1 lb
1	onion	1
1 clove	garlic	1 clove
1 tbs	soya (soy) sauce	1 tbs
1 tsp	cornflour (cornstarch)	1 tsp
2 tbs	water	2 tbs
2 tbs	vegetable oil	2 tbs

1 Shred the cabbage and chop the onion and garlic finely.
2 Heat the oil in a heavy frying pan, add the onion and garlic and sauté until they begin to soften.
3 Add the cabbage, increase the heat and stir constantly for 3-6 minutes.

4 Combine the cornflour (cornstarch), water and soya (soy) sauce in a small cup. Pour this mixture over the vegetables in the frying pan, stir well until thoroughly mixed and thickened and serve.

Note: A traditional Chinese method of cooking vegetables can be used for side dishes too.

Broccoli with Almonds, Onions and Garlic

900g (2 lb)	broccoli	2 lb
90ml (3 fl oz)	vegetable oil	⅓ cup
45g (1½ oz)	blanched almonds	⅓ cup
2 cloves	garlic	2 cloves
1 small	onion	1 small
3 tbs	capers	3 tbs
As required	sea salt	As required
As required	freshly ground black pepper	As required

1 Prepare the broccoli and cook it in lightly salted water until just tender. Set aside to drain well.
2 Slice the almonds, chop the onion and finely chop the garlic.
3 Sauté the onion, garlic and almonds in oil until browned.
4 Add the broccoli, capers and seasoning to the pan and cook over a high heat for 1 minute, stirring well, and serve.

Note: Capers add an unusual tang to this dish.

Cauliflower Romagna-style

1	cauliflower	1
30g (1 oz)	vegan margarine	2 tbs
3 tbs	vegetable oil	3 tbs
1 clove	garlic	1 clove
2 tbs	chopped parsley	2 tbs
As required	sea salt	As required
As required	freshly ground black pepper	As required
6 tbs	water	6 tbs
1 tbs	tomato purée (paste)	1 tbs

1 Divide the washed cauliflower into individual florets. Crush the garlic.
2 Heat the margarine and oil in a saucepan and fry the garlic and parsley for a few moments.
3 Add the cauliflower, stir and cook for several minutes, then add the seasoning, water and tomato purée (paste). Cover the pan and cook over a low heat until tender (about 15-20 minutes).

Note: This Italian style of cooking transforms the humble cauliflower.

Baked Tomatoes with Potatoes

455g (1 lb)	potatoes	1 lb
680g (1½ lb)	tomatoes	1½ lb
2 cloves	garlic	2 cloves
2 tsp	dried oregano or thyme	2 tsp
285ml (½ pt)	soya (soy) milk	1⅓ cups
15g (½ oz)	vegan margarine	1 tbs
As required	sea salt	As required
As required	freshly ground black pepper	As required
2 tbs	chopped parsley	2 tbs

1 Cook the potatoes (or use leftover cooked potatoes) and peel them, if desired.
2 Skin the tomatoes. Slice the potatoes and tomatoes into fairly thick slices.
3 In a casserole, place a layer of potatoes, a little crushed garlic, a dot or two of the margarine, a sprinkling of herbs, and so on until the ingredients are used up, ending with a layer of tomatoes.
4 Pour the milk over the vegetables.
5 Cover the dish and cook in the centre of a moderate oven at 350°F/180°C (Gas Mark 4) for about half an hour. Before serving sprinkle some chopped parsley over the top.

Note: Instead of plain boiled or roast potatoes with a nut roast, try these instead.

Bubble and Squeak

455g (1 lb)	cabbage, cooked	1 lb
455g (1 lb)	potatoes, cooked	1 lb
2	onions	2
2-3 tbs	vegetable oil	2-3 tbs
As required	sea salt	As required
As required	freshly ground black pepper	As required

1 Use either leftover cooked cabbage and potatoes, or cook them freshly. Chop both the cabbage and the potatoes quite finely.
2 Chop the onions and sauté in the oil until tender. Add the potatoes and stir well over a moderately high flame until the onions and potatoes begin to brown. Then add the cabbage, and continue stirring. Season well.

Note: This traditional British dish is vegan. With cabbage and potato left over from a previous meal (and stored in the refrigerator), it takes no time at all to make.
Quick and Easy. Suitable for One.

Potatoes Niçoise

455g (1 lb)	potatoes	1 lb
2	onions	2
3 cloves	garlic	3 cloves
4 tbs	olive oil	4 tbs
1 small	green pepper	1 small
4-6 (depending on size)	very ripe tomatoes	4-6 (depending on size)
4 tbs	finely chopped parsley	4 tbs
12	black olives	12
As required	sea salt	As required
As required	freshly ground black pepper	As required

1 Cook the potatoes (or use leftover cooked potatoes).
2 Chop the onions and chop the garlic finely. Sauté in the oil in a frying pan and cook for a few minutes, stirring frequently, until just tender.
3 Cut the green pepper into thin slivers. Add to the frying pan for a minute or two.
4 Cut the potatoes (peeled if desired) into small cubes. Add to the frying pan and cook for a few minutes, stirring frequently, until they begin to brown.
5 Skin and chop the tomatoes. Add to the frying pan together with the parsley, turn the heat up, and cook for 2-3 minutes longer.
6 Finely chop the olives. Stir into the potato mixture along with the seasoning.

Note: This is a lovely Mediterranean side dish as well as a good way of using leftover potatoes.
Quick and Easy. Suitable for One.

Stovies

3 or 4	onions	3 or 4
2 tbs	vegetable oil	2 tbs
900g (2 lb)	potatoes	2 lb
285ml (½ pt)	hot water	1⅓ cups
As required	sea salt	As required
As required	freshly ground black pepper	As required
55g (2 oz)	medium oatmeal	½ cup

1 Slice the onions thinly. Heat the vegetable oil in a large pan and sauté them for a few minutes.
2 Scrub the potatoes and slice them thickly. Add them to the pan, and pour the hot water over them. Season to taste. Lower the heat, cover and simmer until tender for about half an hour.
3 In the meantime spread the oatmeal under the grill (broiler) and toast until lightly browned. Sprinkle the oatmeal over the dish before serving it.

Note: This is a vegan version of a traditional Scottish dish.

Princess Potatoes

680g (1½ lb)	potatoes	1½ lb
30g (1 oz)	nutritional yeast	1 oz
55g (2 oz)	vegan margarine	¼ cup
285ml (½ pt)	soya (soy) milk	1⅓ cups
115g (4 oz)	tofu	½ cup
As required	sea salt	As required
As required	freshly ground black pepper	As required

1 Cook the potatoes (or use leftover potatoes). Slice them thickly (peel if desired).
2 Layer the sliced potatoes in a greased casserole with the yeast and half the margarine. Pour half the milk over the top and bake at 425°F/220°C (Gas Mark 7) for 10-20 minutes (the shorter time if freshly cooked; longer if they have been refrigerated).
3 Blend the remainder of the milk with the tofu in a liquidizer and season with salt and nutmeg.
4 Pour the tofu mixture over the potatoes and dot with the remaining margarine. Return to the oven for 15 minutes longer.

Note: This is a version of the kind of potato dish served in some expensive restaurants.
Suitable for a dinner party.

Greek-style Green Beans

455g (1 lb)	fresh or frozen green beans	1 lb
1	onion	1
1 clove	garlic	1 clove
5 tbs	tomato purée (paste)	5 tbs
4 tbs	vegetable oil	4 tbs
285ml (½ pt)	water	1⅓ cups
As required	sea salt	As required
As required	freshly ground black pepper	As required

1 If using fresh beans, top and tail them. Put them in a saucepan (if the beans are long they can be snapped in two).
2 Chop the onion and garlic finely.
3 Add the tomato purée (paste), the oil, onion, garlic and water to the beans, and bring to the boil, stirring well. Season.
4 Cover the saucepan, lower the heat and leave to simmer for about 15 minutes, stirring occasionally, until the beans are tender.

Note: In Greece a vegan might have this as a main dish, but it also makes an appealing side dish.

Heated Avocado Purée

2	avocados	2
1 tsp	lemon juice	1 tsp
Pinch	sea salt	Pinch
Sprinkling	paprika	Sprinkling
1 tsp	grated lemon rind	1 tsp
1 tbs	minced chives or spring onions (scallions)	1 tbs

1 Peel and mash the avocados.
2 Put them into a saucepan with all the other ingredients. Put the saucepan over a large pan of boiling water (or use a double boiler) and heat the avocado mixture.

Note: Avocados are generally used in cold dishes, but here they make an unusual side dish.
Quick and Easy.

Lettuce and Peas

225g (½ lb)	lettuce leaves	½ lb
225g (½ lb)	fresh (shelled) or frozen peas	½ lb
2 tbs	water	2 tbs
30g (1 oz)	vegan margarine	2 tbs

1 Wash the lettuce leaves thoroughly and shred them.
2 Put the shredded lettuce leaves in a saucepan with the peas and water and bring to the boil. Lower the heat and simmer, covered, for 3-5 minutes.
3 Drain the vegetables and return to the pan with the margarine. Cover and cook for a minute or two more and serve.

Note: I am not keen on eating the outside leaves of lettuce but hate waste. I remembered hearing of this combination but couldn't find any simple recipe for it, so I tried cooking them very simply and it worked.
Quick and Easy.

Sauce for vegetables

45g (1½ oz)	vegan margarine	3 tbs
3 tbs	wholewheat flour	3 tbs
Dash	freshly ground black pepper	Dash
200ml (⅓ pt)	soya (soy) yogurt	¾ cup
3 tbs	soya (soy) sauce	3 tbs
120ml (4 fl oz)	vegan mayonnaise	½ cup
Dash	paprika	Dash
As required	lightly cooked green beans, cabbage, Brussels sprouts or broccoli	As required

1 Melt the margarine in a small saucepan over the lowest possible heat. Add the flour and pepper.
2 Stir in the yogurt and soy sauce. Continue stirring constantly to avoid lumps until the sauce thickens.
3 Gently stir in the mayonnaise and continue cooking briefly until heated through.
4 Pour the sauce over the vegetables and garnish with paprika.

Note: This is a creamy sauce that can be used for a variety of vegetables.

15

Fresh Fruit-based Desserts

Special Rhubarb Crumble

340g (¾ lb)	rhubarb	¾ lb
3 tbs	water	3 tbs
160-225g (6-8 oz)	raw cane sugar	1-1⅓ cups
115g (4 oz)	wholewheat flour	1 cup
55g (2 oz)	rolled oats	½ cup
55g (2 oz)	desiccated (shredded) coconut	⅔ cup
2 tsp	powdered ginger	2 tsp
115g (4 oz)	vegan margarine	½ cup

1 Chop the rhubarb and place in an oiled ovenproof dish with the water. Sprinkle about a third to a half of the sugar over it.
2 Put the rest of the sugar in a large bowl with the flour, oats, coconut and ginger. Mix well then add the margarine and blend in well with the fingers.
3 Pile the crumble mixture on top of the fruit and bake at 400°C/200°C (Gas Mark 6) for about half an hour. Check after about 20 minutes and if the top is browning too quickly, turn the oven down to a low heat for the remaining 10 minutes.

Note: Served after a very light meal, or to those with large appetites, this will make four servings, but otherwise it is really enough for six.

Lemon and Chocolate Treats

55g (2 oz)	vegan margarine (preferably unsalted)	¼ cup
55g (2 oz)	icing (powdered) sugar	½ cup
½	medium lemon	½
85g (3 oz)	vegan chocolate	3 oz
4	ripe bananas	4
15g (½ oz)	desiccated (shredded) coconut	1/6 cup

1 Grate the lemon and squeeze out the juice. Cream the margarine and sugar in a bowl and add the lemon rind and juice. Place the bowl in the refrigerator for half an hour or more.
2 Put the chocolate in a small basin. Place the basin over a pan of hot water over gentle heat until the chocolate has melted.
3 Peel and halve the bananas lengthwise. Spoon the lemon mixture between banana halves to sandwich them together. Spoon the melted chocolate over them and sprinkle the coconut on top.

Note: The idea for this – a perennial favourite in our household – came from a woman's magazine about twenty years ago. Plamil chocolate is available at health food stores; otherwise look for vegan chocolates amongst the high-quality Continental ones (they will always list ingredients). Most British 'plain' chocolates contain butterfat and so are not vegan.
Quick and Easy.

Fruit Custard

455g (1 lb)	seedless grapes	1 lb
2 large	sweet oranges	2 large
570ml (1 pt)	soya (soy) milk	2½ cups
2 tbs	custard powder	2 tbs
3-4 tbs	raw cane sugar	3-4 tbs
4 tbs	desiccated (shredded) coconut	4 tbs

1 Wash the grapes and remove them from their stems. Peel and segment the oranges. Put the fruit into four serving dishes.
2 Make up the custard with the milk and powder and as much sugar as required. Leave it to cool briefly.
3 Sprinkle the remainder of the sugar and the coconut over the fruit. Pour the custard over the top.
4 Cool and then chill before serving.

Note: Children who do not eat enough fresh fruit might be coaxed by this dessert. It is also useful because most of the ingredients will be found in every larder so it takes little advance planning. Americans who cannot find custard powder could use cornstarch and a few drops of vanilla essence.

Baked Banana Rolls with Lemon Sauce

For the rolls:

	Pastry made from 115g (4 oz/½ cup) wholewheat flour etc. (see p.41)	
4 small	bananas	4 small
2 tbs	raw cane sugar	2 tbs
As required	cinnamon	As required

For the sauce:

85g (3 oz)	raw cane sugar	½ cup
200-225ml (7-8 fl oz)	water	¾-1 cup
Juice of 1	lemon	Juice of 1
1 tbs	cornflour (cornstarch)	1 tbs

1 Make the pastry and roll out into 4 oblong shapes.
2 Peel the bananas and place one on each of the pastry oblongs. Sprinkle each with ½ tbs sugar and a little cinnamon, then fold over the pastry to enclose the banana. Place on a greased tray and bake for 15 minutes at 400°F/200°C (Gas Mark 8).
3 Meanwhile, put the sugar and water in a saucepan, and bring to the boil slowly. Mix the cornflour (cornstarch) with the lemon juice and stir it into the saucepan. Continue stirring constantly until the mixture has thickened. Simmer briefly so that any raw floury taste has disappeared.
4 Serve the pastry parcels with sauce poured over them.

Frozen Raisin and Pecan Dessert

4	peaches or	4
½	pineapple	½
2 large	bananas	2 large
200ml (⅓ pt)	pineapple or orange juice	¾ cup
170g (6 oz)	raisins	1 cup
115g (4 oz)	pecans	¾ cup

1 Chop the peaches or pineapple and bananas and place the pieces in the freezing compartment of the refrigerator until frozen.
2 Pour the juice into the liquidizer, add the raisins and pecans and blend thoroughly.
3 Add the frozen fruit, a little at a time, blending thoroughly after each addition. Serve immediately.

Note: The next chapter includes a section on vegan ice creams made in an ice cream maker. This and the following recipes are for frozen fruit desserts that can be made without one.
Sugar-Free.

Fruit and Coconut Ice Cream

Juice of 2	lemons	Juice of 2
Juice of 2	oranges	Juice of 2
2	bananas	2
170g (6 oz)	raw cane sugar	1 cup
570ml (1 pt)	hot water	2½ cups
85g (3 oz)	creamed coconut	⅓ cup
55g (2 oz)	cashews	½ cup
2 tbs	vegetable oil	2 tbs

1 Grind the cashews finely.
2 Place all of the ingredients in a liquidizer (in stages if necessary) and blend until thoroughly mixed.
3 Freeze for at least 2 hours. Transfer to the refrigerator for 15-20 minutes before serving.

Blackcurrant Sorbet

455g (1 lb)	fresh blackcurrants	3 cups
Juice of 2	lemons	Juice of 2
85-115g (3-4 oz)	raw cane sugar	½-⅔ cup

1 Top and tail the blackcurrants.
2 Purée the fruit (in 2 batches if necessary) in a liquidizer.
3 Add the lemon juice to the sugar and stir well. Mix this in with the fruit purée.
4 Freeze the mixture in the ice compartment of the refrigerator. If desired, when almost stiff, purée again in a liquidizer just before serving.

Banana Cream Pie

1	pre-baked pastry case (pie shell)	1
115g (4 oz)	cashews	¾ cup
170g (6 oz)	stoned dates	1 cup
4 tsp	arrowroot	4 tsp
Pinch	sea salt	Pinch
1 tsp	vanilla essence	1 tsp
285ml (½ pt)	water	1⅓ cups
2	ripe bananas	2

1 Chop the dates and place them in a liquidizer with the cashews, arrowroot, salt, vanilla and water. Blend thoroughly.
2 Pour into a saucepan and heat gently, stirring constantly, until thickened. Allow the mixture to cool.
3 Slice the bananas into the pie shell. Cover them with the cashew-date mixture; chill and serve.

Note: To make the pastry for this dessert see p.41. Sugar-Free.

Fresh Fruit Trifle

225g (½ lb)	plain sponge cake (see p.131)	½ lb
570ml (1 pt)	soya (soy) milk	2½ cups
As required	custard powder	As required
As required	raw cane sugar	As required
455g (1 lb)	fresh fruit	1 lb
1 packet	vegan fruit jelly	1 packet

1 Crumble the cake into the bottom of the dish.
2 Chop the fruit and put it on top of the cake.
3 Make up the jelly according to the directions on the packet and pour it over the cake and fruit.
4 Make up a thick custard with the milk and when the jelly has set, spread this over the top.
5 Leave in the refrigerator for several hours before serving.

Note: This is a dessert which most people who become vegan think they will never eat again.

Strawberry Shortcake

225g (½ lb)	wholewheat flour	2 cups
4 tsp	baking powder	4 tsp
1 tsp	sea salt	1 tsp
1 tbs	raw cane sugar	1 tbs
30-55g (1-2 oz)	vegan margarine	2 tbs- ¼ cup
140ml (¼ pt)	soya (soy) milk	⅔ cup
As required	mock cream (see p.12) or vegan whipped cream (see p.12)	As required
As required	fresh strawberries	As required

1 Mix the flour with the baking powder, salt and sugar.
2 Add the margarine, cut into small pieces, with a pastry blender, two knives, or the fingers, and mix until thoroughly blended. (The larger amount of margarine will make a richer dessert.)
3 Make a well in the centre and pour in the milk. Stir in vigorously for the shortest possible time then turn the dough out on to a floured board.
4 Cut the dough in half and roll out each half. Bake in two sandwich tins in a hot oven at 425°F/220°C (Gas Mark 7) for 12-15 minutes.
5 Leave to cool, then sandwich and top the layers with cream and strawberries (sweetened if desired).

Apple Mousse

455g (1 lb)	Bramley apples	1 lb
115g (4 oz)	raw cane sugar	⅔ cup
Juice of 1	lemon	Juice of 1
285ml (½ pt)	water	1⅓ cups
1 tsp	agar-agar	1 tsp
85g (3 oz)	cashews	⅔ cup

1 Grind the cashews finely.
2 Peel and slice the apples and cook them with the sugar in just enough of the water to cover. When tender, add the rest of the water and bring to the boil.
3 Sprinkle the agar-agar carefully into the saucepan and cook for 1 minute.
4 Pour the mixture into a liquidizer. Add the lemon juice and ground cashews and blend them thoroughly.
5 Pour into a serving dish or four individual dishes and leave the mousse to cool, then chill before serving.

Note: Cooked apples, lemon and cashews are a very appealing combination.

Nutty Apples

55g (2 oz)	vegan margarine	¼ cup
85g (3 oz)	raw cane sugar	½ cup
55g (2 oz)	wholewheat flour	½ cup
30g (1 oz)	flaked (slivered) almonds or chopped walnuts	3 tbs
4	Bramley apples	4

1 Cream the margarine with the sugar then mix in the flour and nuts.
2 Peel and core the apples and halve them. Arrange them, flat side up, in a greased baking dish. Spoon some of the sugar mixture on top of each.
3 Bake the apples uncovered in a moderate oven, 350°F/180°C (Gas Mark 4) for about half an hour until the apples are soft.

Note: This is a good dessert to make when using the oven for a savoury dish (it is much quicker than conventional baked apples and needs a much lower oven heat). Serve with a vegan cream or custard.

Summer Fruit Cup

200ml (⅓ pt)	orange juice	¾ cup
200ml (⅓ pt)	water	¾ cup
55g (2 oz)	raw cane sugar	⅓ cup
½ tsp	cinnamon	½ tsp
2 small	oranges	2 small
2 ripe	peaches	2 ripe
170-225g (6-8 oz)	strawberries	6-8 oz
30g (1 oz)	chopped almonds	3 tbs

1 Cook the orange juice, water, sugar and cinnamon until it begins to thicken into a syrup. Set aside to cool.
2 Peel and segment the orange; slice the peaches and strawberries.
3 Combine the fruit in a bowl and pour the syrup over them. Sprinkle with the almonds. Chill before serving.

Note: A vegan with a sweet tooth can get pretty fed up with being offered nothing but fruit salads for dessert, but this one is in a class of its own.
Suitable for a dinner party.

Hot Blackberry Soup

680g (1½ lb)	fresh blackberries	1½ lb
1140ml (2 pts)	water	5 cups
55g (2 oz)	vegan margarine	¼ cup
1½ tbs	wholewheat flour	1½ tbs
55g (2 oz)	raw cane sugar	⅓ cup
30g (1 oz)	chopped almonds	3 tbs

1 Put the water in a saucepan and add the berries. Bring to the boil and simmer until tender, then put them through a sieve. Return the sieved berries to the cooking liquid; discard the pulp.
2 Heat the margarine in a pan and stir in the flour. Add the soup gradually, stirring constantly to avoid lumps. Sweeten (the amount given is only a rough guide as berries vary so much in sweetness) and simmer for about 10 minutes.
3 Serve hot, sprinkled with almonds.

Note: On the Continent fruit soup is often eaten as a starter in summer, but it seems more appropriate to me as a dessert. This recipe also works with raspberries or loganberries and is usually eaten with biscuits (cookies).

Avocado Dessert

85-115g (3-4 oz)	raw cane sugar	½-⅔ cup
2	avocados	2
Juice of ½	lemon	Juice of ½

1 Place the sugar in a liquidizer (or coffee grinder) and grind to a fine powder.
2 Peel and dice the avocados.
3 Combine all the ingredients in the liquidizer and blend thoroughly.

Note: Although the avocado is a fruit it is usually served as a savoury starter or in a salad. This and the recipes which follow show how well it works in desserts.
Quick and Easy.

Avocado and Gooseberry Fool

455g (1 lb)	fresh gooseberries	1 lb
140ml (¼ pt)	water	⅔ cup
1	avocado	1
As required	raw cane sugar	As required
55g (2 oz)	vegan chocolate	2 oz

1 Top and tail the gooseberries.
2 Cook with the water until tender. Cool the gooseberries.
3 Peel and dice the avocado and put in a liquidizer with the gooseberries. Blend thoroughly, adding raw cane sugar to taste.
4 Chill the mixture. Shortly before serving grate the chocolate over the top.

Spiced Plums with Avocado Topping

140ml (¼ pt)	water	⅔ cup
115g (4 oz)	raw cane sugar	⅔ cup
1 large	cinnamon stick	1 large
6	whole cloves	6
455g (1 lb)	plums	1 lb
1	avocado	1
1	lemon	1
2 additional tsp	raw cane sugar	2 additional tsp

1 Gently heat the water, sugar, cinnamon and cloves until the sugar has dissolved.
2 Add the plums and simmer until cooked.
3 Cool the plums, then remove the cinnamon and cloves. Chill in the refrigerator.
4 Just before serving, peel and mash the avocado. Grate the lemon rind into it, squeeze the juice of the lemon into it, and finally add the additional sugar. Beat the mixture well.
5 Serve the plums with the avocado topping.

Avocado, Ginger and Apple Crumble

55g (2 oz)	vegetable margarine	¼ cup
85g (3 oz)	rolled oats	¾ cup
2 tbs	Demerara sugar	2 tbs
3 large pieces	crystallized stem ginger	3 large pieces
1	avocado	1
285ml (½ pt)	apple purée (applesauce)	1⅓ cups
140ml (¼ pt)	vegan whipped cream (see p.12)	⅔ cup

1 Melt the margarine, add the oats and sugar and mix well.
2 Grease a shallow baking pan and spread the oat mixture on the bottom.
3 Place in a moderate oven at 350°F/180°C (Gas Mark 4) for about 10 minutes, until lightly toasted. Run a fork through the mixture and leave to cool.
4 Chop the ginger finely. Peel and mash the avocado.
5 Combine the avocado, ginger and apple purée (applesauce).
6 Place in a serving dish and top with the oat mixture.
7 Spoon the whipped cream on to the top of the dessert.

Sugar-Free.

Avocado, Coconut and Apple Dessert

2	dessert apples	2
Juice of ½	lemon	Juice of ½
Juice of ½	orange	Juice of ½
55g (2 oz)	creamed coconut	¼ cup
55g (2 oz)	stoned (pitted) dates	⅓ cup
30g (1 oz)	walnut pieces	3 tbs
1	avocado	1

1 Peel and chop the apples. Place in a liquidizer with lemon and orange juice.
2 Grate the coconut. Chop the dates. Add both to the liquidizer together with the walnuts.
3 Peel and chop the avocado. Add the liquidizer and blend thoroughly.

Sugar-Free.

Baked Bananas and Oranges

30g (1 oz)	vegan margarine	2 tbs
45g (1½ oz)	raw cane sugar	¼ cup
2	oranges	2
4	bananas	4

1 Grate one of the oranges. Cream the margarine and sugar together, and mix in the grated rind.
2 Peel and slice the oranges. Peel and slice the bananas. Layer the fruit and the margarine mixture in an oven dish, and bake at 425°F/220°C (Gas Mark 7) for 10 minutes.

Note: If you are using the oven for a savoury dish, when you remove it just pop this in for a simple dessert.

Quick and Easy.

Apple Strudel

455g (1 lb)	cooking apples	1 lb
85g (3 oz)	raw cane sugar	½ cup
55g (2 oz)	raisins or sultanas (golden seedless raisins)	⅓ cup
30g (1 oz)	flaked (slivered) almonds	¼ cup
½ tsp	cinnamon	½ tsp
55g (2 oz)	vegan margarine	¼ cup
4 sheets	filo pastry (thawed)	4 sheets

1 Peel the apples and chop them finely. Put them in a bowl with the sugar, raisins, almonds and cinnamon; mix well.
2 Melt the margarine. Mix about half of it into the apple mixture.
3 Brush each of the filo pastry sheets with some of the remaining margarine, then put a quarter of the apple mixture on it and roll the dough up.
4 Bake the strudel at 375°F/190°C (Gas Mark 5) for about half an hour. Serve warm if possible.

Note: Traditionally, apfel strudel used to be made with egg, so when I became a vegan I never thought I would be able to eat it again. But nowadays, with frozen filo pastry so easily available, it has become something you can prepare yourself in no time at all. This is nice with a little icing (powdered) sugar sprinkled over the top and/or some vegan whipped cream.

16
Miscellaneous Desserts

Tofu Cheesecake 1

455g (1 lb)	tofu	2 cups
3 tbs	soya (soy) flour	3 tbs
1 tsp	vanilla essence	1 tsp
Juice and grated rind of 2	lemons	Juice and grated rind of 2
2 heaped tsp	agar-agar	2 heaped tsp
170g (6 oz)	raw cane sugar	1 cup
1 heaped tsp	baking powder	1 heaped tsp
115g (4 oz)	vegan cornflakes or wheat flakes	¼ tsp
30g (1 oz)	vegan margarine	2 tbs
1 tsp	cinnamon	1 tsp
2 tbs	desiccated (shredded) coconut	2 tbs

1 Mash the tofu. Add the soya (soy) flour, vanilla essence, lemon juice and rind, agar-agar, baking powder and sugar – leaving about 2 tbs of the sugar aside. Mix very thoroughly.
2 Melt the margarine. Crush the flakes and mix them with the melted margarine. Turn into a flan tin (pie dish) and smooth down to make a pie crust.
3 Pour the tofu mixture into the shell.
4 Mix the remaining sugar with the coconut and cinnamon and sprinkle this over the tofu mixture.
5 Bake in a slow oven 275°F/140°C (Gas Mark 1) for an hour and a half. Cool slightly (or completely) before serving.

Note: When I first became a vegan I thought I had given up for life one of my favourite foods: cheesecake. Some years later I learned, to my delight, that delicious 'cheesecakes' can be made from tofu.

Tofu Cheesecake 2

170g (6 oz)	vegan digestive biscuits (Graham crackers)	6 oz
55g (2 oz)	vegan margarine	¼ cup
455g (1 lb)	tofu	2 cups
3 tbs	tahini	3 tbs
115g (4 oz) plus 2 tbs	raw cane sugar	⅔ cup plus 2 tbs
4 tsp	lemon juice	4 tsp
Pinch	sea salt	Pinch
1½ tsp	vanilla essence	1½ tsp
285ml (½ pt)	soya (soy) yogurt	1⅓ cups
¼ tsp	cinnamon	¼ tsp

1 Melt the margarine, crush the biscuits (Graham crackers) and mix them with the melted margarine. Place the mixture in a flan tin (pie dish) and form into a crust.
2 Purée the tofu then mix it with the tahini, 115g (4 oz) of the sugar, the lemon juice, salt and half of the vanilla essence.
3 Pour the mixture into the shell and bake in a moderate oven at 350°F/180°C (Gas Mark 4) for about half an hour. Remove from the oven.
4 Mix the yogurt, remaining sugar and vanilla essence, and the cinnamon together. Spoon this mixture on top of the cheesecake, and bake at 425°F/220°C (Gas Mark 7) for 5 minutes. Allow to cool, then chill thoroughly until ready to serve.

Maple Pecan Tofu Cheesecake

115g (4 oz)	crunchy muesli (granola)	1 cup
30g (1 oz)	vegan margarine	2 tbs
340g (¾ lb)	tofu	1½ cups
30g (1 oz)	vegetable oil	2 tbs
225g (½ lb)	maple syrup	¾ cup
55g (2 oz)	pecans	½ cup

1 Grind the granola in a liquidizer. Melt the margarine and mix with the muesli (granola). Transfer to a flan tin (pie dish) and press down well.
2 Blend the tofu, oil and maple syrup in a liquidizer. Chop the nuts and stir them in.
3 Pour the tofu mixture over the granola crust and bake at 350°F/180°C (Gas Mark 4) for 30-40 minutes until well risen and turning golden brown. Cool and then chill before serving.

Note: To avoid raw cane sugar, for the base of this cheesecake use a granola that has none added. Sugar-Free.

Coconut Milk Vanilla Ice Cream

1 tin (c.400ml/ 14 fl oz)	coconut milk	1 can (c.14 fl oz)
30g (1 oz)	wholewheat flour	2 tbs
30-55g (1-2 oz)	raw cane sugar	1/6-⅓ cup
1 tsp	vanilla essence	1 tsp

1 Empty the contents of the can into a liquidizer, add the flour and sugar and blend thoroughly. Transfer to a saucepan and heat gently till slightly thickened and simmering. Remove from the heat, cool and chill thoroughly.
2 Stir the vanilla essence into the mixture, then pour into ice cream maker as per manufacturer's instructions.

Note: Vegan ice creams are now available at many health food shops, but for greater scope an ice cream maker is a great advantage. If you want to try one of these recipes without one, then while the mixture is freezing, take it out every 15-20 minutes and stir it well.

Soya Ice Cream

570ml (1 pt)	flavoured soya (soy) milk	2½ cups
2 tbs	cornflour (cornstarch)	2 tbs
2-3 tbs	vegetable oil	2-3 tbs

1 Pour nearly half the milk into a saucepan and bring to the boil. Meanwhile, mix 2-3 tbs milk with the cornflour (cornstarch) in a bowl. Pour the heated milk into the bowl, mix well, return to the saucepan, and heat until boiling and thickened. Cool, then chill thoroughly.
2 Combine the thickened milk with the remaining milk and the oil in a liquidizer and blend.
3 Pour the mixture into an ice cream maker or follow the instructions above.

Note: Many flavoured soya (soy) milks are now available – strawberry, banana, chocolate, carob – and any of them can be used to make a simple frozen dessert.

Mint Chocolate Chip Ice Cream

55g (2 oz)	peppermint stick	2 oz
140ml (¼ pt)	soya (soy) milk	⅔ cup
140ml (¼ pt)	Snowwhip Topping	⅔ cup
15g (½ oz)	vegan chocolate	½ oz

1 Crush the peppermint stick (I put the sticks in a plastic bag and just use a hammer on them!) Soak the crushed peppermint stick in the soya (soy) milk for several hours.
2 Add the Snowwhip Topping to the soya (soy) milk mixture and stir well. Chop the chocolate into very small pieces and add it to the mixture.
3 Proceed according to the instructions on your ice cream maker.

Note: This is not by any stretch of the imagination a 'wholefood' recipe, but I think that once in a while it is nice to indulge in something like this. Children (of all ages) will love it. If you check the ingredients of most peppermint sticks you will find they are vegan.
(See p.12 for Snowwhip Topping.)

Jellied Pudding

570ml (1 pt)	soya (soy) milk	2½ cups
2 tbs	cocoa powder	2 tbs
2 tsp	powdered agar	2 tsp
55g (2 oz)	almonds	½ cup
55-85g (2-3 oz)	raisins	⅓-½ cup
55g (2 oz)	dates	⅓ cup
2-3 tbs	chopped mixed peel	2-3 tbs
85g (3 oz)	raw cane sugar	½ cup
2-3 tsp	cinnamon	2-3 tsp

1 Mix about 4 tbs of the milk with the cocoa powder in a small bowl. Put the rest of the milk in a saucepan.
2 Chop the almonds and dates. The raisins can either be left whole or chopped.
3 When the milk is nearly at boiling point stir in the cocoa mixture and mix in well. Then stir in the agar. When the mixture has come to the boil, lower the heat and let it simmer for a minute or two. Remove from heat and add all the rest of the ingredients. Pour into moulds, cool and then chill.

Note: This is a bit like a chilled, light-textured Christmas pudding. Serve with vegan cream if desired.

Bread and 'Butter' Pudding

5-6 slices	wholewheat bread	5-6 slices
As required	vegan margarine	As required
85g (3 oz)	raisins or sultanas (golden seedless raisins)	½ cup
30-55g (1-2 oz)	raw cane sugar	1/6-⅓ cup
4 tbs	water	4 tbs
2 tbs	soya (soy) flour	2 tbs
½ tsp	baking powder	½ tsp
570ml (1 pt)	soya (soy) milk	2½ cups
As required	grated nutmeg	As required

1 Spread margarine on the slices of bread and cut them into strips. Layer the strips in an ovenproof dish with the dried fruit and sugar.
2 Beat the soya (soy) flour and baking powder into the water with a fork.
3 Heat the milk in a saucepan but remove from the heat before it boils. Beat in the soya (soy) flour mixture. Pour this over the bread. Grate some nutmeg over this and leave to soak for 20-30 minutes.
4 Bake at 350°F/180°C (Gas Mark 4) for about half an hour.

Note: I used to love this traditional sweet, so I experimented and came up with a vegan version. I prefer it with bread made from 81% or 85% wholewheat flour.

Carob Pudding

285ml (½ pt)	water	1⅓ cups
30g (1 oz)	soya (soy) flour	¼ cup
85g (3 oz)	sunflower seeds	3/5 cup
4 tbs	carob powder	4 tbs
85g (3 oz)	pitted dates	½ cup
2 tsp	vanilla essence	2 tsp

1 Place all the ingredients in the liquidizer and blend thoroughly.

Note: This is fast, simple and highly nutritious. Quick and Easy. Sugar-Free.

Baked Date and Coconut Pudding

340g (12 oz)	stoned dates	2 cups
85g (3 oz)	shredded (desiccated) coconut	1 cup
115g (4 oz)	creamed coconut	½ cup
1 tsp	agar-agar	1 tsp
285ml (½ pt)	boiling water	1⅓ cups

1 Chop the dates finely. In an oiled casserole, place alternate layers of chopped dates and shredded coconut.
2 Grate or finely chop the creamed coconut and put it in a liquidizer with the agar-agar. Pour in the boiling water and blend thoroughly.
3 Pour the liquid over the dates and coconut.
4 Bake in a slow oven at 300°F/150°C (Gas Mark 2) for about 30 minutes or until brown on top. Serve hot.

Note: This is a rich dessert sweetened only by the dates. Sugar-Free.

Creamy Date Pudding

170g (6 oz)	stoned dates	1 cup
1 tsp	vanilla essence	1 tsp
115g (4 oz)	creamed coconut	½ cup
285ml (½ pt)	hot water	1⅓ cups

1 Grate or chop the creamed coconut finely and add it to the hot water in a saucepan.
2 Chop the dates and add them to the saucepan.
3 Cook the mixture over the lowest possible heat, stirring occasionally, until the dates have dissolved and the mixture is thick and creamy. Add the vanilla essence.
4 Chill thoroughly before serving.

Note: This too is sweetened only by dates but it is a refreshing cold dessert. Sugar-Free.

Carob and Date Ice Cream

425ml (¾ pt)	water	2 cups
170g (6 oz)	stoned dates	1 cup
4 tbs	vegetable oil	4 tbs
30g (1 oz)	carob powder	¼ cup
2 tsp	vanilla essence	2 tsp
2 cartons (125g) each	soya (soy) cream	2 cartons

1 Soak the dates in the water for several hours (not absolutely necessary, but it does make blending easier). Blend all the ingredients in a liquidizer and place the mixture in the freezing compartment of the refrigerator for at least 3 hours, stirring occasionally.

Note: In my book *Vegan Cooking*, this recipe was made with powdered soya (soy) milk, which no longer exists. However, there are now soya (soy) creams available in cartons at British health food stores, and I found that they worked in this. As before, the recipe has no added sugar, but the cream is already sweetened. It was created in the days before I had an ice cream maker and works well without one.

Cloutie Dumpling

85g (3 oz)	medium oatmeal	¾ cup
85g (3 oz)	wholewheat flour	¾ cup
85g (3 oz)	hard vegetable fat	⅓ cup
85g (3 oz)	raw cane sugar	½ cup
115g (4 oz)	sultanas (golden seedless raisins), raisins, currants, or a mixture	
1 tsp	ground cinnamon	1 tsp
½ tsp	bicarbonate of soda (baking soda)	½ tsp
115-140g (4-5 oz)	soya (soy) yogurt	½-⅔ cup
As required	water	As required

1 Put the oatmeal and flour in a mixing bowl. Grate the fat into the bowl. Add the sugar, dried fruit, cinnamon and soda, and mix well.
2 Add the yogurt and enough water to make a thick batter. Spoon the batter into a greased pudding bowl and steam for 2-3 hours. Serve with custard.

Note: This is based on a traditional recipe and is perfect for a cold winter night. It makes four servings for those with large appetites; otherwise it could easily serve six.

Steamed Date Pudding

170g (6 oz)	wholewheat self-raising flour	1½ cups
Pinch	sea salt	Pinch
85g (3 oz)	hard vegetable fat	⅓ cup
30g (1 oz)	raw cane sugar	2 tbs
115g (4 oz)	dates	⅔ cup
140ml (¼ pt)	soya (soy) milk	⅔ cup
Grated rind of 1	lemon (use the juice for a sauce)	Grated rind of 1

1 Chop the dates finely.
2 Grate the fat and mix it in with the flour, salt and sugar. Add the dates and lemon rind.
3 Make a well in the centre and add enough milk to give a soft dropping consistency.
4 Place in a greased basin, cover with greased greaseproof paper or foil and steam for 1½-2 hours.
5 Serve with a lemon sauce (see p.120).

Note: This and the following recipe are two more traditional steamed puddings.

Steamed Jam Pudding

170g (6 oz)	wholewheat self-raising flour	1½ cups
55g (2 oz)	soya (soy) flour	½ cup
55g (2 oz)	raw cane sugar	⅓ cup
85-115g (3-4 oz)	vegan margarine	⅓-½ cup
As required	soya (soy) milk	As required
As required	sugar-free or raw-sugar jam	As required

1 Mix the flour and sugar and rub in the margarine.
2 Add enough milk to make a soft dough.
3 Put some jam at the bottom of a pudding basin and add the pudding mixture.
4 Cover with greaseproof (greased) paper or tin (aluminium) foil and steam for 1 hour.
5 Serve with custard if desired.

Baked Raisin Pudding

115g (4 oz)	raw cane sugar	⅔ cup
30g (1 oz)	vegan margarine	2 tbs
85-115g (3-4 oz)	raisins	½-⅔ cup
12 tbs	boiling water	12 tbs
1 tsp	vanilla essence	1 tsp
30g (1 oz)	chopped nuts	3 tbs
85g (3 oz)	wholewheat flour	¾ cup
1 tsp	baking powder	1 tsp
Approx 5 tbs	soya (soy) milk	Approx 5 tbs

1 First make a syrup by putting half the sugar, half the margarine and the raisins in a small saucepan with the boiling water. Heat slowly until the sugar dissolves, then boil steadily for 10 minutes. Add the vanilla essence.
2 Meanwhile, cream the rest of the sugar and margarine, add the flour mixed with the baking powder, and stir in enough milk to make a thick batter consistency.
3 Turn the mixture into a greased ovenproof dish and pour the hot sauce over the top with a sprinkling of nuts.
4 Bake in a moderate oven at 350°F/180°C (Gas Mark 4) for 30 minutes. Serve immediately.

Note: This is another winter pudding, but this time cooked in the oven, therefore requiring less time.

Coconut Cream Pie

1 carton	soya (soy) vanilla dessert	1 carton
85g (3 oz)	desiccated (shredded) coconut	1 cup
1	pre-baked flan case (pie shell)	1

1 Empty the contents of the carton into a saucepan and heat gently to boiling point. (Be careful not to burn it.) Simmer for a few minutes, then remove from the heat and stir in the coconut.
2 Leave the mixture to cool for a few minutes, then pour into a flan case (pie shell) and refrigerate until ready to serve.

Note: Cartons of soya (soy) based desserts are available under at least two different brands in virtually every health food store in the UK. They are delicious on their own, but the vanilla one, in particular, may be used as the basis for other desserts. For an authentic finish to this one, top it with vegan whipped cream (see p.12).

Banbury Tart

115g (4 oz)	raisins	¾ cup
115g (4 oz)	currants	¾ cup
30g (1 oz)	vegan margarine	2 tbs
1 tsp	cinnamon	1 tsp
½ tsp	freshly grated nutmeg	½ tsp
285ml (½ pt)	water	1⅓ cups
1 heaped tbs	cornflour (cornstarch)	1 heaped tbs
Rind and juice of ½	lemon	Rind and juice of ½
1	pre-baked flan case (pie shell)	1

1 Put the dried fruit, margarine, cinnamon, and nutmeg, in a saucepan. Pour in all but 3 or 4 tbs of the water, bring to the boil, lower the heat and simmer for a few minutes.
2 Mix the cornflour (cornstarch) with the remaining water and stir it into the saucepan. When the mixture has thickened remove it from the heat and add the lemon rind and juice.
3 Cool it for a few minutes then pour it into a pre-baked flan case (pie shell). Refrigerate until serving time.

Note: For those who cannot do without a little bit of sugar, one or two tablespoons may be added to this dessert. Serve it with a vegan cream.
Sugar-Free.

Oliebollen

170g (6 oz)	wholewheat flour	1½ cups
2 tsp	dried yeast	2 tsp
1	apple	1
About 285ml (½ pt)	soya (soy) milk	1⅓ cups
55g (2 oz)	raisins	⅓ cup
55g (2 oz)	currants	⅓ cup
30g (1 oz)	candied mixed peel	1 oz
3 tsp	lemon juice	3 tsp
Pinch	sea salt	Pinch
As required	raw cane sugar	As required

1 Put the flour in a bowl. If using "easybake" yeast it can be added straight to the bowl; otherwise dissolve it in a little of the milk.
2 Peel and chop the apple. Heat the milk to lukewarm.
3 Add the dried fruit, lemon juice, lemon, salt and milk to the bowl. (The dough should be thick, so add the milk slowly and if it looks like becoming thin do not use the full amount.)
4 Cover the bowl and leave it in a warm place for an hour.
5 Drop spoonfuls of the dough in hot oil until lightly browned. Serve warm, sprinkled with sugar.

Note: This is a traditional Dutch New Year's Eve dish which although sugar-free is traditionally served with sugar over it (I prefer to use sieved icing sugar).

Maple Raisin Tart

120ml (4 fl oz)	water	½ cup
1½ tbs	cornflour (cornstarch)	1½ tbs
340g (12 oz)	maple syrup	1 cup
170g (6 oz)	raisins	1 cup
	Pastry made from 225g (½ lb/2 cups) wholewheat flour (see p.41)	

1 Blend the water and cornflour (cornstarch) in a liquidizer and pour it into a saucepan. Stir in the maple syrup and raisins, and bring to the boil, stirring constantly until it thickens, then continue cooking over a very low heat for two or three minutes more, until it becomes transparent.
2 Roll out most of the pastry and place it in a pan. Cool the mixture slightly and pour it into a pastry case. Cover with a lattice top made from remaining strips of pastry.
3 Bake for about 20 minutes in a hot oven 425°F/225°C (Gas Mark 7) until the pastry is lightly browned. Serve warm.

Note: This recipe allows you to indulge in something as yummy as pure maple syrup and yet feel virtuous because you are not eating sugar.
Sugar-Free.

Maple Cobbler

225g (½ lb)	wholewheat flour	2 cups
4 tsp	baking powder	4 tsp
Pinch	sea salt	Pinch
55g (2 oz)	vegan margarine	¼ cup
About 140ml (¼ pt)	soya (soy) milk	About ⅔ cup
455g (1 lb)	maple syrup	1⅓ cups

1 Combine the flour, baking powder and salt in a bowl. Mix in the margarine. Add the milk and stir just enough to moisten the dry ingredients. (Different flours require different amounts of liquid, so if it is too dry to knead into a dough then add a little more milk.)
2 Knead the dough gently, then roll it out to a thickness of about ½ inch, and cut it into squares, rectangles or circles.
3 Heat the syrup to boiling point and pour it into a baking dish. Put the dough pieces on top of the syrup and bake uncovered in a hot oven 425°F/225°C (Gas Mark 7) for 15-20 minutes, until the surface is golden brown, basting once with the syrup before the end of the cooking time.

Sugar-Free.

Baked Jam Delight

85g (3 oz)	wholewheat self-raising flour	¾ cup
85g (3 oz)	rolled oats	¾ cup
115g (4 oz)	raw cane sugar	¾ cup
85g (3 oz)	vegan margarine	⅓ cup
170g (6 oz)	raw sugar or sugar-free jam	½ cup

1 Put the dry ingredients in a mixing bowl. Rub in the margarine until the mixture is crumbly.
2 Place half the mixture in the bottom of a greased baking tin. Spread with jam. Cover with the remaining mixture.
3 Bake at 350°F/180°C (Gas Mark 4) for about half an hour.

Note: The useful thing about this recipe is that in the first instance it is served hot – topped, if desired, with a vegan cream – and if there is any left over it can be left to cool and then sliced into squares and served as biscuits (cookies).

17

Cakes and Biscuits

Christmas Cake

85g (3 oz)	soft vegetable fat	⅓ cup
115g (4 oz)	raw cane sugar	⅔ cup
Juice of	oranges	Juice of
2 small		2 small
115g (4 oz)	wholewheat flour	1 cup
1 tbs	mixed spice	1 tbs
455g (1 lb)	mixed dried fruit	3 cups

1 Cream the fat and sugar together.
2 Add the rest of the ingredients and mix thoroughly.
3 Bake in a tin lined with greased greaseproof paper for
   3 hours in a slow oven at 300°F/150°C (Gas Mark 2).
4 Allow to cool completely before storing.

Note: This cake is best made several weeks before required and kept, well wrapped, in a cool place. Top with marzipan made from a mixture of ground almonds, soya (soy) flour, lemon juice and almond extract, and ice with a white glacé icing.

Plain Sponge Cake

55g (2 oz)	vegan margarine	¼ cup
55g (2 oz)	raw cane sugar	⅓ cup
1 tbs	soya (soy) flour	1 tbs
2 tbs	water	2 tbs
Few drops	vanilla essence	Few drops
100g (3½ oz)	wholewheat self-raising	¾ cup plus
	flour	1 tbs
½ tsp	baking powder	½ tsp
15g (½ oz)	cornflour (cornstarch)	1 tbs
3-4 tbs	soya (soy) milk	3-4 tbs

1 Cream the margarine and sugar together until fluffy.
2 Mix the soya (soy) flour into the water with a fork. Mix it into the margarine mixture, a little at a time. Add the vanilla essence.
3 Mix the flour, baking powder and cornflour (cornstarch) together. Add them to the bowl, together with enough milk to make a batter of dropping consistency.
4 Put the batter into two 7 inch sandwich tins (cake pans) and bake at 375°F/190°C (Gas Mark 5) for about 20 minutes, until it is firm to the touch and beginning to shrink away from the pan.

Note: This can either be sandwiched with jam and sprinkled with sugar, or sandwiched with a 'butter' filling made from vegan margarine and icing (powdered) sugar or finely ground raw cane sugar and iced with caramel icing (see recipe below).

Caramel Icing

140g (5 oz)	raw cane sugar	5/6 cup
4 tbs	soya (soy) milk	4 tbs
55g (2 oz)	vegan margarine	¼ cup
½ tsp	vanilla essence	½ tsp

1 Mix the sugar, milk and margarine in a saucepan.
2 Bring to the boil, stirring constantly. Boil for 2-3 minutes.
3 Remove from the heat and beat until lukewarm.
4 Add the vanilla essence and beat to a spreading consistency.

Orange Cake

115g (4 oz)	raw cane sugar	⅔ cup
½ tsp	sea salt	½ tsp
200g (7 oz)	wholewheat flour	1¾ cups
1 tsp	bicarbonate of soda (baking soda)	1 tsp
4 tbs	vegetable oil	4 tbs
2 tbs	pure orange juice	2 tbs
Grated rind of 1 small	orange	Grated rind of 1 small
200ml (⅓ pt)	water	¾ cup

1 In a large bowl mix together thoroughly the flour, sugar, salt and soda.
2 Add the oil, juice, rind and water. Mix with a fork until all the dry ingredients are moist. Do not beat.
3 Pour the mixture into two greased (and, if desired, lined with greaseproof paper) sandwich tins.
4 Bake in a moderate oven at 350°F/180°C (Gas Mark 4) for 30 minutes, or until the top of the cake springs up when lightly pressed. Leave to cool thoroughly.

Note: This cake tastes good sandwiched with margarine mixed with raw cane sugar and pure orange juice and topped with an orange-flavoured glacé icing.

Chocolate Cake

115g (4 oz)	raw cane sugar	⅔ cup
4 tsp	cocoa or carob powder	4 tsp
½ tsp	sea salt	½ tsp
170g (6 oz)	wholewheat flour	1½ cups
¾ tsp	bicarbonate of soda (baking soda)	¾ tsp
90ml (3 fl oz)	vegetable oil	⅓ cup
1 tsp	vanilla essence	1 tsp
2 tsp	cider vinegar or wine vinegar	2 tsp
200ml (⅓ pt)	cold water	¾ cup

1 Mix thoroughly the sugar, cocoa (or carob), salt, flour and soda in a mixing bowl.
2 Add the oil, vanilla essence and vinegar and pour cold water over the mixture.
3 Combine well with a fork, but do not beat.
4 Pour into two greased sandwich tins (lined if desired) and bake in a moderate oven at 350°F/180°C (Gas Mark 4) for 30 minutes or until the cake springs back when lightly pressed. Leave to cool thoroughly.

Note: This cake may be sandwiched with vegan margarine creamed with sugar and vanilla essence or chocolate, and iced with chocolate icing, if desired (see recipe below).

Chocolate Icing

55g (2 oz)	vegan margarine	¼ cup
30g (1 oz)	cocoa or carob powder	¼ cup
4 tbs	soya (soy) milk	4 tbs
140g (5 oz)	raw cane sugar	5/6 cup
1 tsp	vanilla essence	1 tsp

1 Combine the first four ingredients in a saucepan and bring them to the boil slowly, stirring constantly.
2 Boil for 1 minute.
3 Remove from the heat and beat until cool. Add the vanilla essence and spread the icing on the cake.

Date and Pecan Cake

225g (½ lb)	dates	1⅓ cups
55g (2 oz)	pecans	⅓ cup
85g (3 oz)	vegan margarine	⅓ cup
285ml (½ pt)	water	⅓ cup
115g (4 oz)	raisins	¾ cup
½ tsp	cinnamon	½ tsp
½ tsp	nutmeg	½ tsp
Pinch	sea salt	Pinch
225g (½ lb)	wholewheat flour	½ lb
1 tsp	baking powder	1 tsp
1 tsp	bicarbonate of soda (baking soda)	1 tsp

1 Chop the dates and pecans.
2 Put the dates, margarine, water, and raisins in a large saucepan. Bring to the boil and then let it boil for a couple of minutes.
3 Remove from the cooker, and stir in the remaining ingredients, mixing thoroughly. Turn the mixture into a cake pan, and bake at 375°F/190°C (Gas Mark 5) for about 45 minutes.

Note: This old-fashioned-style wholemeal cake is very quick and easy to make.
Sugar-Free.

Applesauce Cake

170g (6 oz)	cooking apples	6 oz
115g (4 oz)	dates	¾ cup
3 tbs	water	3 tbs
55g (2 oz)	vegan margarine	¼ cup
1 tsp	bicarbonate of soda (baking soda)	1 tsp
170g (6 oz)	self-raising wholewheat flour	1½ cups
1 tsp	cinnamon	1 tsp
Grating	nutmeg	Grating

1 Peel and chop the apples. Chop the dates. Put the chopped apple and dates into a saucepan with the

water. Bring to the boil, then lower the heat, cover and cook until the apple is tender. Cool slightly then put the mixture into a liquidizer and blend thoroughly.

2 Return the apple mixture to the saucepan and heat again over a very low flame. Add the margarine and stir until it is melted. Remove from the heat and immediately stir in the soda.

3 Add the flour, cinnamon and a good grating of nutmeg to the pan and stir quickly just until it is all mixed.

4 Transfer the batter to a cake pan and bake at 350°F/180°C (Gas Mark 4) for about 40 minutes.

Note: If you do not object to using sugar, then a plain glacé icing is nice on this cake.
Sugar-Free.

Gingerbread

170g (6 oz)	wholewheat flour	1½ cups
85g (3 oz)	raw cane sugar	½ cup
1 tsp	baking powder	1 tsp
1 tsp	bicarbonate of soda (baking soda)	1 tsp
1 tsp	ginger	1 tsp
½ tsp	cinnamon	½ tsp
½ tsp	nutmeg	½ tsp
Pinch	sea salt	Pinch
55g (2 oz)	vegan margarine	¼ cup
170g (6 oz)	molasses, black treacle, golden syrup, or a mixture	½ cup
4 tbs	water	4 tbs

1 Mix all the dry ingredients together.

2 In a large saucepan gently heat the margarine, treacle/syrup and water until it has all melted. Remove from the heat and stir in the dry ingredients.

3 Turn the mixture into a square or rectangular baking tin and bake at 375°F/190°C (Gas Mark 5) for 20-30 minutes.

Note: Gingerbread can refer to anything from a loaf-type cake to a biscuit (cookie). This is sort of in-between, baked flat but with a cake-like texture. It has a tendency to fall apart but, nevertheless, tastes fine.

Peanut Butter Oaties

55g (2 oz)	vegan margarine	¼ cup
55g (2 oz)	peanut butter	¼ cup
Pinch	sea salt	Pinch
½ tsp	vanilla essence	½ tsp
55g (2 oz)	raw cane sugar	⅓ cup
2 oz	wholewheat flour	½ cup
55g (2 oz)	rolled oats	½ cup
¼ tsp	bicarbonate of soda (baking soda)	¼ tsp
2 tbs	water	2 tbs

1 Put the margarine and peanut butter in a mixing bowl and beat well. Add the salt, vanilla and sugar and beat until light.

2 Add the flour, oats, soda and water to the bowl. Mix thoroughly and turn out into a greased pan, pressing down to ¼-½ inch.

3 Bake for 15-20 minutes at 375°F/190°C (Gas Mark 5). Remove from oven and let cool before slicing into bars.

Note: Making biscuits (cookies) can be fiddly, but with the 'bar' kind there is no need to shape them before baking.

Coconut Refrigerator Cookies

55g (2 oz)	vegan margarine	¼ cup
45g (1½ oz)	raw cane sugar	¼ cup
115g (4 oz)	wholewheat flour	1 cup
Pinch	sea salt	Pinch
½ tsp	baking powder	½ tsp
60ml (2 fl oz)	soya (soy) milk	¼ cup
45g (1½ oz)	desiccated (shredded) coconut	½ cup

1 Cream the margarine and sugar in a bowl until light. Mix together the flour, salt and baking powder. Add the milk to the margarine mixture, and then the flour mixture. Mix well, then knead into a dough.

2 Form the mixture into a large roll (like an oversized sausage), and cover with cling-film or foil. Put the roll into the refrigerator and chill thoroughly.

3 When ready to bake, remove the roll from the refrigerator, and slice it into ¼ inch rounds. Place the rounds on a greased baking tray, and bake for about 10 minutes at 325°F/170°C (Gas Mark 3).

Note: 'Refrigerator cookies' are a great American invention. They save rolling out dough, and most of the preparation is done well in advance (they can be kept refrigerated for anything from a few hours to a few days).

Oaty Chocolate Treats

115g (4 oz)	raw cane sugar	¾ cup
55g (2 oz)	vegan margarine	¼ cup
60ml (2 fl oz)	soya (soy) milk	¼ cup
30g (1 oz)	cocoa or carob powder	¼ cup
30g (1 oz)	nuts	¼ cup
30g (1 oz)	raisins	2 tbs
170g (6 oz)	rolled oats	1½ cups
Few drops	vanilla essence	Few drops

1 Mix the sugar, margarine, milk and cocoa in a pan. Bring to the boil over a medium heat, stirring frequently, then lower the heat to minimum and leave it to boil for three minutes.
2 Chop the nuts (or use cashew pieces). Chop the raisins if desired.
3 Remove the pan from the heat and stir in the oats, nuts, raisins and vanilla. Drop by spoonfuls on to a greased pan or plate to form walnut-sized balls (20-25). Leave to cool. (If it is a warm day then store in the refrigerator.)

Quick and Easy.

Appendix
Directory of Recipes

Quick and Easy Recipes

These are dishes which take under half an hour to prepare, though they may require certain ingredients – rice, potatoes or beans – to be pre-cooked

Curried sweetcorn (corn) soup
Avocado and cashew soup
Curried pea soup
Cream of peanut butter soup
Chilled avocado and tomato soup
Curried avocado soup
Coconutty sweetcorn (corn) and red pepper soup
White bean and black olive soup
Caribbean salad
Chick pea (Garbanzo bean) and walnut salad
Curried butter bean (lima bean) salad
Stuffed pear salad
Stuffed banana salad
Chick pea (Garbanzo bean) salad with tahini dressing
Fruit and nut coleslaw
Macaroni and avocado salad
Mediterranean-style pasta salad
Tomato and onion savoury
Mushroom spread
Grilled garlic mushrooms
Hummus
Haricot bean (navy bean) and olive dip
Chick pea (garbanzo bean) spread
Guacamole
Curried avocado spread
Eggless Egg Sandwich Spread
Vegan rarebit
Fried peanut butter sandwiches
Curried vegetable rice
Nasi goreng

Short-cut risotto
Creamy curried sauce on bulgur
Gnocchi alla Romana
Bulgur wheat and chestnut bake
Quick pizza
Stir-fried vegetables with barley
Barley lentil savoury
Oaty burgers
Fried polenta
Spaghetti with tahini sauce
Spaghetti All' Alfredo
Bean and potato stew
Macaroni and bean 'hot-pot'
Chick pea (Garbanzo bean) stroganoff
Chick pea (Garbanzo bean) burgers
Italian macaroni and beans
'Hummus' patties
Masoor dahl
Quick and easy chilli
Kidney bean burgers
Potato kephtides
Potato-paprika
Tomato and sweetcorn (corn) savoury
San Clemente curry
Avocado à la king
Hazelnut and potato patties
Chestnut burgers
Tofu and onions
Sweet and sour tofu and vegetables
Mushroom stroganoff
Tofu 'scrambled eggs'

Scrambled tofu and mushrooms
Tofu and pea curry
Tofu burgers
Crispy fried sea-flavoured frozen tofu
Smoked tofu, courgette (zucchini) and corn risotto
Smokey duvec
Smoked tofu and mashed potato cakes
Tempeh burgers
Nutmeat stew
Quick 'sausage' pie
Bolognese sauce for spaghetti
Arame and peanut stir-fry

Kedgeree
Oriental-style fried rice with tofu and nori
Bubble and squeak
Potatoes Niçoise
Heated avocado purée
Lettuce and peas
Lemon and chocolate treats
Avocado dessert
Baked bananas and oranges
Carob pudding
Oaty chocolate treats

Suitable for One

These are dishes which are particularly easy to make up for one portion only; use a quarter of the ingredients given in the recipe.

Brussels sprouts salad
Curried butter bean (lima bean) salad
Stuffed pear salad
Stuffed banana salad
Chick pea (Garbanzo bean) salad with tahini dressing
Grilled garlic mushrooms
Vegan rarebit
Fried peanut butter sandwiches
Curried vegetable rice
Short-cut risotto
Creamy curried sauce on bulgur
Gnocchi alla Romana
Bulgur wheat and chestnut bake
Stir-fried vegetables with barley
Barley lentil savoury
Oaty burgers
Fried polenta
Spaghetti All' Alfredo
Butter bean (Lima bean) and potato stew
Macaroni and bean 'hot-pot'

Chick pea (Garbanzo bean) stroganoff
Chick pea (Garbanzo Bean) Burgers
Italian macaroni and beans
'Hummus' patties
Megadarra
Quick and easy chilli
Kidney bean burgers
Potato-paprika
Potato gnocchi
Hazelnut and potato patties
Tofu 'scrambled eggs'
Scrambled tofu and mushrooms
Tofu burgers
Tempeh burgers
Quick 'sausage' pie
Toad in the hole
Kedgeree
Bubble and squeak
Potatoes Nicojse

Suitable for a Dinner Party

These are dishes which are likely to appeal to those who are not vegan, or even lacto-vegetarian.

Avocado vichyssoise
Cream of mushroom miso soup
Avocado and mushroom salad
Aubergine (Eggplant) and tahini dip
Baked noodles and aubergine (eggplant)
Baked vegetable curry and coconut rice casserole

Nut crunch and mushroom cream
Chestnut and mushroom pie
Tempeh croquettes with mushroom sauce
Princess potatoes
Summer fruit cup

Sugar-Free

These are desserts and cakes which do not contain cane sugar.

Frozen raisin and pecan dessert
Banana cream pie
Avocado, coconut and apple dessert
Maple pecan tofu cheesecake
Carob pudding
Baked date and coconut pudding

Creamy date pudding
Banbury tart
Maple raisin tart
Maple cobbler
Date and pecan cake
Applesauce cake

Index

By the same author . . .

The Tofu Cookbook

Easy to cook, deliciously versatile and wonderfully healthy, tofu is now readily available in supermarkets and health stores everywhere.

A soya-based bean-curd which has been used for cooking in the Far East for centuries, it absorbs flavours easily and can be used in more interesting and varied ways than any other single food.

Leah Leneman explains how it's made, the different types of tofu, how to store it and how to cook creatively with it – for successful results every time. Her recipes are dairy-free versions of international favourites, including classic dishes such as English shepherd's pie, Mexican tacos, savoury Mediterranean-style risotto as well as soups, salads and desserts from every corner of the world.

High in protein, low in calories and completely cholesterol-free, tofu can be used as a substitute for eggs, dairy products and meat. It is fun to cook and the ideal food for the future.

The Single Vegan

If you are a vegan then the chances are that you will have to cook for yourself. Maybe you live alone, or you are the only vegan member of your family. Are you tired of eating the same tried and tested food night after night, simply because you cannot find vegan recipes in most cookery books that can be divided to make them suitable for one person? Perhaps you are relying on convenience foods – all right for emergencies but rather expensive for everyday requirements.

Help is at hand! Here is a mouth-watering selection of quick and easy-to-prepare vegan menus, all suitable for one person. Savour the delights of Smoked Tofu à la King, Vegetable Pilau Special, Jambalaya or Nutty Plum Crumble. Of course, you may not always want to dine alone, so all of these recipes can be easily increased to suit your numbers. Includes:

- Weekly shopping lists for perishable items to be used up over the week's menus.
- Lists of 'staple' foods to be kept in the store cupboard.
- Seasonal menus to make the most of cheaper ingredients.

THE TOFU COOKBOOK	0 7225 2587 7	£5.99 ☐
THE SINGLE VEGAN	0 7225 1454 9	£5.99 ☐
THE SINGLE VEGETARIAN	0 7225 1358 5	£5.99 ☐
365+1 VEGETARIAN MAIN MEALS	0 7225 0895 6	£5.99 ☐
365+1 VEGETARIAN STARTERS, SNACKS, AND SAVOURIES	0 7225 2686 5	£5.99 ☐
THE VERY BEST OF VEGETARIAN COOKING	0 7225 2619 9	£8.99 ☐
COLIN SPENCER'S SUMMER COOKING	0 7225 2653 9	£9.99 ☐
CORDON VERT	0 7225 2621 0	£9.99 ☐

All these books are available at your local bookseller or can be ordered direct from the publishers.

To order direct just tick the titles you want and fill in the form below:

Name: _____

Address: _____

_____

_____ Postcode: _____

Send to: Thorsons Mail Order, Dept 3, HarperCollins*Publishers*, Westerhill Road, Bishopbriggs, Glasgow G64 2QT.
Please enclose a cheque or postal order or debit my Visa/Access account —

Credit card no: ☐☐☐☐ ☐☐☐☐ ☐☐☐☐ ☐☐☐☐

Expiry date: _____

Signature: _____

— to the value of the cover price plus:
UK & BFPO: Add £1.00 for the first book and 25p for each additional book ordered.
Overseas orders including Eire: Please add £2.95 service charge. Books will be sent by surface mail but quotes for airmail despatches will be given on request.

**24 HOUR TELEPHONE ORDERING SERVICE FOR ACCESS/VISA CARDHOLDERS —
TEL: 041 772 2281.**